MW00851890

DZOGCHEN
DEITY PRACTICE

Rangjung Yeshe Books ♦ www.rangjung.com

PADMASAMBHAVA ♦ *Treasures from Juniper Ridge* ♦ *Advice from the Lotus-Born* ♦ *Dakini Teachings*

PADMASAMBHAVA AND JAMGÖN KONGTRÜL ♦ *The Light of Wisdom, Vol. 1, Vol. 2, Vol. 3, Vol. 4, & Vol. 5*

PADMASAMBHAVA, CHOKGYUR LINGPA, TULKU URGYEN RINPOCHE, ORGYEN TOBGYAL RINPOCHE, AND LAMA PUTSI PEMA TASHI ♦ *Dispeller of Obstacles*

YESHE TSOGYAL ♦ *The Lotus-Born*

DAKPO TASHI NAMGYAL ♦ *Clarifying the Natural State*

TSELE NATSOK RANGDRÖL ♦ *Mirror of Mindfulness* ♦ *Empowerment* ♦ *Heart Lamp*

CHOKGYUR LINGPA ♦ *Ocean of Amrita* ♦ *The Great Gate* ♦ *Skillful Grace* ♦ *Great Accomplishment*

TRAKTUNG DUDJOM LINGPA ♦ *A Clear Mirror*

JAMGÖN MIPHAM RINPOCHE ♦ *Gateway to Knowledge, Vol. 1, Vol. 2, Vol. 3, & Vol. 4*

TULKU URGYEN RINPOCHE ♦ *Blazing Splendor* ♦ *Rainbow Painting* ♦ *As It Is, Vol. 1 & Vol. 2* ♦ *Vajra Speech* ♦ *Repeating the Words of the Buddha*

ADEU RINPOCHE ♦ *Freedom in Bondage*

KHENCHEN THRANGU RINPOCHE ♦ *King of Samadhi* ♦ *Crystal Clear*

CHÖKYI NYIMA RINPOCHE ♦ *Present Fresh Wakefulness*

TULKU THONDUP ♦ *Enlightened Living*

ORGYEN TOBGYAL RINPOCHE ♦ *Life & Teachings of Chokgyur Lingpa*

DZIGAR KONGTRÜL RINPOCHE ♦ *Uncommon Happiness*

TSOKNYI RINPOCHE ♦ *Fearless Simplicity* ♦ *Carefree Dignity*

DZOGCHEN TRILOGY COMPILED BY MARCIA BINDER SCHMIDT ♦ *Dzogchen Primer* ♦ *Dzogchen Essentials* ♦ *Quintessential Dzogchen*

ERIK PEMA KUNSANG ♦ *Wellsprings of the Great Perfection* ♦ *A Tibetan Buddhist Companion* ♦ *The Rangjung Yeshe Tibetan-English Dictionary of Buddhist Culture & Perfect Clarity*

MARCIA DECHEN WANGMO ♦ *Confessions of a Gypsy Yogini* ♦ *Precious Songs of Awakening*

CHOKGYUR LINGPA, JAMGÖN KONGTRÜL, JAMYANG KHYENTSE WANGPO, ADEU RINPOCHE, AND ORGYEN TOBGYAL RINPOCHE ♦ *The Tara Compendium Feminine Principles Discovered*

DZOGCHEN
DEITY PRACTICE

MEETING YOUR TRUE NATURE

Padmasambhava
Chokgyur Lingpa
Tulku Urgyen Rinpoche
Orgyen Tobgyal Rinpoche

Translated by
Erik Pema Kunsang

Rangjung Yeshe
PUBLICATIONS

Rangjung Yeshe Publications
Box 395
Leggett, CA, 95585 USA

Address letters to:
Rangjung Yeshe Publications
C/O Above
www.rangjung.com
www.lotustreasure.com

Copyright © 2016 Rangjung Yeshe Publications & Erik Pema Kunsang

All rights reserved. No part of this book may be reproduced in any form or by any means, electronic or mechanical—including photocopying, recording, and duplicating by means of any information storage and retrieval system—without written permission from the publisher.

1 3 5 7 9 8 6 4 2

First paperback edition published in 2016
Printed in the United States of America

Distributed to the book trade by:
Publishers Group West

Publication data: ISBN13: 978-0-9909978-3-2 (pbk)

Title: Dzogchen Deity Practice: Meeting Your True Nature
Padmasambhava, Chokgyur Lingpa, Tulku Urgyen Rinpoche, Orgyen Tobgyal Rinpoche, & Marcia Binder Schmidt
Translated from the Tibetan by Erik Pema Kunsang (Erik Hein Schmidt). Compiled and edited by Marcia Binder Schmidt.
1. Vajrayana/Yidam—Tradition of Pith Instructions
2. Buddhism—Tibet
Photos courtesy of Graham Sunstein, Phillipe O'Sullivan, & Marcia Binder Schmidt

Cover Art by Maryann Lipaj

First Edition

CONTENTS

PREFACE: Marcia Dechen Wangmo   vii

INTRODUCTION

    A Jewel in the Crown Ornament:
        Orgyen Tobgyal Rinpoche   ix

ORIGIN: Tulku Urgyen Rinpoche   I

    Dzogchen Key Points   3
    Background   9
    Intent: To Recognize Mind's Nature   II

APPLICATION: Tulku Urgyen Rinpoche   15

    Structure of the *Kunzang Tuktig*
        Cycle of Teachings   17
    Train in Indivisibility   19
    Lineage Supplication   31
    From the Beginning   43
    Preliminaries, with Questions & Answers   53
    The Main Part, with Questions & Answers   69
    Conclusion and the *Zurgyen*,
        with Questions & Answers   83

TEXTS   157

    The Brilliant Concise Meaning, Extract:
        Karmey Khenpo Rinchen Dargye   159

CONTENTS

The Mind Ornament of Samantabhadra, Extract:
    Dilgo Khyentse Rinpoche   161
The Destroyer of All Evil Deeds and Obscurations,
    General Empowerment Text:
    Padmasambhava, revealed by
    Chokgyur Lingpa   171
The Excellent Path to True Goodness:
    Karmey Khenpo Rinchen Dargye   181
Self-Manifest Luminosity: Chokgyur Lingpa   201
The Manifest Essence:
    Padmasambhava, revealed by
    Chokgyur Lingpa   207
Short Dharmapala Petition: Padmasambhava   221
The Inexhaustible Garland of Lightning:
    Künzang Gyurmey Tsewang Drakpa
    Ngedön Drubpey Dorje   223

ENGLISH BIBLIOGRAPHY   227

TIBETAN SOURCE MATERIAL   229

ENDNOTES   231

Peaceful and Wrathful Deities

PREFACE

Marcia Dechen Wangmo

Some years ago, I overheard a conversation between two great Nyingma masters, who were privately discussing sadhana practice, with its various characteristics, components, and qualities. In fact, one of the lamas was actually questioning the other about application of ritual. The lama who was responding outlined and then explained in-depth all aspects of development and completion stages, in regard to a sadhana. From the onset, the lama being questioned emphasized that to truly engage in these two practices, one needed to unfold the sadhana from within the recognition of the view of all-encompassing purity, the application being an expression of awareness. Explaining the special stylistic qualities of the Nyingma development stage practice, beginning with the samadhi of suchness up until the recitation, he stressed the intent of the tantras and the way to unfold that in practice. It was an extraordinary teaching that very closely reminded me of the way in which both Tulku Urgyen Rinpoche and Dungse Trinley Norbu Rinpoche elucidated the key points of this training.

Toward the end of the discussion, the second lama—who was unduly impressed, awed, and inspired—said, "No one these days teaches like this. Please share this wisdom with others. It is essential for practitioners to know the correct view, meditation, and conduct!" The first lama just laughed, saying, "There is no way that I will teach this openly, because few can really understand and even fewer will be able to put it into practice."

My heart seized, remembering how freely Tulku Urgyen Rinpoche had offered such experience and realization. He deeply believed that people should get the whole view and apply it in a genuine way, to the extent of their capacity. I am not reproaching the first lama or brazenly praising my teacher but simply observing how things evolved. I also feel very dejected that so few masters these days have the courage to teach in this way. I have had the overwhelming impression that such a precious tradition is on the verge of fading away, which has made me even sadder. This is not a veiled criticism of today's teachers. The first lama was probably correct in assessing that few can hear such teachings, assimilate them, and have the confidence to put them into practice—because training like this takes an immense storehouse of merit and stability in awareness. Nevertheless, the conversation motivated me to compile this book of Tulku Urgyen Rinpoche's teachings, which exactly define the development and completion stage practices from the Dzogchen perspective, as the first lama described.

I am fairly certain that I do not need to tell people who Tulku Urgyen Rinpoche was, but only to remind them that he was one of the greatest Dzogchen masters of the last century. His teaching style was direct, simple, and powerful. His compassionate humility created a comfortable ambiance that opened one up to being able to absorb his profound words. He was fearless in teaching the view, meditation, and conduct of the Great Perfection, due to the strength of his realization. He was like a general who ordered his soldiers to take no prisoners. In regard to the view, one either recognized it or not—and if not, no place to hide, nothing to capture! When I listen to or read his teachings, very often I have to stop and catch my breath, recalling how fortunate we have been that such a great being graced our world and that so many of us were able to connect with him personally or though his books, recordings, and videos. What was so easy for him, he made easy for others, with a flair for divine showmanship and humor. He never gave up on us, repeating the same thing again and again, almost relentlessly, till at least we could understand intellectually.

So, fearing that such a teaching style may die out and determined to prevent that from happening, I offer *Dzogchen Deity Practice*. In the context of my series on the Three Roots practice books, this one can be categorized under *yidam* practice; but once again, this is a mere label, as it can be a lama or *dakini* practice as well. The key point here is how to engage in sadhana practice as a pure Dzogchen yogi or yogini. These explanations are repeated in numerous ways on various occasions to make an indelible impression on our minds. Increasing the repetitious effect, a good deal of this book is based on questions that I and other dharma friends raised over the course of twelve years, while searching for other angles, as many of these teachings

do not fit into our narrow minds' framework! Of course, whether we've recognized and stabilized mind's nature or not, Tulku Urgyen Rinpoche never
deviates from the underlying principle, as he explains how to practice.

I need to make one apology in regard to this compilation, although I
am sure I will need to confess many more later. Tulku Urgyen Rinpoche
did not give me permission to openly share teachings on the "ground." So,
here, teachings on the ground have either been edited out or highly veiled. I
retained some reference in order to give a complete picture, so the reader can
get a full sense of the material. When encountering these places, please be
aware of this omission and make the effort to seek these instructions from
your personal teacher.

Although *Dzogchen Deity Practice* uses the peaceful and wrathful terma
of *Kunzang Tuktig* as its basis, these teachings on development and completion stage practices apply with equal efficacy to many other sadhanas as well.
Also, this compilation does not strive for complete consistency and minute
accuracy in the various descriptions of the deities' forms. I am not being
sloppy. The intent of this offering is to mirror Tulku Urgyen Rinpoche, who
placed more emphasis on the deep meaning and underlying principles of
Vajrayana than on specific details. While these details are also important,
the reader should seek them from a different style of teacher and from
external sources that can later be incorporated into practice.

Sincere hearthfelt thanks and appreciation are offered to the dynamic
team who worked on this book: the incomparable Dzogchen lotsawa, Erik
Pema Kunsang; the yogi, Graham Sunstein, who corrects and seamlessly
prepares photos; my amazing editor, Anne Paniagua; my steadfast book
designer, Joan Olson; my creative and adaptable cover creator, Maryann
Lipaj; my resolute proofreaders, Lynn Schroeder and Michael Yockey; and
to my kind printing sponsor, Richard Gere. As an enthusiastic lover of Dzogchen, I proffer these precious teachings by the incomparable master Tulku
Urgyen Rinpoche, as a conduit to captivate, support, and guide future realized beings. May all faults I have committed be forgiven and all blessings
abound. With great joy and trepidation, I present butter to the lamp of the
Dzogchen teachings, so they may continue to burn with brilliance, reaching
and benefiting the innumerable yogis and yoginis who can carry that flame
all the way to enlightenment!

May it be auspicious!

A Jewel in the Crown Ornament

Orgyen Tobgyal Rinpoche

It is impossible for one person to truly judge another, so we can never really know how great a master Tulku Urgyen was. Only a buddha like Shakyamuni can fully know another being. However, during the twentieth century, a few masters were unanimously accepted to be like the Buddha appearing in person. Along with the sixteenth Gyalwang Karmapa, Rangjung Rigpey Dorje, and Kyabje Dudjom Rinpoche, who was the emissary of Guru Padmasambhava, there has also been Kyabje Dilgo Khyentse Rinpoche. Within the contemporary Kagyü and Nyingma schools, no one has been more extraordinary, with so immense an impact on the Buddhadharma, than they have. Yet, these three all accepted Tulku Urgyen among their root gurus. If they respected Tulku Urgyen as their crown ornament, I, too, feel we should regard him as someone special.

Tulku Urgyen Rinpoche upheld both the teaching and family lineages of Chokgyur Lingpa. He kept this lineage of empowerment, instruction, and reading transmission alive, not only by practicing it himself but also by passing it on to the Karmapa and Dudjom Rinpoche, as well as countless others. His activity on behalf of this dharma lineage is an immense kindness that I regard as very special. Tulku Urgyen's family lineage comes through Chokgyur Lingpa's daughter, Könchok Paldrön, and her son, Chimey Dorje, who was Tulku Urgyen's father. Thus, he descended directly from the great *tertön*.

On one occasion, Könchok Paldrön asked for advice from both Jamyang Khyentse and Jamgön Kongtrül as to whether it would be better to become a nun or get married. Both masters replied, "You should take a husband; in the future it is through your bloodline that someone will appear to benefit beings. This is very important."

Accordingly, she married a son of the Tsangsar family. The couple had many children, including Tulku Urgyen's uncle, the great master Samten Gyatso, who brought great benefit to the continuation of the Tersar teachings and was able to carry out great deeds. This lineage continues through Tulku Urgyen's many sons, who are all still alive and well. Although they have their individual titles and bear the responsibility to uphold their respective lineages, I hope that they will also personally practice and transmit the terma teachings of Chokgyur Lingpa, their father's own lineage.

Many people these days hold the opinion that Tulku Urgyen Rinpoche was just a Dzogchen yogi, who only stayed up in his mountain hermitage, Nagi Gompa, and practiced one-pointedly—concluding that he was a good lama with high realization. Since he downplayed his talents, not many people seem to know the details of his qualities beyond these simple facts. But when I reflect on what I personally know, I feel that he was also a great scholar.

Tulku Urgyen was not someone famed for being learned. But if we begin to investigate in detail, starting from reading skills, we see he was a scholar, able to read many kinds of scripts, including even the rare *lantsa* and *wardu* variety. He was proficient in grammar, poetry, and the general sciences, so it is difficult to find anything about which he was ignorant. Concerning the inner knowledge of Buddhism, he had met many very educated and learned masters, and he was especially well-versed in the *Ngakso*, the *Lamrim Yeshe Nyingpo*, and the *Guhyagarbha Tantra*. He was a great calligrapher, very knowledgeable about many scripts that have been practically forgotten today. Taking all this into consideration, I personally consider him very learned.

Tulku Urgyen Rinpoche was also a skilled craftsman. He could make original statues—unlike professional sculptors, who usually just repeat themselves—thus, his sculptures of deities often had much finer proportions. Some of these can be seen in the shrine rooms for the dharma protectors at Ka-Nying Shedrub Ling.

When it came to mundane discussions, he was extremely skillful. Even if people put their heads together, they are often still unable to decide what to do. But Rinpoche was always able to make a decision that was in harmony with both spiritual and social conventions. He always seemed to know what the best course of action would be, giving advice without hesitation. Often people would find that his solution was something they hadn't even thought of, and upon hearing it, they felt, "Well of course!" His decision would put their minds at ease, and they felt confident that this was the best solution. This is another example of the power of his intelligence.

There is a famous Kagyü saying, "Devotion is the head of meditation." Devotion is based upon one's guru, so to have the trust and devotion that one's guru is the Buddha in actuality is a most eminent method. To fulfill one's guru's wish to the letter and to serve him in whatever way possible is the proper way to apply the oral instructions. In this regard, Tulku Urgyen's sense of trust, loyalty, and samaya with other masters was constant. He regarded his own teachers as the Buddha in person. Once he had connected with a teacher through receiving empowerment or oral instructions, his trust was unwavering. If the opportunity came to carry out his guru's wish, he was willing to give unstintingly of whatever wealth was in his possession, without any concern for personal hardship. If it came to it, I feel that he would even have been ready to sacrifice his own life without any hesitation or regret.

Tulku Urgyen Rinpoche was someone who could back up his words with action. In both spiritual and secular affairs, he wouldn't just talk about what needed to be done, he would go ahead and do it. Nor did he get involved in a lot of doubt and hesitation about the tasks at hand, worrying about whether something would be successful or not. He wouldn't get caught up in a web of concepts; instead, he would make a decision free of doubt and never waver. That's the kind of man he was.

When speaking of the Buddhist scriptures—the Middle Way, Prajnaparamita, and so forth—the "exposition lineage" focuses on explaining the syntax and intent. But being learned is not just a matter of knowing the words and their meaning; there is also the transmission of the real meaning. Tulku Urgyen was a *pandita* in the true sense of the word.

At one time, I went to see Tulku Urgyen Rinpoche to ask him to clarify a verse from the ninth chapter of Shantideva's *Bodhicharya Avatara* (*The Way of the Bodhisattva*):

> *When concreteness or inconcreteness*
> *Does not remain before the intellect,*
> *At that moment there is no other mental form,*
> *And so, there is utter peace without conceptions.*

I had studied it many times and asked many khenpos about it but still felt that none of them had given me an adequate explanation. I also asked Tulku Urgyen about certain points in the Prajnaparamita teachings, in which the fact of emptiness is established, such as the statement that emptiness has no form, no sound, and so forth. Only Tulku Urgyen was able to prove the reality of these statements in a reasonable way. His logic established emptiness in actuality for me, while the other scholars merely established emptiness in words.

At some point, the reincarnation of Neten Chokling, Tulku Pema Wangyal, and a few of us went up to Nagi Gompa and spent a few days asking questions. During this time, Tulku Urgyen clearly laid out the logic of establishing emptiness. Everyone was amazed at his clarity. Explaining how all sentient beings have buddha-nature also proves that buddha-nature is an intrinsic quality. This is especially done in the higher Middle Way School, known as Shentong. In the biographies of many great lamas, you find that they would bow down to and circumambulate even old dogs to show their respect for buddha-nature, while saying, "I take refuge in the buddha-nature."

Tulku Urgyen had confidence and utterly pure trust, based on his personal, direct understanding that buddha-nature really is present in every sentient being. Just like oil is present in each and every sesame seed, any sentient being can realize the awakened state and thus has the basis for enlightenment. Therefore, Tulku Urgyen showed respect for every sentient being and didn't turn against anyone. He felt this not as mere platitude, but from the core of his heart.

Tulku Urgyen also showed vast insight about the meaning of the *Uttaratantra, Hevajra Tantra,* and the *Profound Inner Meaning,* which are favored in the Kagyü lineage. Within the Nyingma School, he was incredibly well-versed in both the root text of the *Lamrim Yeshe Nyingpo,* as well as Jamgön Kongtrül's commentary on it. He knew most of the root text by heart and had repeatedly studied the commentaries by Rinchen Namgyal and Khenpo Jokyab. He was very knowledgeable in Vajrayana, having studied the *Guhyagarbha Tantra, The Secret Essence of the Magical Net.* In a discussion with Dilgo Khyentse Rinpoche, it became apparent to me that Tulku Urgyen also had a complete grasp of the *Guhyagarbha Tantra.*

During the first *Ngakso drubchen* held at Ka-Nying Shedrub Ling, I had the chance to ask Tulku Urgyen questions about the tenfold meaning of mantra. He gave very clear explanations that made me appreciate his learnedness in the *Guhyagarbha Tantra.* He also had an in-depth knowledge of many other tantras. He was especially insightful when defining the *kayas* and wisdoms and the "chakras of syllable clouds," the sounds and meaning of mantra. In short, he exactly fit the title, Pandita of Definitive Meaning.

Concerning tantric ceremonies, Tulku Urgyen Rinpoche was extremely competent in the mandalas for vast activities, knowing their proportions and the accompanying rituals of sacred dance and exorcism. He was a skilled *torma* maker as well as an expert *umdzey*, "chant master." He had a remarkable grasp of architecture and all other necessary fields of knowledge connected to Tibetan Buddhist practice. While some umdzeys merely sing ceremonies from beginning to end, Tulku Urgyen's singing carried a certain blessing that could move the listener to devotion. When he gave an empowerment, even though the ritual may not have involved more than placing a vase on somebody's head, people would feel it was something really special. Even the way he looked at people would give them some understanding that was totally unlike an ordinary person's perception.

When giving empowerment to a gathering of thousands of people, sitting on a throne made of brocade cushions, he never looked out of place. His air and bearing, impressive and dignified, never looked contrived. He was definitely extraordinary.

Rinpoche would always touch heads with whoever came into his presence, even the poorest Nepali worker, and ask, "How are you?" And you could see happiness on the person's face, which far surpassed the joy of receiving thousands of rupees. There is no reason why someone should become so happy just by being asked how they are and touching foreheads, but people were so delighted. Many foreigners changed their whole perspective on life from only one meeting and felt extraordinarily blessed. Practitioners felt that they received blessings, and even ordinary people still felt that something unusual had happened. Whoever came into his presence never felt tired, even after several hours had passed. That is totally unlike being in the presence of some politicians, when you can't wait to get away. Speaking for myself, I never tired of being with Tulku Urgyen—I only felt happy.

In all his conversations, he never mentioned any prejudice. Whether you talked about religious or secular affairs, he always spoke honestly and clearly, never acting pretentiously or ever lying. He also had a sharp memory and spoke of events long past as if they just happened yesterday. Nobody wanted to leave his presence; people always wanted to sit longer—they just wouldn't get out. I've heard that he scolded a few people, but I've never met anyone who actually got scolded. I never heard him say a harsh word. At the same time, anyone who lived near him or knew him for a long time felt a sense of timidity and awe. His very presence was powerful.

The qualities of someone who has completely severed the ties of selfishness and pursues only the welfare of others may not necessarily be visible. But it is hard to find a more unselfish person than Tulku Urgyen Rinpoche. When focusing on benefiting others, our own aims automatically become fulfilled without having to deliberately try. Building a monastery is a very difficult task that sometimes seems insurmountable. But most people are not aware of how many temples Tulku Urgyen built. Nor does anybody know exactly how many years he stayed in retreat, which practices he did, and the number of recitations he completed. People can vaguely say that he did it once or twice in Tibet and once in India; but other than that, no one knows. I figure he spent approximately half of his entire life doing intensive practice in retreat.

There are no accurate records of which empowerments, transmissions, and teachings he received. But he probably received most of the Nyingma Kama and Terma, all the Kagyü teachings, and the Lamdrey from the Sakya school, as well as many other lineages. Every time someone brought up a certain teaching and asked him about it, it seemed he held the transmission for it. He received an ocean of teachings. Tulku Urgyen's unique heart practice was the *Chetsün Nyingtig* and *Kunzang Tuktig*, belonging to the Great Perfection itself. Everyone unanimously accepts him as a great Dzogchen yogi.

It is not really up to me to speak about his attainment of great accomplishment; but in 1985, after a discussion with Dilgo Khyentse Rinpoche, His Holiness told me that Tulku Urgyen had reached the level of "culmination of awareness." When someone has arrived at the culmination of awareness, there is nothing more to realize other than "exhaustion in dharmata." So he was someone who achieved the final realization of the Great Perfection. In short, it is perfectly fine to regard him as a master who was both learned and accomplished.

From a personal point of view, I can say that I haven't met anyone superior to Tulku Urgyen. There has been no one who, in actuality, was better able to carry out the intent of Shantideva's *Bodhicharya Avatara* to the letter. Without any concern for personal hardship, he always aimed to do his utmost to benefit sentient beings. He was also extremely humble and self-effacing—totally in tune with Shantideva's bodhisattva ideal. He treated everyone, whether important or ordinary, with the same affection and attention, teaching everyone equally. In order to bring the highest benefit, he always tried to communicate in the listener's own terms. He clearly reflected the bodhisattva ideal of ocean-like activity, not only in his teaching but also in all his conversations. While I never saw him actually give away his head, arms, or legs, as you hear about in some of the bodhisattva stories, I feel absolutely certain that he was a great bodhisattva, able to do so.

Whether he was giving empowerment, instruction, or reading transmission, he always gave his full attention, taking his utmost care to bring benefit to the recipients—particularly when giving the sublime Dzogchen teachings. He was unlike many teachers who, lacking substance, supposedly give teachings on Dzogchen while only teaching the words. When Tulku Urgyen Rinpoche imparted the pointing-out instruction, he would point out the real thing, nakedly and directly.

Tulku Urgyen Rinpoche's way of giving a general outline of the ground, path, and fruition of the Great Perfection was not extraordinary compared to that of other masters. But if you asked him about one single word, no matter how subtle or profound the connotation, his answer was just as subtle and profound. Both Dzongsar Khyentse and I felt that compared to many months and years of studying books and going through analytical meditation, it was more beneficial to spend just a few hours asking questions of Tulku Urgyen Rinpoche and listening to his answers. I went to see him at Nagi Gompa many times and received various empowerments, but I feel the actual teachings were revealed in ordinary discussion.

These days you find people who say, "I know the teachings but I don't like to practice sadhana in large gatherings. I don't feel like doing all that chanting." Honestly, there are people who have said this to me, and it surely proves their lack of realization. Anyone who truly understands the teachings, especially the Vajrayana, will also know that these teachings are implemented in group sadhana, in development and completion stage training, and in chanting. That is the application of Vajrayana, and if someone talks but doesn't practice, then that person is definitely not learned.

Tulku Urgyen himself knew all about the encompassing activities of the Vajrayana and never belittled their application. He gave great attention to the performance of all the important rituals, including the drubchen ceremonies. In the first half of his life, in order to be of benefit to others, he learned these down to their minutest detail, never missing a single day. He also never belittled the consequence of any karmic action.

Without having to deliberately ask for donations, he managed to raise funds in an apparently effortless fashion. Tulku Urgyen was able to build all the temples and monasteries he intended to construct. Yet all these projects were totally completed on the side; you never saw them as his main aim or occupation.

In the latter part of his life, he basically abandoned all involvement in conceptual activities and didn't put any obvious effort into building. Yet temples still seemed to rise up continuously and many tasks were accomplished. He always spent the money that came during the day, and when the sun went down, he had nothing. He didn't keep a project schedule, and I never saw or heard about him sending out any fundraising letters, which are so plentiful these days. Even so, it seems he was able to build more temples than any other contemporary lama, no matter how much effort they put into it. So I feel confident that he accomplished his aims without hardship.

In terms of Vajrayana, he had perfected the practices of both development and completion. I know he spent at least four three-year retreats doing sadhana and recitation. Later, he remained in what you could call life-retreat at his hermitage, Nagi Gompa. The scriptures mention something called the "threefold gathering" and the "threefold blazing forth," which is achieved upon having perfected the practices of the development and completion stages. I feel he possessed these in entirety and taught these practices from the expanse of the view.

To truly practice development and completion stages and teach them, one needs to have actualized and stabilized the view. The great *dharmadhatu* is free of center and edges, coming and going, outer and inner. Resting in the equanimity of *rigpa*, out of this great emptiness, the unimpeded display, the great compassion, appears as the deity, indivisible and complete—empty but apparent, luminous yet empty. From this unified, empty luminosity, all the characteristics of the deity appear, completely perfect. The appearance is the deity; the mantra is the self-resounding sound; the deity and resounding sound unfold from the nongrasping mind, which is recognized devoid of solid reality. A realized being knows that it is not appearing from outside but from the nature of mind, without elaborations. The deity is the empty essence, the cognizant, clear nature—nonexistent, like an illusion; free of concept; luminous; and liberated upon arising. One's mind, free of elaboration, empty in essence, and luminous in nature is the completeness of the deity. This form unimpededly manifests as empty appearance, from which all phenomena arise; from within this state, the great display unfolds, and the mantra is recited.

The crucial point of the Nyingma teachings is that first the view is ascertained. In the new schools, the view is of the great purity, but it is considered inconceivable, as according to Rangzom Pandit's commentary *Ascertaining Appearances As the Deity*. First, the view has to be established according to the Nyingma way, which is very profound and precise. In the new schools, if the view of the great purity is not ascertained, then what does not exist needs to be created and that is complicated.

All that appears and exists is the great primordial purity, from the beginning. Do not grasp after the words; recognize the meaning. The expanse of the great purity is seeing things as they are: All appearances are the display of the deity. There is nothing to visualize; merely know things to be as they are. For the practitioner, the deity and oneself are the same. There is no big or small, good or bad. For the intellectual, the Dzogchen view just does not fit in their brains. But if it does, that is the way to practice a deity. Vajrayana begins with pure perception, the purity of all. As one's experience of that increases, it brings greater blessings. It is pure phenomena, free of any dualistic grasping, but if impure perceptions obscure this, then one is unable to experience pure phenomena. Some can talk about this but not really know it. The ultimate view in Vajrayana is pure perception. The basis is the buddha-nature, where there is no mention of pure or impure. It is completely pure. If you think that the deity and you are separate, that the deity is pure and you are impure, as a duality, then there is no way to accomplish a deity. All duality needs to be dispersed; once that happens, then one can practice deity yoga. The whole root of deity practice is realization of nonduality. That is the way to practice, and this is how Tulku Urgyen Rinpoche practiced and taught.

I feel certain that there is not the slightest difference between the state of mind of Tulku Urgyen Rinpoche and Samantabhadra. For those who regard him as Vajradhara in person, the perfect root guru and the support for their supplications, he is definitely extraordinary. To summarize, Tulku Urgyen Rinpoche was an incredible master, both learned and accomplished. Teachings should always be given upon request. So, since I was specifically asked, I have said what I personally know and have witnessed.

ORIGIN

Kunzang Yab Yum

Dzogchen Key Points

Tulku Urgyen Rinpoche

Our basic nature is essentially identical with the ground. It has two basic aspects: primordial purity *(kadag)* and spontaneous presence *(lhundrub)*. Our mind's empty essence is related to primordial purity, while its cognizant nature is linked to spontaneous presence.

Spontaneous presence literally means "that which appears and is present by itself." Besides our cognizant nature, it includes the deities that are experienced in the bardo as well as all the *Tögal* displays. In the same way, the pure wisdom realms that unfold out of the expanse of the three kayas, which is the state of rigpa devoid of clinging, are also experienced as a natural presence. To rephrase this, all the self-appearing and naturally present Tögal displays, the kayas and wisdoms, which unfold out of the state of dharmakaya, free of grasping, manifest from the primordially pure essence and spontaneously present nature, kadag, and lhundrub.

This *lhundrub* quality also pertains to samsaric experience. Spontaneous presence includes everything that "appears automatically," due to ignorance of our true nature: the worlds, beings, the three realms, the six classes, and all the rest of samsara. These all appear automatically; we don't need to imagine any of them. In other words, the samsaric states that unfold out of the ignorant dualistic mind are all experienced vividly and clearly. Mind and its objects—the perceived objects in the three realms of samsara and the perceiving dualistic mind with its three poisons—all unfold within the arena of dualistic mind, *sem*. We don't need to visualize our world. The *sems* experiences include the different experiences of the six classes of beings, which are visible yet intangible. Currently our "impure" samsaric experience is clearly present and quite tangible. We can touch the things around us, right? In "pure" awareness, known as the kayas and wisdoms, experience takes place in a way that is visible yet insubstantial. This immaterial or nonphysical quality means that the experience is something you can see but not grasp—like a rainbow.

The *sambhogakaya* buddhas and realms unfold, visible yet intangible; they are insubstantial like a rainbow in the unconfined sky of *dharmakaya*. After you first recognize your basic state of primordial purity and then perfect its strength and attain stability, your body returns to rainbow light. In other words, within this very body, your realization is equal to that of sambhogakaya. All the inconceivable adornments and sceneries belonging to sambhogakaya are then as visible as rainbows in the sky. Unlike sentient beings in samsara's three realms, who experience things in a material way, the displays of kayas and wisdom are immaterial and unconditioned. Have you ever heard of a sambhogakaya buddha needing to visit the toilet? That's because they are insubstantial, not material. The six types of beings, on the other hand, must defecate and urinate after they eat. That's direct proof of their corporeality. Deities are in an incorporeal state, celestial and rainbow-like. You can't eat rainbows and then shit them out! With a rainbow body, there is no thought of food; but ordinary sentient beings, who have material bodies, can't go without food. If they do, they die of starvation. The materiality I am speaking of here has three aspects: the material body of flesh and blood, the material disposition that needs food as fuel, and the material mind that is born and dies, arises, and ceases. The deities' immaterial purity lies beyond those three, beyond every kind of materiality. This is why we say their bodies are made of rainbow light. In short, samsara is material substance and nirvana is insubstantial.

We hear the deities described as having bodies of light and living in an insubstantial mansion in an immaculate realm—but that is only how it appears from our point of view. The notion of being beyond corporeality is an adaptation to the habitual tendencies of samsaric beings, because we live in material places, in material houses, and have material bodies. From the deities' point of view, there is no such concept whatsoever.

The complete aspects of the Dzogchen empowerments authorize the yogi to embark on Tögal practice. But without cutting through with *Trekchö*, one doesn't directly cross with Tögal. Trekchö means that you have the basic state of primordial purity pointed out to you, at which point you must recognize it and then train in stabilizing that recognition.

The way to approach Dzogchen practice is this: Begin with the *ngöndro*, the preliminaries; follow that with yidam practice, for instance, the recitation of the peaceful and wrathful deities of *Kunzang Tuktig*; then continue with the actual training in Trekchö. Later, as an enhancement of Trekchö, there is

Tögal practice. All these Dharma practices should be applied. When training in Trekchö, leave your mind free of clinging. When practicing Tögal, though there is no clinging, one still applies four key points.

For all dharma practice, you need preliminary steps, just like laying the foundation when you construct a house. We begin the Dzogchen path with the ngöndro for this reason. Throughout innumerable past lives, we have created immeasurable negative karma and obscurations. The ngöndro purifies every misdeed and obscuration created through our physical, verbal, and mental actions. Having gone through a complete ngöndro, you come to the main part next, which is like building a palace upon the solid foundation. It may have many stories, but no matter how many there are, they will now all remain stable. The main part is composed of two stages: development and completion. Development stage, in this case, is the visualization of and recitation for one's personal yidam deity. Yidam practice is then followed by the completion stage, which is Trekchö.

Trekchö means recognizing that our essence is primordially pure. The basis for Tögal is recognizing, at the same time, that our natural display is spontaneously present. Then, recognizing that the natural display, the spontaneous presence, is insubstantial and devoid of any self-nature is the ultimate path—the unity of primordial purity and spontaneous presence, which we call the unity of Trekchö and Tögal. Trekchö and Tögal correspond to the two aspects known as the "path of liberation" and the "path of means." By combining Trekchö and Tögal in the Dzogchen system, you experience the natural displays of the peaceful and wrathful deities within this lifetime, without having to wait for the *bardo*. Since the entire path has been traversed during your life, there is nothing more to train in or to purify during the bardo state.

To reiterate, having thoroughly done the ngöndro, you then proceed with the development stage of the yidam deity. The tantras mention that you have to quadruple all practices during our age. Whereas in the past it was sufficient to chant 100,000 mantras for each syllable, these days one must chant 400,000 per syllable. Spend however many months it takes to do the recitation in retreat. Ngöndro practices and recitations have set numbers, but Trekchö has no set number, not even a time limit. One doesn't "finish" Trekchö after a couple of months or years—as long as there is life, there is Trekchö training. You never hear anybody say, "Now I've finished Trekchö!" Throughout one's entire life, the nature of mind must be recognized. On the other hand, you can master or accomplish Trekchö, where you have absolutely no delusion anymore, either day or night. At that point, you can truly say you have gone beyond Trekchö. However, I do believe that for the rest of this life there will be sufficient reason to practice. Read the guidance manuals thoroughly, many times. When you really understand them, you will understand the meaning of Dzogchen.

Neither Trekchö nor Tögal is a formal meditation practice. Trekchö means simply acknowledging that your basic essence is empty, and Tögal is the natural display of what is spontaneously present. The essence and its displays are not our creation; we do not fabricate them by practicing. In both Trekchö and Tögal, you do not create anything with your imagination but merely rest in the natural state.

To express it slightly differently, Trekchö is recognizing that our natural state or basic essence is primordially pure. Tögal is recognizing that the natural displays of this primordial purity are spontaneously present. And recognizing that this natural display is insubstantial—that the natural manifestations of the five wisdoms as five-colored light are not something you can take hold of—is the unity of primordial purity and spontaneous presence. These two aspects, primordial purity and spontaneous presence, are not separate and distinct, like your two arms. They are an indivisible unity, because the empty quality of mind-essence is primordial purity, while the cognizant quality is spontaneous presence. Hence, they are totally indivisible; therefore, Trekchö and Tögal are fundamentally indivisible.

You wouldn't describe Tögal as a meditation practice, but you could say it is a training, because we apply key points. I would like to stress again that Tögal is not a matter of imagining or meditating upon anything; the displays that appear are the expressions of natural purity. If you train properly and apply the key points, all the Tögal displays evolve naturally.

Many Dzogchen teachings are connected to a sadhana involving the peaceful and wrathful deities, like *Kunzang Tuktig*, because the displays include these deities. The practice lets whatever is already present within you become visible; nothing else manifests. Since the peaceful and wrathful deities are already present within your body, they become visible during Tögal practice. The deities in Tögal are the same ones that will appear in the bardo. So, if the complete mandala has manifested during your life, no second mandala needs to appear in the bardo state—it doesn't manifest twice. This is why many Dzogchen teachings emphasize the mandala of the peaceful and wrathful deities.

We can practice the peaceful and wrathful deities on many levels, such as in Mahayoga, Anu Yoga, and Ati Yoga. Chokgyur Lingpa, for instance, revealed sadhanas for all three vehicles. For Ati Yoga, he revealed the *Kunzang Tuktig,* as well as one belonging to the *Dzogchen Desum.* You can also base your Dzogchen practice on the guru principle, since the enlightened master embodies everything. For example, the mind treasure of Jigmey Lingpa, called *Tigle Gyachen,* is based on the single figure of Longchenpa. Thus, there are various approaches, and it is really good to do such practices. Whether you are sitting down or moving about, whatever situation you are in, always remember Trekchö—recognizing the nature of mind. It is the very core, the very heart of Dzogchen practice.

The first experiences we will have at the moment of death are the sounds, colors, and lights; however, these will not be vague, feeble, or limited, as they are now, but intense and overwhelming. The colors then are iridescent hues, while the lights are sharp like needle points, similar to looking directly into the sun. The colors indicate enlightened body, the sounds indicate enlightened speech, and the lights indicate enlightened mind. That is why *The Tibetan Book of the Dead* reminds the dying person, "Do not be afraid of these lights. Do not fear the sounds. Do not be terrified by the colors."

In the bardo, yogis who grew somewhat familiar with Tögal practice during their lives can remain unafraid, free of terror or dread, because they know that the colors, sounds, and lights are their own manifestations—the natural displays of their buddha-nature's body, speech, and mind. These initial manifestations are a prelude to the rest of the bardo. Ordinary people, however, become totally overwhelmed by the immensity of the displays.

The sounds in the bardo are not small noises—they roar like 100,000 simultaneous thunderclaps—and the lights and colors shine with the brilliance of 100,000 suns. Later, when the deities begin to appear, the largest are the size of Mount Sumeru, while the smallest are no bigger than a mustard seed. The deities are vibrantly alive and dance about. Faced with this spectacle, you have two options: either you panic with fright or you recognize them as your natural displays. This is why it is incredibly beneficial to practice in this life, so you grow familiar with your natural displays. Otherwise, facing them in the bardo will result in deep confusion and bewilderment.

Even if you are an accomplished Buddhist scholar who knows a lot of dharma, can debate, and all the rest, without this familiarity you will still become terrified and panic at the awesome display in the bardo. You can't debate with these deities; you can't explain them away. But if you follow the Vajrayana path and grow familiar with the unified path of development and completion, you will surely recognize all this to be your own manifestation—which will be of real benefit.

That is why *The Tibetan Book of the Dead* emphasizes, "Do not be afraid of your own displays." There is no reason to be afraid of yourself, no need to be overwhelmed by your own sounds, colors, and lights. You can also cross the bardo successfully if you have become fully trained in Mahamudra and the six doctrines, but success is guaranteed if you have attained stability in Trekchö and Tögal. Trekchö is recognizing that the *dharmata* of mind and the colors and lights are all dharmata's natural displays and that the sounds are the self-resounding of dharmata. We must recognize that these manifestations, visible yet insubstantial, come from nowhere else. Understand this, truly, and the Lord of Death will have no hold upon you.

It is incredibly important to grow familiar with these displays during this lifetime, by practicing the unity of Trekchö and Tögal, because sooner or later everybody ends up in the bardo and these manifestations will definitely appear. These intense bardo experiences are not exclusive to just a few people or to Buddhists, nor does it help to say, "I don't have to worry about those bardo experiences, because I don't believe in anything after death." The bardo experiences don't care what you think. They appear to everyone. Avoid the sorry fate of most people, who get completely overwhelmed believing the displays of their own buddha-nature to be devils coming to torture them and carry them off to hell. What a pity that would be!

Background

Tulku Urgyen Rinpoche

During the last century, there was a great master named Dzongsar Khyentse Chökyi Lodrö, who was like a replica stamped from the same mold as his predecessor, Jamyang Khyentse Wangpo. He possessed perfect realization and perfect learning and activity. At one point, in Kham, he was renowned as the greatest master. He passed away in Sikkim after fleeing Tibet, where I met him during a visit there. At that time, Chökyi Lodrö was living quietly and not receiving any visitors, except I was able to see him every day and receive teachings. I would ask Chökyi Lodrö questions during these visits.

One day I asked Dzongsar Khyentse what teaching I should practice. "The Great Perfection will blaze like a wildfire during this coming age," he replied, paraphrasing the famous prophesy, "When the flames of the Dark Age rage rampantly, the teachings of Vajrayana will blaze like wildfire."

Dzongsar Khyentse explained that during the early days of Buddhism in Tibet, when the Dharma was just beginning to spread, three masters—Padmasambhava, Vimalamitra, and Vairotsana—brought the teachings of the Great Perfection to Tibet. These teachings flourished widely. Later on, the teachings of the Great Perfection were upheld by means of terma revelations. Terma revelations are like crops that ripen in the autumn. Every year, there's a new crop, and each season it is freshly harvested and enjoyed, as the crop to be used at that time. In the same way, the terma teachings are concealed and revealed at later periods in history. They appear in varying forms appropriate to the different time-periods when they are to be revealed. When the time comes for the various terma teachings to be revealed, great tertöns appear in this world. They are able to dive into lakes, fly up to impossible locations in caves, and take objects out of solid rock. My great-grandfather, Chokgyur Lingpa, was one of those masters who revealed the Lotus-Born Master's hidden treasures.

As Dzongsar Khyentse told me, "Each major tertön must reveal a minimum of three major themes: Guru Sadhana, Great Perfection, and

Avalokiteshvara. In our time, Old Khyentse and Chokling were specifically endowed with seven transmissions."

Dzongsar Khyentse continued explaining that over the centuries, various cycles of Great Perfection teachings came to light and spread among people. The older tradition flourished all the way until the time of Chetsun Senge Wangchuk. Later on, Longchenpa codified the teachings into *The Four Branches of Heart Essence*, which flourished. Later still, there were the Great Perfection teachings of the *Tawa Long-Yang, The Vast Expanse of the View*, revealed by Dorje Lingpa, and Rigdzin Gödem's Dzogchen revelation called the *Gongpa Sangtal, The Direct Showing of the Realization of Samantabhadra*. Jatsön Nyingpo revealed the *Könchog Chidü*, and later on, Jigmey Lingpa revealed the root scriptures of the innermost essence.

The chief termas throughout all these centuries were revealed by the three eminent tertöns: Nyang Ral Nyima Özer, Guru Chöwang, and Rigdzin Gödem, "the vidyadhara with vulture feathers." Each teaching was appropriate for its own age. Recently, Jamyang Khyentse Wangpo, Jamgön Kongtrül, and Chokgyur Lingpa revealed several cycles of the Great Perfection. Chokgyur Lingpa personally revealed seven Nyingtig cycles. But now, during this time period, there are two particular teachings, one revealed by Jamyang Khyentse and one by Chokgyur Lingpa, which will be very influential for the age we are in now. One text is the *Chetsün Nyingtig*, revealed by Jamyang Khyentse Wangpo, while the other is Chokgyur Lingpa's *Kunzang Tuktig*. These practices were personally applied by the two "siddha kings" who lived in recent times, both disciples of Jamyang Khyentse: mahasiddha Shakya Shri and mahasiddha Adzom Drugpa. Both practiced these cycles. Dzongsar Khyentse recommended that I focus on the *Kunzang Tuktig*, because it is very suitable in this day and age. He pointed to the last statement made by Padmasambhava in the *Leyjang* section of the text, where it says, "When the Dark Age arrives, this teaching will cause the heart of Samantabhadra's Dzogchen teachings to spread and flourish."

> *This activity practice, the Manifest Essence,*
> *Which benefits whoever encounters it,*
> *Will spread the heart-teaching of Samantabhadra,*
> *From the conclusion of the Dark Age until the end of this aeon.*

Intent:
To Recognize Mind's Nature

Tulku Urgyen Rinpoche

Kunzang Tuktig belongs to the Great Perfection, and, therefore, its exclusive focus is on recognizing mind-essence. That is the entire intent. The sadhana involving the one hundred peaceful and wrathful *sugatas* is a very precious and profound support for that. The mandala of peaceful and wrathful deities includes any possible yidam, the Three Jewels, the Three Roots, the deities of the three kayas, and so forth, in myriad ways. They are not something different from the inner core of our basic nature. Often they are called the deities naturally dwelling in the mandala of one's vajra body. In other words, through this practice and training, we realize the various aspects of our basic nature.

That is the support of this practice, which is not limited to a retreat situation or a certain stretch of time. This practice of *Kunzang Tuktig* is a sufficient path for our entire life; it is not something we finish after a while.

It is not like that at all; it is for our entire life. Yidam practice means something we bring into our life in any situation, at any moment, not only when we're sitting down. Therefore, the *Kunzang Tuktig* is something you bring along, whether you sit or walk, in whatever you are doing. Don't have the idea that you should stop after a set number of recitations. On the contrary, continue it for your entire life. You may not count in the same way or do the practice with the same number of sessions, but still it would be excellent to do the sadhana at least once a day for your entire life and to do a certain number of recitations in that session.

This is such a profound support, because it contains all the different aspects of Vajrayana practice. Since it belongs to Dzogchen, you're not limited by a material situation; you also have what is mentally created—both materially present as well as mentally created. So the offerings, the praises, all the different aspects you usually find in the Seven Branches—prostrating, apologizing, making offerings, rejoicing, requesting to turn the wheel of dharma, beseeching not to pass into nirvana, and dedicating the merit for all beings—you can train in all these on a mental level. You don't need to have something materially present, and the same is true for all the other aspects of the sadhana that are the support.

To do this practice is an immense great fortune, because the tantras are contained in Mahayoga, which is contained in the scriptures of Anu Yoga, and these are contained in the pith instructions of Ati Yoga. Ati Yoga is contained within the sadhana practice, and the sadhana is contained within the daily, personal application. Mahayoga has an incredibly extensive and profound scope or perspective, which is primarily presented in the eighteen tantras of Mahayoga. Anu Yoga has the four major or grand scriptures. Ati Yoga has the seventeen Dzogchen tantras, in addition to the tantra of *The Brilliant Expanse of the Blazing Sun of Samantabhadri* and a nineteenth one, *The Tröma Nagmo Tantra* of Ekajati. That is the perspective of Ati Yoga, but all of that is included within one sadhana text, and the sadhana text is embodied in one's personal application. To practice a sadhana text such as *Kunzang Tuktig* as a daily sadhana accumulates immense merit and will purify a vast amount of obscurations. It is a great fortune.

When the buddhas teach, they teach in various ways adapted to the different types of recipients. When the recipients are *shravakas,* it is not possible for the buddhas to teach the three principles of deity, mantra, and samadhi. They are not taught to the *pratyekabuddha* type either. To some extent, these three principles are taught, but not completely, to Mahayana type people. Only the Vajrayana has two main aspects, called the outer and inner tantras. The outer tantras—Kriya, Upa, and Yoga—do not give the complete teaching either. The divine principles are introduced, but in Kriya Yoga they always appear as superior to oneself, and one is an inferior ordinary being. In other words, the deity is like a king, and one is like a subject, with an emphasis on the purity of the deity. In Upa, the perspective changes slightly, where the deity becomes like an older brother. In the Yoga Tantra, one is equal to the deity, but it is still dualistic.

In the inner tantras, the perspective is radically different. From the very onset, everything is all-encompassing purity. In other words, this body in itself is a mandala of the victorious ones, in the sense that the five aggregates, in their pure nature, are the five male buddhas. The five elements are the five female buddhas. The sense bases[2], *(ayatanas),* the consciousnesses, and their objects are the male and female bodhisattvas, and so forth. The *nirmanakaya* quality of disturbing emotions, symbolized by the arrival of the buddhas into this world in different realms, is also included. Buddha Shakyamuni, for example, is one of thousands of nirmanakaya buddhas of this aeon, but only in one of the six realms.

In the mandala of the forty-two peaceful deities, all the buddhas of the six realms are represented. In total, there are forty-two peaceful forms. Right now, even without the sadhana, this mandala of deities is present. The mandala of forty-two peaceful deities is present within our own heart; the wrathful forms of these are present inside our skull, within what is called the "bone mansion." In our throat is the mandala of the pure vidyadharas with consorts. In our navel chakra is Vajra Yogini, and in the secret chakra is Vajra Kilaya—not just as a single deity but surrounded by the mandala of the eaters, slayers, sons, and dancers, seventy-two altogether. This is what is called the "original mandala of the victorious ones, the mandala of the human body." This is the extraordinary aspect of Vajrayana.

Vajrayana, in short, is characterized as having an abundance of methods with minor hardships and being suited to people of sharper faculties. This is why Vajrayana is extraordinary. When condensing all the extensive and profound principles into the very basics, then all the mandalas of all deities are included within the sole indivisible unity of emptiness and cognizance. Training in that as the main principle is what will allow you to accomplish all buddhas. Our experience is comprised of two basic aspects, mind and objects, or phenomena. Mind, the doer, is Samantabhadra; objects, the deed, are in essence the female buddha, Samantabhadri. These two represent the nonduality of emptiness and experience, which itself is the primary source, the root of all tantric deities.

The fact that everything perceived, all sights, are of divine nature, is called all appearances are the deity; whatever is heard, all sounds have the nature of mantra; and all activity of mind has the nature of awakened state, samadhi. Bringing this to mind, reminding oneself of this, is to acknowledge things to be as they are. That is the main principle of Vajrayana. But this is relating to things in an external way. Internally, we focus on the main training of recognizing the undivided empty cognizance, which is in fact the three kayas of the awakened state. In this way, the special quality of Vajrayana is to not have any separation between inside and outside in the training of development and completion; in the training of deity, mantra, and *samadhi;* and in the recognition of mind-essence as the three kayas.

When you actually chant it, start with the supplication to the lineage masters, refuge, and bodhichitta all the way down to the mantra, ending with the verse of auspiciousness. Learn how to do the tunes and the traditional application. It is pretty simple.

Vajrayana is also represented as the "four great gates"[3]. The first is the gate of *mudras,* the second is the gate of offerings, the third is the gate of recitation, and the fourth is the gate of samadhi. These are extremely important. When looking at a person who knows these four gates and can manifest or apply them, it seems like a lot of childish play. Practitioners move their hands in the air, carry stuff around, sing different tunes, recite verses and mantras, wear hats and costumes, and so forth. All this looks like childish play, and some people find it extremely superficial and beside the point, whereas the "real thing" is to look into mind-essence. Anyone who says this lacks real understanding, because it is incredibly significant. All four gates are important. Never regard them as pointless or insignificant. It is said that if the three yogas are disconnected from the melodious tunes, the tradition of Vajrayana will fade away and vanish.

One may wonder, "What is the use of practicing a sadhana like the *Kunzang Tuktig*? What is the benefit?" Actually, the words one says aloud are all reminders of the great, naturally existing mandala of deity, mantra, and samadhi. There are no other words than those, and they are all significant. It is an incredibly practical way to embody the intent of the inner tantras as the sadhana application.

APPLICATION

Sambhogakaya Peaceful and Wrathful Deities

Structure of the *Kunzang Tuktig*
Cycle of Teachings

Tulku Urgyen Rinpoche

THE TEXTS

The *Kunzang Tuktig* terma, itself, consists primarily of three termas:

- The sadhana, which is called *Leyjang*;
- The empowerment texts, including both the general empowerment of the peaceful and wrathful ones and the extraordinary empowerment of ground, path, and fruition; and
- The *Triyig*, the guidance manual by the name of *Döntri*.

Over the years, Karma Khenpo, one of the chief disciples of Chokgyur Lingpa and an emanation of Khenpo Bodhisattva, the great master Shantarakshita, who was also an excellent poet, wrote an explanation of the guidance manual. Tersey Tulku, my uncle, added an apology and mending appendix, titled the *Zurgyen*, at the end of the sadhana. Kyabje Dilgo Khyentse also wrote a commentary on the guidance manual, as requested by the Neten Chokling before he passed away in Bir. Finally, there are some writings by Jedrung Rinpoche, a great master from Riwoche Monastery in Kham, a very important Taklung Kagyü Monastery. Jedrung Rinpoche wrote another empowerment text as well as different commentaries. We should understand, however, that the terma itself was revealed in its entirety, unlike some other termas, where a fraction is discovered and left at that. It is complete, in itself; nothing is missing whatsoever. Although it is very concise, it is complete. In the colophon at the end of text, Padmasambhava explains, "This is a complete sadhana condensed from all the tantras. It is simple to apply, concise, and complete. For the benefit of future generations, may it meet with the destined one." The destined one refers to Chokgyur

Lingpa, who later revealed it. The text also mentions that Yeshe Tsogyal should write it down for this purpose and that the Dzogchen teachings will flourish at the end of the Dark Age.

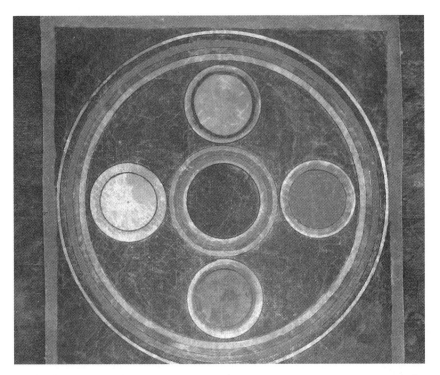

Mandala

Train in Indivisibility

Tulku Urgyen Rinpoche[4]

As I have mentioned numerous times, the way to train in the unity of development and completion is to begin any visualization with the samadhi of suchness, recognizing your own nature and remaining in that. In that very moment, you are actually in the state of the primordially pure essence. The samadhi of illumination then occurs as the natural expression of rigpa. Mind-essence is the unity of being empty and cognizant. The empty aspect is the samadhi of suchness, the primordial purity, the dharmakaya. From this, the spontaneously present phenomena manifest, and this is the second, the samadhi of illumination. The unobstructed cognizant aspect is the samadhi of illumination, the sambhogakaya. Thus, emptiness has a compassionate flavor. The expression of the primordially pure essence, the unconstructed nature, is naturally compassionate. These two—emptiness and compassion—are indivisible. That is the vital point.

To repeat, the empty quality is primordial purity, and the manifest aspect is a spontaneous, compassionate presence. This unity of emptiness and compassion is the basis of all dharma practice, and it is this unity that takes the form of the seed syllable. That is the third samadhi, the samadhi of the seed syllable, which is the nirmanakaya. The unity of being empty and compassionate appears as the seed syllable that is the spiritual life force of the deity you are practicing. For example, if you are practicing Guru Rinpoche, his spiritual life force is HRIH.

Once the seed syllable appears, it sends out E, which is the seed syllable of space, and then YAM for wind, RAM for fire, KAM for water, LAM for earth, SUM for Mt. Sumeru, and finally BHRUM for the celestial palace at the top of Mt. Sumeru. Next, the syllable HRIH descends like a shooting star, lands on the throne within the celestial palace, and transforms into the deity. All this takes place without having to leave behind the state of mind-essence. Without leaving the empty suchness samadhi of rigpa behind, the compassionate illumination of spontaneous presence unfolds unobstructedly from the primordially pure essence. The development stage can take place while recognizing mind-essence, since its expression is unobstructed. If the essence were obstructed, the development stage could not arise; but it isn't so. The development stage is allowed to develop, to manifest, without harming the primordial purity one bit. Without moving away from unchanging primordial purity, the spontaneous presence, the expression of awareness, takes place. This is the indivisibility of primordial purity and spontaneous presence.

This is also why development and completion are basically a unity. The *developed* in development stage refers to "what is formed as an expression of unobstructed awareness." Thought, on the other hand, can obstruct rigpa. When the expression moves as thought, there is delusion. Ordinary thinking is the process of forming one thought, then thinking of something else, and so on, incessantly. The new thought interrupts the previous one, and the next thought interrupts that one. True development stage is not like that at all. The key point lies in this unobstructed quality of rigpa; the samadhi of illumination does not cut off the samadhi of suchness. The seed syllable manifesting in the middle of space doesn't obstruct the compassionate emptiness. In fact, it is the *expression* of compassionate emptiness. Thus, you are not only allowed to let visualization unfold out of compassionate emptiness; it is the real way to practice.

This type of development stage takes place without having to leave behind the state of mind-essence. There is no need to avoid recognizing mind-essence in order to think of these things; let them unfold naturally. Simply allow the visualization to unfold out of compassionate emptiness, the unity of empty cognizance. This is called "letting development stage unfold out of the completion stage." In this way, there is no real separation between them. Otherwise, a common misunderstanding is that the development stage steals the completion stage, and that later you have to kick out the development stage to give the completion stage a chance. Similarly, when you start to think of one thing, the previous thought disappears. That is called "visualizing with dualistic mind."

This is how it may seem in the beginning, when you are being taught, but, really, it isn't like that at all. The reason is that primordial purity and spontaneous presence are a natural unity; they cannot really be divided. If they weren't a unity, you would have only primordial purity, a void state where nothing can take place, or a spontaneous presence that was the same as dualistic mind. There would be a battle between dharmakaya and sambhogakaya. In actuality, there is no conflict, because spontaneous presence is indivisible from primordial purity. You are not only definitely allowed to let the development stage unfold from within the completion stage, but also it is perfectly all right and permissible to do so. There is no conflict between the two. As a famous saying goes, "Some say development stage is right. Others say completion stage is right. They pitch development against completion."

The unity of emptiness and cognizance has an unobstructed capacity. If it were obstructed, we wouldn't be able to know anything. It would be a total blank. If cognizance and emptiness were not a unity, one of them would occur when thinking and the other when not thinking. Conceptual thought obstructs, and confines; this is how development and completion can be obstructed. However, the expression of awareness is unimpeded. If this were not so, rigpa would not have any capacity. But the essence *does* have a capacity. The dharmakaya and sambhogakaya *do* manifest.

Dharmakaya is a totally unconstructed state, and sambhogakaya is the great enjoyment, meaning an abundance of perfect qualities. From the empty essence of primordial purity, the spontaneously present nature manifests unobstructedly. Likewise, we are allowed to practice the development stage unobstructedly. Otherwise, without the samadhi of suchness, development stage would be an imitation. We might even think the wrathful deities were literally angry!

Rainbows give us a very good way to understand this. When a rainbow appears in the sky, it doesn't damage the empty sky at all, and yet the rainbow is totally visible. It doesn't change the sky or hurt it in the slightest. It's exactly the same when recognizing the essence of mind, which has been pointed out as being utterly empty. That is the samadhi of suchness. That recognition doesn't have to be left behind in order for cognizance, the samadhi of illumination, to be present; it is spontaneously present by nature. That is true compassion. The sky is the samadhi of suchness, while the rainbow is the samadhi of illumination, the development stage. There is no fight between space and a rainbow, is there? It's exactly like that. First of all, you need to know the samadhi of suchness. Having recognized that, the expression of awareness arises from the essence as the development stage. It is not like construction work. Like the rainbow appearing in the sky, the expression of awareness is the perfect unity of development and completion stages.

Applying this approach is not always possible for every practitioner. The next best way is when you think of one detail at a time, like the head of the deity, the arms, the legs, the body, the attributes, and so forth. Every once in a while, you'll recognize who is visualizing, and again you'll arrive at the state of original empty wakefulness. Then again think of some visualized details, and again recognize, alternating back and forth between the two. That is called the "next best," the medium way of practicing. The least, or minimum, requirement is to first think that everything becomes empty. Recite the mantra OM MAHA SUNYATA ... and after that say, "From the state of emptiness, such-and-such appears." In this way, think of one thing at a time, and at the end of the sadhana, again dissolve the whole thing into emptiness. These are three ways to practice development and completion together.

However, while again and again recognizing your buddha-nature, you can allow the visualization to take place unobstructedly. There is no law that you have to think of one thing after another. The expression of awareness is unobstructed. It is not like bricklaying, where one puts things on top of each other in a very concrete way. Whatever unfolds out of the samadhi of suchness is like a rainbow. The celestial palace and the deities are all like rainbows. This rainbow manifestation doesn't have to somehow block off the space in which it unfolds. It is not necessary at all. The first two samadhis are the unity of primordial purity and spontaneous presence. In the seed samadhi, the word *seed* means it is the "source" or "origin" of the whole mandala and all the deities. The seed syllable is also called the "life-essence of the mind," the deity's mental life force. As mentioned before, for Guru Rinpoche, that is the syllable HRIH, which begins the visualization. But remember, this HRIH and whatever follows are not tangible or material.

The authentic way of practicing is to let visualizations of the development state unfold out of the samadhi of suchness. That is the best, foremost way. The samadhi of suchness is the dharmakaya state. The samadhi of illumination is the sambhogakaya state, and the seed samadhi is the nirmanakaya state. In actuality, all of samsara and nirvana unfold from the expanse of the three kayas. This is the example for the unity of development and completion stages.

Here is another way to understand development stage. All things take place from within the space of the five mothers, meaning the five female buddhas. The five elements are empty yet the cognizant quality knows them. This perceiving quality is the male buddha Samantabhadra, the *yab*, while the empty quality is the female buddha Samantabhadri, the *yum*. The outer objects, the five elements, are not the perceivers; they are the empty aspect. In actuality, the five elements are the five female buddhas. In the impure state, we perceive them as being earth, fire, water, wind, and space, but they are, in fact, the properties of the five female buddhas. In this way, everything in this world is already the mandala of the five female buddhas. Within this type of celestial palace is the pure nature of the five aggregates, the five male buddhas. We are not inventing anything here; this is our basic state as it is. Mind and phenomena, the experiencer and the experienced, are Samantabhadra and consort. In the development stage, we don't perpetuate ordinary impure perception in any way whatsoever. Everything is regarded as the pure wisdom deities, the unity of experience and emptiness.

All phenomena are already, by nature, the unity of experience and emptiness. All experiences, all things in this world and in your life, are already the unity of experience and emptiness. There is nothing that is not empty. The essence of development is the experiencing aspect. The essence of completion is the empty aspect. These two are primordially a unity. There is nothing impure whatsoever. This is how everything already is. Therefore, everything already takes place as the unity of development stage and completion stage. When practicing development and completion stages, you are training yourself in seeing things as they actually are. You are seeing *as it is*, not as pure fantasy that has no basis whatsoever.

Dzogchen has two quintessential principles: primordial purity and spontaneous presence. Primordial purity is the empty aspect and spontaneous presence is the experiencing aspect. These are an original unity. When training in development stage and completion stage, we train in manifesting as a pure form, which is already the case. This is the basic situation of everything, how it really *is*. Reality is already the unity of male and female buddhas, in the sense of the indivisibility of primordial purity and spontaneous presence. The whole mandala with the deity is a display of primordial purity indivisible from spontaneous presence.

This indivisible unity also appears as the deities in the bardo. Likewise, the deities in Tögal practice are the unity of primordial purity and spontaneous presence. In these two instances, the mandala of the deities of your own body arise, or manifest, like rainbows in the sky. These deities are five-colored lights, as a sign of the indivisibility of primordial purity and spontaneous presence. In both cases, these things are as they are; you don't need to think that what isn't, is. Your own deities appear to you.

From the perspective of the manifest aspect of buddha-nature, the deities can be said to abide in our body. These deities of the development stage *do* appear to us in the bardo and in Tögal practice. Our own deities manifest to us. In terms of the essence of our mind, nonexistence is primordial purity; existence is spontaneous presence. Our essence is the unity of existence and nonexistence. The deities are the experienced aspect; this is how things are. This is the preciousness of development stage; it is not an unimportant point.

If, in the state of primordial purity, there were no aspect of experiencing spontaneous presence, nothing would happen. However, this is not the case, because these two, primordial purity and spontaneous presence, are a unity. *Primordial purity* means the "absence," no concrete thing, the empty quality, whereas *spontaneous presence* means the "presence." It is not a case of having "only absence" or "only presence;" they are indivisible. The primordial indivisibility of absence and presence is a very good example. Experience and emptiness are a unity. The experiencing aspect is development, and the empty aspect is completion. The rainbow in the sky is not tangible, but it's still visible. There is no "thing," and yet there is something. That is a very good example. Also, rainbows only appear in the sky. You don't have rainbows in wood or in stone, and so on.

All phenomena are the unity of existence and nonexistence. Primordial purity and spontaneous presence are a unity. The kayas and wisdoms are a unity. There is a quote that goes, "All the scriptures say that everything is empty, but the fact that our nature is not empty of the kayas and wisdoms, that is the real tradition of the Buddha." This is how it really is. In the second turning of the wheel of dharma, the Buddha said that everything, from the aggregate of form all the way up to and including omniscient enlightenment, is empty and devoid of self-entity. Of course that is correct, but it is not the full truth; that statement emphasizes the empty quality. Liberation is only possible through realizing the basic unity of emptiness and experience. Like space, the empty aspect cannot get liberated.

All phenomena are the unity of experience and emptiness. Without the experience aspect, the kayas and wisdoms would be hidden and would never manifest. Kayas and wisdoms are very important principles. It is said, "If the kayas and wisdoms are empty, there is no fruition." If the state of fruition is empty, it is just like space, which is called "nothing whatsoever." *Just like space* means there's "nothing to understand, nothing there." Think about this. Everything is of course empty, but not empty of the kayas and wisdoms, in the sense that they are nonexistent or absent. If the kayas and wisdoms were absent, there would be no twenty-five attributes of fruition. If they were absent, how could there be five kayas, five types of speech, five wisdoms, five qualities, and five activities? The twenty-five attributes of fruition are not some kind of concrete material substance. There is ground, path, and fruition—not only ground and path. If everything were empty, there wouldn't be the two kayas of dharmakaya and rupakaya. The dharmakaya—free from constructs, like space—is defined as "dissolved yet unobscured." *Dissolved* here means "totally free of all disturbing emotions." At the same time, *wisdom,* meaning "original wakefulness," is unobscured. That is the meaning of *dissolved yet unobscured. This is also called the "dharmakaya of basic brilliance."* Dharmakaya is not empty or devoid of a cognizant quality.

Furthermore, in terms of experience, dharmakaya is primordially the unity of experience and emptiness. Primordial purity is the empty aspect, while spontaneous presence is the experience aspect. These two are a unity. That is why we say that the kayas and wisdoms are a unity. Dharmakaya is a body of space, free from constructs. Sambhogakaya is a body like a rainbow. The five buddhas of the five families are called the "bodies of the wisdoms of distinguished characteristics"—white, red, yellow, green, and blue, the five lights.

Once again, first there are two kayas: dharmakaya and *rupakaya.* The rupakaya consists of two types: the sambhogakaya, which is of rainbow light, and the nirmanakaya, which is a material body of flesh and blood possessing the six elements.

If we claim everything is empty, then who would there be to know that? There wouldn't be anything. There would be no wisdom, no original wakefulness. The wakefulness knowing the original nature is a type of knowing that does not depend on an object. Thought, on the other hand, cannot stir without depending upon an object. When you say *original wakefulness, (yeshe,)* or wisdom, by definition it signifies "a knowing that has no object." When you say *thought, (namshey,)* it signifies "a knowing that has the structure of subject and object." Yeshe is a knowing that doesn't fixate in a dualistic way, whereas our ordinary knowing is dualistic fixation. Dualistic fixation should be destroyed. That is the whole reason why we strive so diligently in meditation and recognize mind-essence. Yeshe is primordial knowing. We get used to primordial knowing by recognizing our essence as primordial purity. Nondualistic wakefulness destroys dualistic fixation. When dualistic fixation is destroyed, deluded experience falls apart, and all conceptual activity collapses. We should become completely clear and resolved about this.

Ultimately, the vital point is the difference between consciousness and wakefulness, namshey and yeshe. Consciousness is a way of knowing in which there is subject and object and in which the subject gets involved in the object. The state of realization of all the buddhas, on the other hand, is a primordial knowing that is independent from an object. Trekchö training reveals this state of realization. If we, on the other hand, believe that our basic state is only empty, a blank empty state, this emptiness wouldn't possess any qualities. But the qualities are primordially present. This original wakefulness, yeshe, is inconceivable. The Dzogchen teachings describe it either as the unity of being empty and cognizant or as the unity of being aware and empty. Of course, the dualistic consciousness is also empty and cognizant, but it is suffused with ignorance, with unknowing. *Ignorance* means "not knowing rigpa." Yeshe is empty cognizance suffused with knowing.

In actuality, all that appears and exists, all worlds and beings, are the mandala of the five male and female buddhas, the mandala of the victorious ones. This is simply how it already is, and that is how we train ourselves in seeing things, by means of the development stage. To recognize rigpa is the true way to acknowledge what is, *as it is.* At that moment, experience, in itself, is already the mandala of the male and female buddhas, without us having to think it is. When we don't recognize rigpa, then *it isn't,* even though, essentially, *it is.* When we merely think it is, that is only a pretense—even though, based on this pretense, called "ordinary development stage," we can realize rigpa, in actuality, since whatever appears and exists is already the mandala of the victorious ones.

Development stage is a training in *what really is.* The perceiving quality is the yab and the empty quality is the yum. These two are an indivisible unity. This is the fundamental mandala of all the victorious ones, of all buddhas. This unity of experience and emptiness is also the source of the ordinary body, speech, and mind of sentient beings. Sentient beings, however, are not simply ordinary body, speech, and mind. We possess the enlightened body, speech, and mind as well; we just don't recognize this. Still, it is not enough to pretend this is so. We can pretend to be a buddha, but still we won't be enlightened by thinking, "I am a buddha." We need to authentically acknowledge what *actually is.* Even though our world is a nirmanakaya buddhafield, we need to also know it.

There are the six munis, one for each of the six realms of samsara. There is Dharmaraja for the hell beings, Khala Mebar for the hungry ghosts,

26

Senge Rabten for the animals, Shakyamuni for the humans, Taksangri for the demigods, and Shakra for the gods. Each of the six realms of samsara is in fact a nirmanakaya buddhafield. Even though this is so, beings don't know it. We need to know that our nature is an unconfined empty cognizance. Knowing this to be *as it is* is the mandala of the victorious ones—just as the buddhas know it to be. However, we have fallen under the power of wrong views and distorted concepts, and we are wandering about in the confused states of samsara.

The four lines for ultimate bodhichitta, included in the preliminary practices of *Kunzang Tuktig*, say,

> *Namo*ः
> *I and the six classes of beings, all living things,*ः
> *Are buddhas from the very beginning.*ः
> *By the nature of knowing this to be as it is,*ः
> *I form the resolve towards supreme enlightenment.*ः

By the nature of knowing this to be as it is,ः means "seeing reality as it is." It means that whatever appears and exists is already all-encompassing purity, the mandala of the victorious ones. It is not only something we pretend it to be. However, it only becomes true when recognizing the natural state. Otherwise, we don't see it as it really is. Our ignorance of the unknowing, grasping at duality, and getting involved in the three poisons obscures the all-encompassing purity of what appears and exists. The difference lies entirely between knowing and not knowing. When we recognize our nature as pointed out by a master, then we know *what is* to be *as it is.* We then train in this, in the state of original wakefulness unspoiled by dualistic fixation.

To recognize self-existing wakefulness is to see things as they are. This is unlike taking a white conch shell to be yellow; there is no way that this is so. When you have jaundice, you see a conch as being yellow. The conch definitely isn't yellow; it never was, but the gall in the body makes your eye yellow, so you see white as yellow, even though it isn't. This exemplifies confusion, the mistakenness of sentient beings. We don't see things as they really are.

Since I and all other sentient beings are buddhas from the very beginning, I resolve to attain supreme enlightenment by the power of recognizing this to be *as it is,* by the ultimate bodhichitta. This is the way of acknowledging the all-encompassing purity of all that appears and exists. All-encompassing purity abides within us.

According to the Dzogchen teachings, the state of primordial enlightenment has never been confused. The basic state of buddhas is like pure gold that is not covered by any dirt. Dirt is an example of the confused thinking that temporarily takes place. If the gold always remains pure, there is no cleaning to be done and there is no achievement of purity, because it already is like that from the beginning. The state of primordial enlightenment is analogous, because self-existing wakefulness was never confused. If there is no being confused, how can we use the phrase *being liberated?* It is impossible, because liberation is totally dependent upon having been confused. Since the awakened state of the buddhas is not confused, you cannot really say that buddhas become liberated either. We can clear up confusion because we've been mistaken. Unless there is confusion, it is not possible to be liberated.

We sentient beings have the same self-existing wakefulness as the buddhas. There is no difference whatsoever in our natures. However, the self-existing wakefulness of the buddhas, all the infinite qualities, never became confused, like the gold that never became tainted. Even though we possess the same gold, ours fell in the dirt. Not knowing this dirty gold to be intrinsically pure, we fell under the power of confused thinking. This is what obscured us: our thinking. The gold of the buddhas was known to be what it is. Buddhas do not have discursive thinking. It won't help us sentient beings to act as if we were primordially pure gold, if we have already become confused and are now unaware of our own nature. It doesn't become true. We have to apply the practice we have, of first recognizing the view, then training in meditation, and acting in accordance with that as the conduct—thus realizing it fully as fruition. This practice is like the special chemicals that clean away dirt from gold. In other words, view, meditation, and conduct remove the confusion.

In recognizing our nature, the confusion is liberated. For buddhas, neither the words *confusion* nor *liberation* apply. The word *confusion* connotes "bewilderment, being mistaken, deluded." Confusion is nothing other than the expression of rigpa that has moved in a mistaken way. As long as you are confusing yourself by your awareness being extroverted, nobody else can *ever* solve that. There is only you, right? Otherwise, confusion goes on and on. That is exactly what samsara is, confusion going on and on. Even though we sentient beings are buddhas, we are like the dirt-encrusted gold; we don't recognize the gold for what it is, due to deluded thinking. In our basic essence, there is no thinking; the essence is wakefulness that is pure from the beginning. By recognizing your buddha-nature, the three kayas become an actuality.

The empty essence is dharmakaya, and the cognizant nature is sambhogakaya—awareness and the expression of awareness. We need to allow the expression of awareness, of rigpa, to be liberated. It is said that nirmanakaya recognizes sambhogakaya, which in turn recognizes dharmakaya. In awareness itself, there is neither the word *liberation* nor *confusion*. It is the expression that has fallen into conceptualizing. If the expression of rigpa recognizes itself, it dawns as knowledge, *sherab*. This is not the ordinary knowledge that is the outcome of learning, reflecting, and meditating. It is the real *prajnaparamita*, "transcendent knowledge," the expression of awareness recognizing itself. In that moment, the expression of awareness dissolves back into awareness, and there is only the state of rigpa, which is identical to the state of primordial enlightenment of all buddhas, the state that never strayed from itself.

A famous and important quotation describes this, "When the expression moves as thinking, it is confused. When the expression dawns as knowledge, it is liberated." That doesn't mean there was ever any difference in the state of the essence, rigpa. The state of rigpa, buddha-nature itself, is never confused and never liberated. The confusion and liberation can only take place in the expression.

The state of original enlightenment is the essence itself, where there is no confusion and no liberation. The state of sentient beings is to be constantly absorbed in confused thinking. It is the expression, the thinking that can be liberated again. Yet, all the time, the essence was never different from that of any other buddha. That is the important point: recognize your own essence. That is also the key point in the first samadhi of suchness. Real development stage practice is not possible without the samadhi of suchness, and this suchness is not recognized without first having the nature of mind pointed out.

Lineage Supplication

Tulku Urgyen Rinpoche

First of all, the foundation for the Vajra Vehicle of Secret Mantra is called "tantra, scripture, and instruction"—in Tibetan, *gyü lung menngag*. In this context, tantra means Mahayoga, scripture means Anu Yoga, and instruction means Ati Yoga. The way in which these are interconnected is called the "fourfold linkage" or the "fourfold relatedness." Thus, the tantras are combined or contained within the scriptures, the scriptures are contained within the instructions, the instructions are contained within the application, and the sadhana is contained in the application. *Application* means the "way of chanting, the actual sadhana practice."

Regarding sadhanas, there are different ways to practice a mandala. In tantra Mahayoga, the mandala is called the "mandala as a reflection or form that is external." At best, it is made of colored sand; next best is painted canvas; and, at minimum, it is assembled from heaped grains. By taking the support of an external mandala, the practitioner accomplishes the deity. In scripture Anu Yoga, the mandala is internal, meaning it is "within the vajra body." The vajra body mandala is called the "three seats of completeness," the *densum tsangwey kyilkhor*. In instruction Ati Yoga, the mandala is mental, or the mandala of mind. Here, *mind* refers to "buddha-nature," which is present in everyone. This is the mandala used to accomplish the deity. So the intent of Mahayoga is related to or contained within the application of Anu Yoga, while the intent of Anu Yoga is contained within Ati Yoga. And, then, Ati Yoga is contained within the application of a sadhana.

Within Ati Yoga, there are different aspects: the Mahayoga aspect of Ati, the Anu aspect of Ati, and the Ati of Ati. Using a sadhana practice from the Ati Yoga perspective is called the Mahayoga of Ati, or Maha-Ati. That is the practice of the peaceful and wrathful deities we have before us here. So this practice is a sadhana that belongs to the Mahayoga section of Ati Yoga. We combine the peaceful and wrathful deities, the *Shitro*, with Ati Yoga, because later on, during the practice of Tögal or Direct Crossing, these peaceful and wrathful deities will unfold within our vision. Moreover, at the time of death, while in the bardos, the peaceful and wrathful deities—the intrinsic mandala—will manifest. That is the purpose of combining the peaceful and wrathful deities within a sadhana practice.

There are different ways of practicing the *Shitro*, according to Mahayoga, Anu Yoga, and Ati Yoga. Chokgyur Lingpa had *Shitro* practices for each of the three levels of inner tantras. The Mahayoga version of the *Shitro* sadhana is called *Gyutrül*, meaning *The Magical Net*. Chokgyur Lingpa's terma for this is extremely extensive and yet totally identical with that of the Kama tradition, the Nyingma oral tradition. The sadhana for the *Gyutrül Shitro* has separate practices for both the peaceful and wrathful deities, as well as one for the combined mandala of the forty-two peaceful and fifty-eight wrathful deities. Moreover, he had a terma for the Anu Yoga version of the *Shitro*, called *Narak Dongtruk*. The terma Chokling revealed for Ati Yoga is the *Kunzang Tuktig*.

This sadhana is extremely condensed, yet nothing is missing. It is identical with another Ati Yoga *Shitro* terma, the *Karling Shitro*, revealed by Karma Lingpa. This terma is quite famous, and the *Bardo Tödröl* comes from it. The *Kunzang Tuktig* differs from the *Karling Shitro* only in size, not in essence. In fact, you will have a difficult time finding any sadhana more condensed or shorter than this one. It's only a couple of pages long, disregarding the major sections of confessions and mending and the lineage-masters' supplication written by Chokgyur Lingpa. Yet, nothing is missing. It is complete; everything is contained. The deities themselves, although their attributes and details are not spelled out, are exactly the same as those found in the *Karling Shitro*. Nothing is omitted. The *Leyjang* is extremely condensed. According to the intent of the instructions, the extensive one is Mahayoga. Anu is more profound, while Ati Yoga is extremely profound.

Traditionally, one always supplicates the masters of a lineage before beginning a sadhana practice. The lineage supplication is never included in the terma, because we never know precisely what will happen in the future. Therefore, the supplication is composed after the revelation and after having seen through whom the line passed. Chokgyur Lingpa, himself, wrote this very short lineage supplication.

The name of the supplication to the lineage masters is called *Ösel Rangshar*, meaning *Self-Manifest Luminosity*. The imagery of the shining sun is very significant. The sun's radiance is not created or formed by anyone. It shines naturally. In the same way, the basic state of awareness, the buddha-nature present within everyone, is manifest or radiant all by itself—it is self-existing, naturally and spontaneously present. No one made it; it is totally uncreated. This is the basic intent of the Dzogchen teachings, which were transmitted first in the divine realms of Akanishtha, Tushita, and the realm of the thirty-three deva kings on the summit of Mt. Sumeru. Afterward, these teachings appeared in the human realm.

It starts out with EMA HO, which means "how amazing!" The first three verses in the lineage supplication are linked with the meaning of ground, path, and fruition. Here, the word *tantra* is used for "ground, path, and fruition." The very meaning of *tantra* is "continuity or ceaselessness," in the sense that buddha-nature is uninterrupted throughout ground, path, and fruition. In the first verse, referring to the ground, it says, *within the dharmadhatu realm of Akanishtha*. Here, *Akanishtha* means "unsurpassable, the unexcelled, the highest, not beneath anything else." It is *densely arrayed*, meaning that all the qualities of complete enlightenment are spontaneously present, such as the attributes, the scenery, the qualities, and so forth. They are present in a dense array—nothing is missing; it is utterly perfect. Within this realm, *I supplicate Samantabhadra Vajradhara*. Sometimes we think of Samantabhadra and Vajradhara as two different buddhas, but actually they are identical. They are not two at all.

Concerning path, *mind* is "unified, empty cognizance." The second verse refers to the cognizant quality of mind, as the appearing aspect. It is often said that the identity is Samantabhadra, the appearance is the five buddhas, and the manifestation is the buddhas of the six realms. This indicates the relationship among dharmakaya, sambhogakaya, and nirmanakaya. This is known as "identity, appearance, and manifestation." The identity is Samantabhadra; the appearance is the five buddha families; and the manifestation is the munis, or buddhas of the six realms. This is also called "not different and not separate."

The first four lines are about the continuity of ground, which is primordial purity. The second verse, which asks to *grant your blessings for realizing the continuity of path*, refers to spontaneous presence. *May we perfect the path*, in the third verse, is about fruition. When the ground manifestation arose, the buddhas of the six realms appeared. This is related to nirmanakaya. One of the realms includes the one thousand buddhas of the Good Aeon. In this sense, manifesting as nirmanakaya is compared to the fruition—may we realize it.

The first three verses are general, while the fourth verse begins with the word *khyepar,* meaning "in particular." So, in particular, *in the buddha-field of True Joy, Abhirati,* the pure land of Vajrasattva—who is identical with Akshobhya, one of the five buddhas—we ask for the blessing to realize the view of Trekchö. Next, we supplicate to realize the view of Tögal. The next four lines are a supplication to Garab Dorje to attain certainty in, or to establish with certainty, the inseparability of space and awareness, which is the basis for Tögal practice.

In the next verse, *grant your blessings that experience and visions may increase,* we pray to Manjushrimitra, asking for the blessing to realize the second of the four visions.

Among the four visions, the first is called the "actuality, or the direct perception, of the innate nature of dharmata." The second one pertains to this experience increasing further and further. In the third, experience reaches fullness and is completely manifested—the culmination of awareness.

The next verse is a supplication to Padmasambhava, residing in his magically created pure land called the Palace of Lotus Light, located atop the Glorious Copper-Colored Mountain, situated southwest of Bodhgaya. We invoke him, praying, *Grant your blessings that we may reach the exhaustion of phenomena.*

The next verse addresses Yeshe Tsogyal, Prince Lhasey, and his consort, requesting them to *please bestow your blessings to ripen and liberate my being.* This signifies that empowerment brings us to maturity, while the instructions and reading transmission liberate us. The verse mentions Yeshe Tsogyal by name, but the *prince and consort* actually refers to the royal ruler, King Trisong Deütsen and his sons.

The first of the next three verses supplicates Chokgyur Lingpa, the revealer of this terma. *Wherever he resides is the wishfulfilling origin or source of the teachings* honors him as the regent, or emissary, of Padmasambhava, indicating his mere presence in the world ensures the authentic transmission of the teachings.

The next verse invokes the place of revelation, a mountain in Kham called Namkha Dzö, the Sky Treasury mountain. The *Kunzang Tuktig* teachings were revealed in a cave on the slopes of this mountain. Padmasambhava and his twenty-five close disciples flew through the sky, landing on this mountain. It is where he disclosed the mandala of *Kadü Chökyi Gyatso, The Dharma Ocean Embodying All Teachings.*

The following verse is a supplication to the dharma protectors, especially the great dakini in wrathful form, who is the manifestation of Ekajati. Primordial purity and spontaneous presence, and the seventeen Dzogchen tantras are entrusted to this protectress of mantra. She is the wrathful form of Samantabhadri, who pervades all places and remains everywhere the wheel of dharma is turned.

The next verse supplicates our dharma friends, wherever they may be. Their place of practice, *the cave where luminosity continually manifests,* is depicted as a place of "unceasing experience." As in the past, with all the Kagyü and Nyingma practitioners, the guru foretells the place. Naropa told Marpa where he should practice to attain accomplishment. Marpa told Milarepa to go to such-and-such cave to practice. This is used as a model for a guru telling a disciple to go to such-and-such place to practice until they reach accomplishment. Later, this becomes a sacred place for followers. In this way, one supplicates fellow practitioners and their place of practice to receive blessings from those who will be future buddhas. The idea is also to develop some degree of pure appreciation for fellow practitioners, who have received teachings and practiced—whether they've just embarked, are firmly established, or have already reached fruition on the path to enlightenment. Fellow practitioners are incredibly precious. Thus, we pray *that impartial pure perception may arise.* All have buddha-nature, so there is no basis for impurity and wrong views. One needs pure perception for the path of mantra, in which all forms, sounds, and thoughts are deity, mantra, and samadhi.

It is said that Vajrayana is the path of pure perception. This sacred outlook, or pure perception, is the special quality of Vajrayana. As it is said, "Simply through pure perception, or sacred outlook, half the path is already traversed." This is not complete imagination. *Sacred outlook* refers to "seeing things as they actually are," not in the ordinary deluded way, where we think earth is simply solid matter, water is merely water, wind is wind, and so forth. The five elements, as they appear to us in our ordinary experience, are actually the five female buddhas, the five aggregates are the five male buddhas, and so forth. Therefore, training in pure perception is not a way of convincing ourselves that things are what they are not; rather, we are training in seeing things as they truly are.

That is not the case in the sutra teachings, where we merely think everything is perfect. The Buddha did not teach pure perception, meaning the "correct outlook" in sutra. He saw that people who gravitated to the sutra teachings would not trust the Vajrayana teachings in the same way. It is a special quality of Vajrayana, knowing things to be as they really are. In this sense, since our dharma friends possess buddha-nature, they are dakas and dakinis. It is said that we need to train in pure perception.

Next, we pray to be blessed with faith and trust and to have the intelligence, firm understanding, and ability to take to heart the preciousness of the human body, impermanence, karma, the defects of samsara, and so forth.

The next four lines deal with trusting in the Three Jewels and having compassion for all beings, *my parents*. Bless me to *equalize life and practice*. In short, there are three indispensable things: to have devotion upward toward the buddhas, to have compassion downward toward all beings, and to be diligent in-between.

Next, we supplicate to realize the view of Trekchö. Within the mind-stream of all beings is the self-existing buddha-nature, in the form of the self-appearing peaceful and wrathful ones. The development stage is not something foolish. The second line refers to the fact that the outer world and the inner contents are all peaceful and wrathful buddhas, which is actually Tögal.

In the third line of this verse, the main image of *dharmadhatu* is that of space—*the space of all things*, within which all phenomena manifest, abide, and dissolve. This is similar to physical space, which is like a container, within which the remaining four elements appear, abide, and disappear. These four elements do not come out of any other source; they emerge from space itself. They do not remain anywhere else other than within space; neither do they go anywhere outside of space. In the same way, dharmadhatu is the basic environment of all phenomena, whether they belong to samsara or nirvana. It encompasses whatever appears and exists, including the worlds and all beings. Everything takes place within and dissolves back into the state of dharmadhatu. Dharmadhatu encompasses all of samsara and nirvana. It doesn't include only nirvana and exclude samsara; it's not like that.

External phenomena appear within space, remain within space, and disappear within space again. Is there any place where earth, water, fire, and wind can go that is outside space? Don't they always remain within space? When they disintegrate, don't they dissolve within space? Is there any place at all to go beyond or outside space that is other than space? Please understand very well this symbolic resemblance between dharmadhatu and physical space.

The prayer says, *within the realm of dharmadhatu, which encompasses all of samsara and nirvana.* The relationship among dharmadhatu, dharmakaya, and dharmadhatu wisdom is like the relationship among a place, a person, and the person's mind. If there is no place, there is no environment for the person to exist in; and there is no person unless that person also has a mind dwelling in the body. In the same way, the main field or realm called dharmadhatu has the nature of dharmakaya. Dharmakaya has the quality of dharmadhatu wisdom, which is like the mind aspect.

We also need to clearly understand what is meant by the terms *samsara* and *nirvana. Nirvana* means the "fully realized buddha-nature that consists of body, speech, and mind aspects." The body is the essence that simply is. Speech is its nature, the cognizant quality that is vividly present. Mind is the capacity, which is radiant. These three aspects comprise the basic presence of all buddhas, as their essence, nature, and capacity. All sugatas have this same identity. Similarly, *samsara* is the "body, speech, and mind of all sentient beings." These are the deluded expressions of their essence, nature, and capacity. In this way, dharmadhatu encompasses all of samsara and nirvana.

Dharmadhatu is adorned with dharmakaya, which is endowed with dharmadhatu wisdom. This is a brief but very profound statement, because dharmadhatu also refers to *sugatagarbha* or "buddha-nature." Buddha-nature is all-encompassing: thus it is present, or basic, to all states, regardless of whether they belong to samsara or nirvana. Remember, nirvana refers to the body, speech, and mind of all the awakened ones. Body is the abiding essence, speech is the vividly present nature, and mind is the radiant capacity. These three, the body, speech, and mind of all buddhas, are also known as the three vajras.

This buddha-nature is present just as the shining sun is present in the sky. It is indivisible from the three vajras of the awakened state, which do not perish or change. Vajra body is the unchanging quality; vajra speech is the unceasing quality; and vajra mind is the undeluded, unmistaken quality. So, the buddha-nature, or dharmadhatu, is the three vajras; at the same time, its *expression* manifests as the deluded body, speech, and mind of all beings.

In the normal sense of these words, body refers to something perishable composed of flesh and blood, speech refers to intermittent utterances that come and go and eventually perish, and mind refers to thought states and emotions that continually come and go under the power of dualistic attitude, like beads on a rosary. These mental states are also transient. Everyone agrees that the body, speech, and mind of living beings are constantly changing, continually coming and going. Still, the basis of our ordinary body, speech, and mind is the buddha-nature, the dharmadhatu, which encompasses all of samsara and nirvana. There isn't a single being for whom this isn't so.

Looking from the pure angle, then, this buddha-nature, the expression of the victorious ones, is present in every being, just like the rays of light are present in the sun. The light is emanated by the sun, isn't it? If it weren't for the sun, there wouldn't be any light. Similarly, the origin of the body, speech, and mind of beings is the expression of the buddha-nature, which pervades both samsara and nirvana. It does not pervade only one and not the other. Chokgyur Lingpa's beginning words are quite impressive: *Dharmadhatu encompasses all of samsara and nirvana*—not just the awakened state of nirvana, but everything.

It is said that all sentient beings are buddhas, but they are covered by their temporary obscurations. These temporary obscurations are our own thinking. Dharmadhatu encompasses all of samsara and nirvana—not just the awakened state of nirvana, but everything, every single thing. The ordinary body, speech, and mind of sentient beings temporarily arose from the expression of the qualities of enlightened body, speech, and mind. As space pervades, so awareness pervades. If this were not so, then space would pervade but rigpa wouldn't. Just like space, rigpa is all-encompassing: nothing is outside it. Just as the contents and beings are all pervaded by space, rigpa pervades the minds of beings. Dharmadhatu pervades all of samsara and nirvana.

It is essential to start out with a basic understanding of this profound meaning, in order to authentically practice the teaching of the Great Perfection. Unless we know what is what, at least intellectually, we may perceive sentient beings as disconnected, alien entities, without having any idea where they come from, where they belong, or what they actually are. They are not disconnected at all. The difference between buddhas and sentient beings lies in the latter's narrowness of scope and attitude. Sentient beings confine themselves to their own limited little area of samsara, through their own attitude and thinking.

It is said that the difference between buddhas and sentient beings is like the difference between the narrowness and openness of space. Sentient beings are like the space held within a tightly closed fist, while buddhas are fully open, all-encompassing. Basic space and awareness are innately all-encompassing. Basic space is the absence of mental constructs, while awareness is the *knowing* of this absence of constructs, recognizing the complete emptiness of mind-essence. Space and awareness are inherently indivisible. It is said, "When the mother, the basic space of dharmadhatu, does not stray from her awareness child, have no doubt that they are forever indivisible."

The ultimate Dharma is the realization of the indivisibility of basic space and awareness. That is the starting point, which is pointed out to begin with. It is essential to understand this; otherwise, we might have the feeling that Samantabhadra and his consort are an old blue man and woman who lived aeons ago. It's not like that at all! Samantabhadra and his consort are the indivisible unity of space and awareness.

As you know, the nine gradual vehicles and the four schools of philosophy—Vaibhashika, Sautrantika, Mind Only, and Middle Way—are designed to suit the various mental capacities of different people. The term Great Perfection, on the other hand, implies that everything is included in Dzogchen; everything is complete. Dzogchen is said to be unexcelled, meaning there is nothing higher than it. Why is this? It is because of knowing *what truly is* to be *as it is*—the ultimate, naked state of dharmakaya. Isn't that truly the ultimate? Please carefully understand this.

The Great Perfection is totally beyond any kind of pigeonholing, in any way whatsoever. It is to be utterly open, beyond categories, limitations, and the confines of assumptions and beliefs. All other ways of describing things are confined by categories and limitations. The ultimate destination in Dzogchen is the view of the kayas and wisdoms. Listen to this quote I said earler, "Although everything is empty, the special quality of the Buddhadharma is to not be empty of the kayas and wisdoms." All other systems expound that all things are empty; but truly, the intention of the Buddha is to use the word *emptiness* rather than *empty*. This is a very important point.

For instance, in the Prajnaparamita scriptures, you find the statements, "Outer things are emptiness, inner things are emptiness, emptiness is emptiness, the vast is emptiness, the ultimate is emptiness, the conditioned is emptiness, the unconditioned is emptiness …" *Emptiness* here should be understood as "empty cognizance." Please understand this. The suffix -*ness* implies the "cognizant quality." We need to understand this word in its correct connotation.

Otherwise, it sounds too nihilistic to simply say that outer things are empty. If we understand emptiness as empty or void, rather than as empty cognizance, we are leaning too much towards nihilism, the idea that everything is a big, blank void. This is a serious sidetrack.

The Buddha initially taught that all things are empty. This was unavoidable; indeed, it was justifiable, because we need to dismantle our fixation on the permanence of our experiences. A normal person clings to the contents of his experiences as solid, as being *that*— not just as mere experience, but also as something that is solid, real, concrete, and permanent. But if we look honestly and closely at what happens, experience is simply experience, and it is not made out of anything whatsoever. It has no form, no sound, no color, no taste, and no texture; it is simply experience—an empty cognizance.

The vivid display in manifold colors that you see with open eyes is not mind but "illuminated matter." Similarly, when you close your eyes and see something dark, it is not mind but "dark matter." In both cases, matter is merely a presence, an experience of something. It is *mind* that experiences the external elements and everything else.

An appearance can only exist if there is a mind that beholds it. The beholding of that appearance is nothing other than experience; that is what actually takes place. Without a perceiver, how could an appearance be an appearance? It wouldn't exist anywhere. Perceptions are experienced by mind; they are not experienced by water or earth. All the elements are vividly distinguished as long as the mind fixates on them. Yet they are nothing but a mere presence, an appearance. It is mind that apprehends this mere presence. When this mind doesn't apprehend, hold, or fixate on what is experienced—in other words, when the real, authentic samadhi of suchness dawns within your stream-of-being—"reality" loses its solid, obstructing quality. That is why accomplished yogis cannot be burned, drowned, or harmed by wind. In their experience, all appearances are a mere presence, since fixation has disintegrated from within. Mind is that which experiences, within which experience unfolds. What else is there to experience? *Mind* means "individual experience." All experience is individual, personal.

For instance, the fact that one yogi's delusion dissolves doesn't mean everyone else's delusion vanishes as well. When someone gets enlightened, that person is enlightened, not everyone else. When a yogi transcends fixation, only the deluded individual experience of that one person dissolves. Please think about this. There is, however, another aspect called "other's experience" or the "general experience" of sentient beings.

In all of this seemingly solid reality *(Rinpoche knocks on the wood of his bed)*, there is not a single thing that is indestructible. Whatever is material in this world will be destroyed in fire at the end of the *kalpa;* there is no exception. This fire then vanishes by itself. *(Rinpoche chuckles.)*

Try to spend some time on *Nangjang* training,[5] and you will discover that all of reality is insubstantial and unreal. By means of *Nangjang* training, we discover that all experience is personal experience and that we see personal experience as unreal and insubstantial, when we're not fixating upon it. In this entire world, no created appearance remains, ultimately. Seemingly, external visual forms do not really remain anywhere. These mere perceptions are dependent karmic experiences. All of relative reality is by definition dependent upon something else, upon causes and conditions, isn't it? When explaining relative phenomena, you have to mention their causes and conditions; there is no way around that. In the end, we realize that their nature is ultimately beyond causes and conditions. What is ultimate cannot possibly be made out of causes and conditions.

Only the authentic state of samadhi can purify or clear up this self-created confusion. More appearances and further fixating will not destroy this. This profound state is present in all individuals, if only they would know it! The ultimate nature is already fully present. We give it names like dharmakaya, sambhogakaya, and nirmanakaya. Our deluded state hides this from us, but this is what destroys the delusion. Isn't this really amazing! *(Rinpoche chuckles.)*

Once we attain stability in samadhi, delusion is destroyed, since samadhi dismantles the entire drama of delusion. In other words, this mind has basically created the delusion, but by recognizing the nature of this mind, we clear up our delusion, since, at that moment, no delusion can be recreated. If everyone could just understand this! This is amazing! *(Rinpoche laughs.)* It is the mind, itself, that creates this whole delusion, but it is also the mind, itself, that can let the whole delusion collapse. *(Rinpoche laughs again.)* Besides buddha-nature, what else is there to be free from delusion? Buddha-nature is the very basis for delusion. It is also what dissolves the delusion. Please try to understand this carefully! This is something you *can* understand!

Delusion seems to separate all sentient beings from their buddha-nature. But this very buddha-nature clears up the delusion. It is basically a matter of recognizing it or not. We speak of those who were never deluded: the buddhas and the hundred sublime families of peaceful and wrathful sugatas, including Buddha Samantabhadra. When failing to recognize, one is deluded. Delusion dissolves the very moment you recognize the identity of what is deluded.

Delusion is like becoming possessed by a spirit during a seance, when someone starts to suddenly hop around and do all kinds of crazy things. This is exactly what has happened to all of us. Sentient beings are possessed by the "spirit" of ignorance and the 84,000 disturbing emotions, and they are all dancing around doing incredible things. They have undergone all different kinds of pain and misery for so long, aeons upon aeons. But it is a self-created possession. It is not really something from outside. Buddha-nature has lost track of itself and created samsara, but buddha-nature, recognizing itself, also clears up the delusion of samsaric existence. The moment of recognition is like the spirit leaving. All of a sudden the possession vanishes. We can't even say where it went. This is called the "collapse of confusion."

We have undergone so much misery—oh my! Spinning around on the wheel of samsara, we have suffered so much trouble! Roaming and rambling about among the six classes of beings, of course we have suffered! *(Rinpoche laughs.)* A yogi is like a formerly possessed person, whom the spirit has left. While possessed, this mind thinks and acts in delusion, but the very moment you recognize the nature of this mind—rigpa—the possession immediately vanishes. *(Rinpoche laughs.)*

This may sound like nonsense, but actually there is much meaning here. *Dharmadhatu encompasses all of samsara and nirvana.* Samantabhadra said, "I am devoid of delusion, while from my expression seeming delusion occurs." *I am devoid of delusion* refers to the Buddha, while *from my expression seeming delusion occurs. Delusion occurs* refers to sentient beings. In the moment of recognizing the essence, then the expression, which is sentient beings, dissolves back into the essence, known as the Buddha. It is not necessary to depend on any external technique or remedy, because recognition of the essence destroys the expression. *I am without delusion* means the buddha-nature is speaking, *but out of my expression, seeming delusion takes place.*

From the Beginning

Tulku Urgyen Rinpoche

When we begin any practice, the main thing is our motivation *(kun slong)*. All dharmas depend on our motivation, our attitude. There are two kinds of attitudes, the Mahayana attitude and the Secret Mantra attitude. They are called the "vast" and the "profound." The vast is the sutra aspect, and the profound is the mantra aspect. The chief point of the sutra aspect is the motivation through compassion, where we consider that every single sentient being in the three realms of samsara has been our parent. There is merely a slight difference in terms of the distance from our present parents. All of these parent sentient beings want only happiness. However, their application produces the cause of suffering; thus, they have wandered in endless samsara. By means of the profound development and completion stages, for the sake of enabling all the infinite sentient beings to attain the omniscient and perfect enlightenment, I will practice the profound Dharma. This is the attitude according to sutra.

The attitude according to mantra is that the outer universe is a celestial palace and the inner contents of sentient beings have the nature of male and female deities. There is no impurity whatsoever. Body has the nature of deity, speech has the nature of mantra, and mind has the nature of samadhi. We should practice these two perfect attitudes of sutra and mantra, because the root of all vehicles is the two precious kinds of bodhichitta. According to the sutra path, one accomplishes enlightenment through emptiness and compassion. Emptiness is the path of knowledge *(prajna),* and compassion is the path of means *(upaya).* The true roots of prajna and upaya according to the Sutrayana are emptiness and compassion. According to Mantrayana, upaya is the development stage and prajna is the completion stage; through the development and completion stages, we attain the unified level of Vajradhara. These are the special principles of sutra and mantra. The roots of both kinds of precious bodhichitta, the relative and absolute, are complete within the attitude of compassion. Whether the Dharma carries you onward to a perfect path or not depends on your attitude. First, you should consider the sutra attitude and the mantra attitude, then proceed with your practice.

Begin practice in the morning, starting with guru yoga or the Three Roots, which, in the mantra teachings, are the support for our practice. The root of blessing is the guru and the root of the siddhis is the yidam. The dakinis and dharmapalas, together, are the root of activities. If you can do the practice of the Three Roots as your "back support," you will not fall under the power of obstacles on the paths and *bhumis*. The main hindrances for attaining the state of perfect enlightenment are the obstacles. Some people only hold onto emptiness for pacifying obstacles, thinking, "I will just practice emptiness." That alone will not clear away the obstacles, because upaya and prajna are not combined. As this saying explains, "Prajna without upaya and upaya without prajna are said to fetter the person; therefore, neither of them should be abandoned." If upaya and prajna are separated, it becomes quite difficult to attain the perfect enlightenment, the unified level of Vajradhara.

To reiterate, in the sutra teachings, upaya and prajna are compassion and emptiness. At the mantra level, we combine the development and completion stages as upaya and prajna. In Dzogchen, Ati Yoga, we attain the sambhogakaya in one life within one body through the paths of *Trekchö* and *Tögal*—which are the union of upaya and prajna. If upaya (means) and prajna (knowledge) are separated, it is difficult to attain buddhahood. If you think of it, actually, it is impossible to complete a work, even in this samsaric world, without upaya and prajna. For instance, when making an airplane, if you know through prajna how to construct it, but you don't manage to get the necessary articles together through upaya, your mind alone cannot make an airplane. Also, even if you manage to gather all the parts for the construction of a plane, but you have no knowledge of how to assemble them through prajna, it will never be successful. We have to gather all the plane parts, the nature of upaya; when we also know how to put them together, through prajna, then the plane will be able to fly. It is said that the siddhas of the past could fly through the sky, but it was never the case that five or six hundred people could fly, right? This is only possible through the union of upaya and prajna. Without these two, even all works in samsara would be impossible; nobody could do anything or stay anywhere. How can we attain nirvana, or the state of enlightenment, without the combination of upaya and prajna? With only prajna or upaya, we will not get enlightened.

By compassion alone, without emptiness, it is also a little difficult. Emptiness, unembraced by compassion, is not the perfect path—our dharma will stray onto the wrong track of self-interest.

When realizing the perfect view, the nature, or cognizance aspect, will arise as compassion. After attaining enlightenment, the buddhas never leave sentient beings behind. This is because of the power of compassion; the link between buddhas and beings is made out of compassion. After enlightenment, the buddhas do not have even a hair tip of self-interest. They only accomplish the benefit of others, the benefit of the beings in endless samsara. From the space of dharmakaya comes sambhogakaya, and from the space of sambhogakaya arises (nirmanakaya) rupakaya—because of compassion.

Some people say, "What's the use of development stage? Only completion stage is good!" Development stage is not unnecessary at all. Since the beginning, the development stage is the spontaneous presence *(lhun grub)*, which does not need to be developed. For instance, when practicing Dzogchen and the *Tögal* displays appear, they appear automatically, of their own accord. They do not arise because we produce them, right? They are self-arising, spontaneously present.

First of all, the development stage is indispensable, because *that which is* has two modes: abiding in the ground *(gzhir bzhugs)* and being manifest in the ground *(gzhir gzhengs)*. When the abiding in the ground manifests in the ground, then the development stage unfolds. The empty essence is dharmakaya, and the cognizant nature is sambhogakaya. As essence and nature are a unity, development and completion stage are primordially united. Without understanding that, someone might say, "What is development stage good for? I don't need it!" That is due to wrong understanding. If development stage were unnecessary, then the buddhas, bodhisattvas, and siddhas who appeared in the past would have said there is no need for it, right? They said that one needs development stage. *(Laughs.)* Also, Gyalwa Longchen Rabjam said that both development and completion stage are necessary. It is also not possible to attain enlightenment by development stage alone, if it is not embraced by completion stage.

In short, we should take a yidam practice as our back support, whichever yidam that is, according to our disposition. In the past, many practiced *Kunzang Tuktig* in Kham.

In the early morning, practice guru yoga, and during the daytime, practice a yidam sadhana. In the evening, practice the dakini and dharma protectors. As I mentioned before, the guru is the root of blessings; the yidam is the root of siddhis; and the dakinis and dharmapalas are the root of activities. Thus, you can practice the Three Roots consecutively. Otherwise, the guru is included within *Kunzang Tuktig,* as there is no guru superior to Samantabhadra and the five buddhas. As for the yidams, there are none superior to the infinite peaceful and wrathful victorious ones, right? Concerning dakinis, there are the eight ladies of the sacred places *(gnas ma brgyad)* and of the valleys *(yul ma brgyad).* In that way of practicing, there is nothing improper.

It is said that Tibetans fail because they have too many deities, abandoning one deity after the other. The Indians had "one deity for one person," "one-pointed mind and accomplishment." All the siddhas of the past had one deity and attained accomplishment. However, Tibetans think, "Oh, this one will not do. I must practice some other deity." Then they do some other practice, but again abandon that and look for another, after which they think, "Oh, no good!" Therefore, it is said that Tibetans fail due to too many deities. The expression *one thought, one accomplishment,* in reference to the Indians, means they decide on one excellent thought and stick to it, whether it is good or not. They keep to their initial concern, whether it is white or black. In the past, the Indians were quite stable-minded. I do not know how they are nowadays. Tibetans had very pure perceptions of both men and women from the noble land of India. In the past, most Indians practiced Jetsün Tara, Manjushri, and so forth, and had incredible results—meeting the deities face to face and receiving the supreme and common siddhis. Many became great siddhas. The expression *supreme deity* means the "especially exalted one," the deity with whom one has a connection since past lives.

All the deities are complete within the peaceful and wrathful ones in the mandala of our body. There is no need to search in other mandalas. The buddha-mandala of our body is the real palace of the peaceful and wrathful deities. For this reason, it is amazingly excellent to practice *Shitro.* As I mentioned previously, Khyentse Rinpoche told me the *Kunzang Tuktig* is an extremely profound teaching—the most extraordinary teaching. Jamyang Khyentse Chokyi Lodro said, "*The Chetsün Nyingtig* and the *Kunzang Tuktig* of Chokgyur Lingpa are extremely profound teachings. When practicing *Dzogchen,* they are most excellent."

The opening point we should understand is that everything, all world systems and all beings—whatever appears and exists, meaning the perceived and the perceiver—everything takes place in the sphere of the three kayas. Everything originates from the three kayas, takes place within the sphere of the three kayas, and dissolves back again into the sphere of the three kayas. This is how things appear, remain, and disappear. This is a basic fact as well as the Vajrayana perspective, which is very important to have.

Out of that, the Vajrayana principle of all-encompassing purity is taught. All-encompassing purity refers to the purity of whatever appears and exists. Primordial purity, basic purity, original purity, original freedom, and so forth are all synonyms, and understanding them is extremely important. Based on this perspective, we can actually apply Vajrayana practice. Without this, it becomes just bricklaying, or mental labor.

It is very important to have the right perspective from the start; otherwise, it becomes like an act of superimposing. With the right perspective, Vajrayana practice is not superimposing or imagining something to be what it is not. It is not like trying to convince ourselves that a piece of wood is actually pure gold. It's not like that at all. It's actually the other way around. We first visualize and then acknowledge that pure gold is, indeed, pure gold. Temporarily, we see things as being like a piece of wood; but, in fact, from the very beginning, they have always been, always are, and always will be all-encompassing purity. Due to our ignorance, dualistic fixation, disturbing emotions, and habitual tendencies, we apprehend earth as just being solid earth, water as water, and so forth, and see things as something they are not.

So, in order to train ourselves in seeing things as they truly are, we practice two profound aspects of Vajrayana practice, called development stage and completion stage. All the buddhas teach these in order to correct this error. All sadhanas have a main structure that resembles the way everything evolves, remains, and vanishes. Usually, it is said that development is like a resemblance, like a mask or portrait of the real thing, like the painting of Padmasambhava here on my wall. It's not really Padmasambhava, in person, because he is presently residing in his pure land, the Copper-Colored Mountain, but it is a likeness. In the same way, the development stage is a likeness, or imitation, of the real thing. But, it is not false, because it is an exercise in seeing things as they actually are. It is not seeing them as something other. In actuality, the completion stage is the real thing, the natural state.

A sadhana practice always begins with the three samadhis. The first is the samadhi of suchness, the nature of mind, which corresponds to dharmakaya. Out of dharmakaya, sambhogakaya unfolds—here we say, "Its nature of wisdom embraces all." Out of the unity of emptiness and compassion, nirmanakaya occurs. At the conclusion of a sadhana, there is a reversal. Nirmanakaya dissolves into the sambhogakaya quality, and then that dissolves back into the unconstructed sphere of dharmakaya. This is how everything really is. In order to realize this, we train in that by means of the profound method of sadhana practice.

It is very important to understand these basic principles. In order to accomplish a deity, we must know the nature of the deity we are attempting to accomplish. This is called "identifying the deity to be accomplished." This is the most important point before beginning a sadhana practice; otherwise, everything becomes imagination. First, you sit and imagine there is nothing whatsoever—everything is emptiness. Next, you try to imagine there being a place for the mandala, and then you try to build the mandala, step by step, through your imagination. This becomes a lot of hard work, like laying bricks. Therefore, it is essential to begin by identifying the deity to be accomplished and by understanding that the indivisible unity of primordial purity and spontaneous presence is what we call "deity." This is always the intent of any sadhana practice.

Development stage and completion stage in Vajrayana make all the difference between an ordinary person and a Vajrayana practitioner, because an ordinary person has no development or completion stage practice. In this regard, he is not much different from an ox. Someone who familiarizes him or herself with the two profound stages of Vajrayana will have a great advantage meeting death. The reason why I go on and on about this point, again and again, is because it is very important to understand the principle of primordial purity. In fact, everything has the nature of primordial purity. Everything is of the nature of primordial purity. This is not something we achieve through the practice. We're uncovering how things actually are from the beginning. The minds of all sentient beings are, at every moment, the unity of being empty and perceiving. This is nothing other than Buddha Samantabhadra with consort, also called the "mind and object" (yid, yül).

Our physical body, our experiences—the contents—are composed of the five elements and the five aggregates. In their actual nature, these are none other than the five male and five female buddhas, and so forth. In this way, all worlds, all experience, all sentient beings are already the mandala of the peaceful and wrathful deities. They do not suddenly become this at the moment of accomplishment; it is how things are to begin with. This is the acknowledgment we need to use as the very basis of our practice. Otherwise, it becomes very simplistic in a materialistic sense of constructing a mansion and inviting over beautiful people with rich adornments and special silk garments. Then, in order to impress them, we dish out exotic offerings, we flatter them and make then happy, and they give us something in return. This kind of simplistic view is, of course, totally interwoven with the normal habitual tendencies of mundane people. It will, of course, purify some bad karma, but this is not the profound intent of the Vajrayana. That is why I have repeatedly said that the all-encompassing purity is the main principle to understand.

The name Buddha Vairochana means "manifest form," which refers to all experiences of form. We experience forms, yet they are indivisible from emptiness itself. This nature is called Buddha Vairochana. Speech is Buddha Amitabha, meaning "what is semi-manifest," such as sound and communication indivisible from emptiness. We call this Buddha Amitabha. Mind is Buddha Akshobhya, meaning "unshakable." The nature of cognition, the consciousness aggregate, is indivisible from emptiness, and we call this Buddha Akshobhya. Even though *aggregate* means "group, conglomeration of many parts together," these different aspects all have the same nature, namely the nature of the five buddhas. It is the same with the elements. Everything is composed of elements; therefore, everything is the nature of the five female buddhas. All qualities are Ratnasambhava; all activities and interactions are Amoghasiddhi. In this way, we cannot find anything that is not already the mandala of the five male and female buddhas. This is what the phrase *all-encompassing purity* means. We should pay close attention to it and really try to understand the meaning of the principle of all-encompassing purity.

Please gain full comprehension of the principle of this practice! Materialistic approaches to practicing the development stage are not that effective, like the guy who visualized himself as Yamantaka and then couldn't get out the door of his cave, because his horns were too wide. His guru called for him to come, and he sent back a message, saying, "Sorry! I can't come out! My horns get stuck in the doorway."

From another perspective, which I've also stated several times, these are the deities who appear when we practice Tögal. And, needless to mention, we will all die one day. Then these same peaceful and wrathful deities will appear in our experience. Now, during our lives, we can purify our karmic obscurations and gather the accumulations to be able to realize them.

Once we die, it will not help to try to cover our eyes with our hands, since we won't have hands or eyes either at that time. Everything manifests out of our own nature, so there is no way we can hide the displays; they will unfold. Some deities are as huge as Mt. Sumeru, while others are as tiny as mustard seeds. What occurs is the manifestation of our body, speech, and mind—body refers to the bodily forms and speech refers to the natural sounds of the vowels and consonants, which are sometimes as loud as 100,000 simultaneous thundercracks. The manifestations of mind are the dazzling, radiant, swirling beams of light, which are totally overpowering and confusing for someone in an unstable state of mind. So, here is the chance to grow familiar with and befriend the natural manifestations of body, speech, and mind, which we are bound to encounter at one point or another—there's no escape.

All this is called the "inconceivable display of our innate nature." It is not someone else coming to us. We cannot deny that this experience takes place, because it will happen as though in actuality. Yet, we also cannot claim that these deities truly exist, either, because there is nothing to take hold of really. If we can practice in a way that combines both development and completion stages, then through our development stage practice, we will grow used to manifestations, which are devoid of self-nature and without any solid reality. We will not fear whatever we experience, realizing they are all empty forms without any true existence.

In the bardo state, two types of light appear simultaneously: the overwhelming radiance, which is the unfailing, and the soft, seductive lights of the six realms, which fool us. Sentient beings are again and again attracted to the comforting dim lights of the six realms and take another rebirth. The wisdom deities are radiant, with a light resembling the equivalent of 100,000 suns. Beings unfamiliar with the one hundred peaceful and wrathful deities are overwhelmed with terror. Therefore, they seek shelter in the soft, petty light of the six realms, and thus drag themselves through another rebirth. This is another reason for the deep significance of a practice like this.

Before the deities in the bardo actually take form, the very onset of the manifestations of body, speech, and mind are called the "sounds, colors, and lights." The colors are the manifestation of body, the sounds are the manifestation of speech, and the light-rays are the manifestation of mind. They are incredibly vast in scope, deep in their intensity, and utterly overwhelming. An unprepared person, who is totally unfamiliar with development and completion stage meditation practice, will be completely overcome with fright and panic. If 100,000 thundercracks strike simultaneously, how will that person feel? He or she will faint from terror. It is the same with the light-rays and the intensity of colors, which resemble 100,000 suns shining simultaneously. For most, this is unbearable. So training in the development and completion stage practice has incredibly great benefit. Even without the completion stage of mind-essence, we gain an indispensable advantage from practicing the development stage of a deity, since we train the mind in insubstantiality. Then, when the different visions occur, we will no longer fear being chopped, diced, or disintegrated, because we won't hold onto a solid form. So, even just training in the development stage is of great benefit.

For example, consider a hillbilly from the mountains out here who has never even heard of the concept of a movie or film. If he is taken to a movie theater with a big screen and shown a movie of the Second World War, or an imaginary Third World War, he will be terrified, because he doesn't understand it is just a film. He will see people fighting and shooting and so forth. He will probably sit quaking or perhaps even run away; whereas, perhaps the movie director himself may be present in the same room. He will just laugh, because he knows the whole display is an illusion to begin with. Nothing that appears in the film ever really took place. In the same way, the experiences of the after-death state will definitely occur. That's irrefutable, but how much reality we attach to it depends on how much training we, as practitioners, have had in the development and completion stages. So, there is definitely great benefit in this practice.

If the hillbilly is ill-prepared, or if someone has told him, "We're going to a very scary place. You'll see some frightening things inside this movie hall. It's very dangerous!" then, when he enters the hall, he'll be ready to panic and run away; the other guy will just laugh. A person who has trained only in the development stage will see what he developed or imagined, because whatever one imagines takes place. Another person may think, "Oh, it's all coming from there! Whatever he imagines seems to appear before me," but at the same time he will know that none of it is actually real. There's no substantiality. This manual is a way of preparing ourselves for what we will experience later on in the bardo state, so we'll be able to recognize that the bardo experience is the bardo phenomena and that deluded experience is mere delusion.

Preliminaries

Tulku Urgyen Rinpoche

As we have already covered the supplication to the lineage masters, now I will start to explain the sadhana text. Traditionally, the sequence of instructions begins with the general and specific preliminaries, which we have covered in detail in the past. After completing the preliminaries, with them as backing, we proceed to the main part. Here, it is the sadhana text, and later there are instructions on Dzogchen, the Great Perfection, regarding Trekchö and Tögal. Now, we begin with a brief overview and instruction in the sadhana text. It is not the correct approach to immediately jump into Trekchö and Tögal without the support of the sadhana text.

When you want to build a temple, you must begin with a solid foundation. If the foundation is firm and steady, you can build a temple with many stories on top of that and everything will remain stable. In exactly the same way, the practice of Dzogchen must have the solid foundation of the preliminaries. Sentient beings, in fact, are obscured by karma and disturbing emotions. For example, although the sun shines unceasingly in the sky, clouds can temporarily cover it. Similarly, sentient beings possess the enlightened essence, buddha-nature; nevertheless, they become obscured by the different veils of karma and disturbing emotions. In order to remove these veils, we do the preliminary practices of "gathering the accumulations" and "purifying obscurations."

Buddha-nature is also defined as the "unity of space and wisdom," *ying* and *yeshe*. *Ying* refers to the absence of all constructs, meaning "space that is unconstructed." *Yeshe,* or wisdom, refers to the "primordially awake state beyond being obscured and cleared." Unchanging, this indivisible unity of space and wisdom is present as the nature of mind of all sentient beings. In order to realize this, there are the inner Vajrayana teachings that can be applied in the so-called fourfold combination or linkage. To reiterate, the Mahayoga teachings are combined within Anu Yoga, the Anu Yoga are combined within Ati Yoga, the Ati Yoga are combined within sadhana, and sadhana is combined within our application. When applying a sadhana text of this type, which is within the different levels of Ati Yoga, it is called the Maha of Ati, meaning it is a sadhana with peaceful and wrathful deities.

Like completely refined gold, this is the heart essence of all tantras, scriptures, and instructions; the source of all the supreme and ordinary siddhis; and the single supreme path traversed by all the victorious ones throughout the three times.

Tantras (rgyud) refer to the tantras of Mahayoga, *scriptures (lung)* to the scriptures of Anu Yoga, and *instructions (man ngag)* to the instructions of Ati Yoga. This text is the essence of all of these—the root, just like the root or the basic part of the body is the heart. This is like the blood within the heart or like refined gold. The most pure gold in the world is called the "river gold of Jambu continent."

The supreme siddhi is self-existing wakefulness, and the ordinary siddhis are the eight siddhis or accomplishments. This is the place from which all these siddhis originate. This method of sugatagarbha is the path through which all the buddhas of the past, present, and future—thus, all the victorious ones—have attained enlightenment. There has been no other path whatsoever.

Its name is *The Manifest Essence,* which is the general practice manual for the peaceful and wrathful ones, according to the heart-essence of Samantabhadra, the Pure Gold Great Perfection. The name in Tibetan is *las byang,* as written on the title page. *Leyjang* is an abbreviation of *las kyi byang bu,* which means "practice manual." *Las* is the same word as karma, the activities, of pacifying, increasing, magnetizing, and subjugating —plus a fifth activity, which is the spontaneous accomplishment of the other four. *Jangbu* means a "manual or text," but not an extensive one, a short text. It is called "general" because it is the Mahayoga aspect of Ati Yoga, not because it is a superficial or relative practice. This means it conforms with Mahayoga, since it is a development stage practice. This is the sadhana of the peaceful and wrathful deities, according to *Kunzang Tuktig.*

As I discussed previously, Mahayoga is usually accomplished by means of the three types of mandalas: at best, the mandala of colored powder or sand; next best, the mandala of painted canvas; or, at least, a mandala of heaps of grains. In Anu Yoga, the mandala is the body, itself, called the "body-mandala." The Ati Yoga mandala is the mandala of the primordially pure state of original wakefulness. But in this case, the Mahayoga practice is condensed into, or combined within, the body-mandala of Anu Yoga. The Anu Yoga body-mandala is contained within the Ati Yoga mandala of primordially pure wisdom. The primordially pure wisdom mandala of Ati Yoga is condensed within the sadhana practice, which is then contained within our application. In this way, there is a fourfold condensation, which is extremely profound.

Regarding the three levels of the inner tantras of Maha, Anu, and Ati, which are also called "tantra, scripture, and instruction," each yoga is progressively more profound than the previous one. Compared to Mahayoga—which is usually the "mandala of the support and supported," meaning the celestial palace and the deities—Anu Yoga is more profound, since the mandala consists of the structured *nadis*, or "channels," the *pranas*, or "moving winds," and the arrayed *bindus*, or "essences." By nature, these are the vajra body, speech, and mind. But the mandala of primordially pure wakefulness itself, wherein all deities and mandalas are naturally contained, is even more profound. Here, we have all levels at once, since it is the Maha aspect of Ati Yoga. This mandala of deities is still within Ati Yoga. Later on, there is Ati Yoga proper, the teachings of Trekchö and Tögal.

The first four characters are symbolic script. They are dakini letters, placed there to show that this teaching comes from an authentic source. It is not just the writing of any ordinary person. That is why there is the tradition of placing symbolic script at the beginning. Placing the dakini script at the beginning of the text shows its pure origin and also proves it was not composed by any intellectual who cannot grasp or decode the script itself. This means the text derives from an extraordinary being, a great tertön, who then wrote down the entire teaching based just on these (four) characters.

It is said that symbolic script is nirmanakaya, because you can see it with your eyes in actuality. It is also enlightened speech, since you can hear it. Since its meaning can be understood by means of these letters, it is also enlightened mind. In this way, the script is enlightened body, speech, and mind. The teaching presented here arose in its entirety from these four characters.

Only a tertön can perceive the meaning through the symbolic script—no one else can. He (or she) then decodes the secret language, writing it out in understandable letters. It is said that even if he makes a spelling mistake, the terma letters will remain in his experience until he notices the mistake, corrects it, and continues. That is why it's always correct.

NAMO GURU MAHANIDHI SAMANTABHADRAYA

This is Sanskrit. NAMO means "I pay homage," GURU is "master," MAHA means "great," and NIDHI SAMANTABHADRAYA means "I pay homage to Samantabhadra."

The Tibetan word for *guru*, or mahasiddha, is *lama;* one explanation is that *la* refers to the vital force of all sentient beings, while *ma* is the mother of all sentient beings. This demonstrates that it is the essence as well as the source of all sentient beings. Another explanation is that *la* means "unexcelled, unsurpassable, nothing higher than that."

From another approach, Samantabhadra is both the teacher and the teaching itself. Furthermore, it is said that Samantabhadra is everything that encompasses all of samsara and nirvana. In terms of being, appearance, and manifestation, the being itself is Samantabhadra, who is present throughout all states of samsara as well as nirvana. The appearance is the form of the five buddha families, while the manifestation refers to the buddhas of the six realms as well as all the buddhas of the Fortunate Aeon. All of this, in essence, is Guru Samantabhadra.

So, what is Samantabhadra? The real Samantabhadra is the *tongsal rangjung yeshe*, meaning "empty, cognizant, self-existing wakefulness," which is the very heart, or essence, of all of samsara and nirvana. When we look for the ultimate core or nature of everything—the very essence of any state whatsoever, whether it belongs to samsara or nirvana—we find none other than the unity of empty cognizance and self-existing wakefulness. That unity, itself, is known as the real Samantabhadra. That is the reason why Samantabhadra is mentioned at the outset of the text. Samantabhadra, who is the nature of mind of all sentient beings, is here called Guru Samantabhadra, to whom we pay homage or respect.

Sometimes we phrase this in a more lengthy way, saying, "Homage to Glorious Samantabhadra, the forefather of all buddhas." In the old school, or Nyingma school, the dharmakaya buddha is called Samantabhadra, while in the new schools, the Sarma schools, the dharmakaya buddha is called Dorje Chang, or Vajradhara. However, these are not two different buddhas. They are, in fact, the same, just two different manifestations.

When expressing simplicity, the absence of constructs, the dharmakaya buddha is presented in a form without ornamentation or garments, which demonstrates unconstructed primordial purity. When demonstrating the densely arrayed, spontaneously present qualities, the same buddha is dressed in jewel ornaments and silken garments. This is, in fact, the sambhogakaya aspect of the dharmakaya manifested in this form, but they are not two different buddhas. It is said that the dharmakaya of dharmakaya is called Buddha Samantabhadra, while the sambhogakaya of dharmakaya is called Vajradhara. The nirmanakaya of dharmakaya is called Vajrasattva. They are not three totally separate entities but three aspects of the same identity.

Samantabhadra's hands are in the gesture of equanimity, and this gesture symbolizes having totally relinquished all hope and fear—attempts to accept or reject, adopt or avoid. Samantabhadra is deep blue, like the color of the sky. His legs are crossed in vajra-posture. He is totally naked, not wearing anything whatsoever. Samantabhadra's consort is Samantabhadri. *Bhadra* means "excellent," while *bhadri* is its feminine form. *Samanta* means "in all aspects, in all ways whatsoever." There are no negative qualities at all, so altogether, *Samantabhadra* means "ever-excellent."

Don't think of Samantabhadra and Samantabhadri as human beings, because they are not. They are definitely not some fellow with his wife. Don't even think of them as male and female deities. We certainly understand that Buddha Samantabhadra and his consort are not human beings, but we may think that they are two deities or divine personages. Don't think this either. The male represents the manifest quality, while the female represents the empty quality—just as you know the nature of mind is, basically, the unity of being empty and cognizant, right? It is not only empty; if our nature were just like space, how could any good qualities manifest? Also, our nature is not some material substance that is somehow conscious; we cannot hold this thing that perceives with our bare hands. It is not like this. To symbolize the unity of empty cognizance, we are shown the Buddha Samantabhadra with consort. The union of the male and female is a symbol that illustrates the empty, cognizant unity of the nature of mind.

To elaborate further, buddhas' mind is an empty, cognizant unity with a core of knowing, while sentient beings' mind is an empty, cognizant unity with a core of unknowing. This is the meaning of the original protector, Samantabhadra. Earlier, I mentioned "being, appearance, and manifestation." Samantabhadra is the *being* aspect, which appears as the buddhas of the five families. Just as the sun rising in space manifests or shines, Samantabhadra shines or manifests the buddhas of the six realms. *Being* is dharmakaya that appears as sambhogakaya and manifests as nirmanakaya. Within the six realms of sentient beings, six buddhas manifest and are called the six munis. Just as the trunk of a tree has branches and, finally, leaves, the trunk of the tree is Buddha Samantabhadra, the branches are the five buddha families, and the leaves are the nirmanakaya buddhas of the six realms. This is how we should understand it.

It may seem to us as though the six realms of samsara are impure states, but they are in fact buddhafields, because the buddhas of the six realms do appear. Although we fail to recognize our own nature, and, therefore, every experience is a mistaken experience or delusion, we are nevertheless living in a buddhafield, because the realms of the six classes of sentient beings are where the buddhas manifest. So we must recognize our own nature by means of the Trekchö view. The moment we recognize our own nature, we recognize the *being* aspect, Buddha Samantabhadra, himself.

Here we find two terms: *tamer* and *those to be tamed*. *Tamer* refers to the teacher, while *those to be tamed* are the disciples, the recipients, or practitioners. The first sentence, *with faith and karmic connection, having attained empowerment and possessing pure samayas*, means that those who practice this teaching should have faith and devotion in the teaching. Possessing the pure link, they should have received the empowerment and be keeping its samaya in a pure manner.

Among the different types of faith—admiration, longing, and confident trust—we should possess the third type, confident trust. We must also have received three types of transmission: the ripening empowerment, the liberating instruction, and the supportive reading transmission. The scriptures state, "Transmission is received through empowerment but retained through keeping the samayas." Even though we may have received the empowerments, unless we are keeping the samayas, we are not really retaining the empowerment.

The second sentence says, *This is how to carry out the practice.* Since this is an Ati Yoga teaching, carrying out the practice means bringing our own nature into actual experience, recognizing our own nature through the practice. This is what we should do.

In a place of solitude, take a comfortable seat. Here, *solitude* means "isolation of body, speech, and mind." *Solitude of body* means going a couple of furlongs away from the normal village setting of worldly people, so we rise above or distance ourselves from the ordinary ways of human beings. *Solitude of speech* means stopping ordinary conversation. In a remote area, with no one to talk to, we are removed from ordinary conversations. *Solitude of mind* means giving up any involvement in past, present, and future thoughts.

A comfortable seat means we should sit on a seat that does not create any cause of illness, since our illusory body is still composed of flesh and blood, and, thus, is susceptible to disease. If we have already gained mastery over the nadis, pranas, and bindus, like Lord Milarepa, then we can sit on solid rock, and it will not disturb us. Yet, since we are beginners with a corporal body that can fall ill, we should be sure to sit in a place that will not cause illness. Although the place of solitude should be remote, it should be free of three kinds of dangers: enemies, wild animals, and bandits.

The text says, *Having prepared the mandala and gathered the practice materials*. How should we prepare the shrine? Since this is the Mahayoga aspect of Ati Yoga, we should know how to arrange the shrine. First, the mandala should, at best, be made of colored sand, but this is a very intricate task, so we can forget about that. Next best is a painted canvas, or picture, which is possible. The mandala structure is identical to what is known as the *Karling Shitro,* the peaceful and wrathful mandala according to Karma Lingpa, as revealed in *The Tibetan Book of the Dead*. It is perfectly all right to use that illustration, since this practice has the same intent as the longer version. Or, we should at least place the five heaps or draw five circles on canvas or paper.

We do this as follows: In the center is a blue circle. Create a rainbow ring around this, consisting of five colors. In front of this blue circle, create a white circle with an encircling rainbow. To the blue circle's right, create a yellow circle with an encircling rainbow. To the blue circle's left, create a green circle with an encircling rainbow, and behind the blue circle, create a red circle with an encircling rainbow. Altogether, there are five circles. This is the minimum requirement for a mandala.

Above this, place a tripod and put a traditional *bum-pa,* or "vase," on the tripod. Place a skull-cup on top, and above that place a mirror marked with *sindhura* powder. Place a crystal on top of this. These four articles—the vase, skull, mirror, and crystal—are representations of the four empowerments, which are the basic intent of Vajrayana. So, they should be placed above the mandala.

There are practice materials as well. In front of the mandala, place the seven general offerings of Argham padyam pushpe dupe, and so forth. To the right and left of the mandala, place small vessels for *amrita* and *rakta*. In front, again in the middle, is the *torma* called the *mey-jung torma,* meaning the Wondrous Torma. You should have one of these. Behind, place the representations of body, speech, and mind: Body is represented by either a *thangkha* or a statue; speech is represented by a scripture—or you can use a text called the *Sangye Seychig, The Only Child of the Buddhas.* If you have that text, which is printed in the form of a blue square, it can be used as the support for both speech and mind aspects rolled into one. As a representation of mind, you can use a crystal, a stupa, or other such objects. The shrine should be arranged in this way. In short, the shrine arrangement should be: a mandala; a tripod with a vase, skull cup, mirror, and crystal; the seven general offerings in front; vessels of amrita and rakta at right and left; the Wondrous Torma in the center; and representations of body, speech, and mind behind.

Train in the preliminary, main, and concluding sections. The whole sadhana is structured in three parts: the five preliminary parts, the five main parts, and the five concluding sections.

First, the preliminaries have five points, which are the general points of the preliminary part of a sadhana: refuge and bodhichitta, a torma to the obstructing forces, a protection circle, and consecration of the offerings. This will all be explained.

There is a line that is usually added in here:

The wisdom wheel of natural experience manifests, filling space.

While repeating that line, acknowledge that your personal experience is the continuity of wisdom. The continuity of wisdom, literally *wisdom-wheel*, means that whatever you experience as sights, sounds, and thoughts is none other than the primordial nature of deity, mantra, and wakefulness. Bringing this to mind, start the practice.

The first aspect of the preliminaries is taking refuge. In all Tibetan teachings, we always begin by first taking refuge. In any case, we practice the three yanas in the very same sitting. The ultimate intent of taking refuge embodies all the Hinayana teachings. In this way, we first take refuge. We should never act pretentious and say, "I'm a Dzogchen practitioner. I don't need to take refuge." We never find Dzogchen teachings that omit refuge taking. The objects of refuge are: outwardly, the Buddha, Dharma, and Sangha; inwardly, the guru, yidam, and dakini; and innermost, the dharmakaya, sambhogakaya, and nirmanakaya. Together, these are called the "ninefold objects of refuge", which include all objects of refuge.

Since this practice is a Dzogchen teaching, the refuge is the refuge of ultimate, or true, meaning. The bodhichitta is the bodhichitta of the real meaning. It's like this all along the way—although the other ways of taking refuge are naturally contained within the refuge of true meaning, or ultimate refuge. They are condensed within that.

Here we say,

> *In the empty essence, dharmakaya,*
> *In the cognizant nature, sambhogakaya,*
> *And in the manifold capacity, nirmanakaya,*
> *I take refuge until enlightenment.*

What are we taking refuge in here? First of all, the empty essence of mind, which is, in itself, dharmakaya; then, in mind's cognizant nature, which is sambhogakaya; and in the capacity of mind, which is nirmanakaya. We take refuge in these three aspects, meaning in all the deities and buddhas who represent these three. We take refuge until enlightenment.

We take refuge in these three aspects until we reach enlightenment, meaning the state of buddhahood itself. This is the ultimate way of taking refuge. In the ultimate style of refuge, all other types of refuge are included—nothing is left out. This is the ultimate refuge because, ultimately, everything originates from and within the sphere of the three kayas. Everything takes place within the sphere of the three kayas. Everything is liberated or purified within the sphere of the three kayas—dissolving into them again. That is why the *long* or "sphere of the three kayas" is the ultimate refuge. It is said that all phenomena belonging to samsara and nirvana originate from, abide within, and dissolve back into, or are liberated within, the sphere of the three kayas.

At the end of this verse, imagine that the field of refuge emanates rays of light toward all sentient beings, including you. Then the field of refuge dissolves into light that is absorbed into you. That was the refuge section.

Now for bodhichitta. The word *Ho!* is a means of calling, or requesting, someone's attention; in Nepali, the word is *Hajur!* It's actually *Hey!*, but in a more respectful approach. How would you call someone politely?

Student: You'd say, "Excuse me."

What is the bodhisattva resolve exactly aimed at here? It's aimed at the infinite number of sentient beings, who are like space in number. Why is space used as an example, where it says, *equal to the sky?* Because wherever there is space, there are sentient beings. Wherever there are sentient beings, there are disturbing emotions and karma. Wherever there are disturbing emotions, there is also buddha-nature. In this way, just as space is all-encompassing, so is buddha-nature. This is the reference of the bodhisattva resolve.

The word *space* means "that which has no center, no edge, no limit and is not confined in any direction." *Space*, meaning "all-pervasiveness," is always full of sentient beings, because karma and disturbing emotions are infinitely present throughout space. Wherever karma and disturbing emotions exist, there are sentient beings. And the essence of sentient beings is buddha-nature. This is what is meant by *all beings equal to the sky*. For sentient beings, in general, there is no end to samsara. It never finishes. But for sentient beings, individually, there is an end to samsara.

Here's an explanation of the three-kaya buddhafields, according to the unexcelled aspect of Mahayana, which is Vajrayana. First of all, dharmakaya is defined as being like space—all-encompassing, unconstructed, and present everywhere—but sambhogakaya manifests, without leaving the state of dharmakaya.

Among the different types of sambhogakaya, the first one is called the "greater sambhogakaya," which is explained as the fivefold mandala of the Buddha Immense Ocean. In the center is Vairochana Immense Ocean, who is a buddha seated in vajra-posture. In his hands, he holds a begging bowl. Within the begging bowl is a great lake called Immense Ocean. In the center of this lake, there is a lotus flower growing—twenty-five in all, growing, in turn, one above the other. Each lotus flower has a thousand petals, and in the center there are a thousand pistils, or anthers. One trillion nirmanakaya realms exist at the tip of each one of these thousand anthers. Likewise, there are trillions of nirmanakaya realms on each of the other anthers, as well as in each pore of this buddha's body. The pores of his body also number in the trillions.

The world we presently reside in is situated on the thirteenth lotus flower, which is exactly at the level of Buddha Immense Ocean's heart. Among the thousands times trillions of nirmanakaya realms, we are just one realm, within which one thousand buddhas will appear in this aeon. The sphere of simultaneous activity of one nirmanakaya buddha is sometimes referred to as one billion, or one hundred times one hundred times one billion, or a trillion worlds. There is an infinite amount.

As a reminder, from this angle, we should consider ourselves as being in a nirmanakaya buddhafield right now, since buddhas do appear here and influence beings in the world we occupy. This is the framework from the Vajrayana perspective.

However, there is not only one Vairochana Immense Ocean—in the eastern, southern, western, and northern directions, there is a Buddha Immense Ocean of the other four buddhas of the five buddha families. Not only that, the Vajrayana point of view sees it this way, as is found in the *Lamrim Yeshe Nyingpo* terma revealed by Chokgyur Lingpa. In the commentary, it is said that Yeshe Tsogyal once asked Guru Rinpoche to reveal just a fraction of his sphere of activity, of the manner in which he manifests in different world-systems. He then revealed himself in the ultimate form as Buddha Immense Ocean. But at the same time, an infinite number of other worlds with other manifestations of himself appeared within each pore of his body. This was just too much—it blew her mind and she fainted. So, this is the structure of the three kayas.

Furthermore, it is said that while dharmakaya is all-pervasive, like space, sambhogakaya appears like the light of the sun and moon. Nirmanakaya emanations act for the welfare of beings, like a rainbow in the sky, appearing in the form of flesh and blood, so people can meet them. Understand this as being inconceivable—that is what is meant by *all beings equal to the sky*.

In order to establish all beings equal to the sky in the state of buddhahood, means even though all sentient beings have buddha-nature, the enlightened essence, they roam about endlessly in samsaric existence, because they don't recognize their own nature, due to ignorance and delusion.

> *In order to establish all beings equal to the sky*
> *In the state of buddhahood,*
> *I will realize dharmakaya of self-existing awareness,*
> *Through the teachings of the Great Perfection.*

This means that, by actualizing the self-aware state of wisdom, which is the nature of all beings, within our own experience, we can liberate all sentient beings. The way to do this is through the teachings of the Great Perfection, Dzogchen, which are the ultimate confluence of all the dharma teachings of all buddhas. In this way, both refuge and bodhichitta are formulated here from the ultimate point of view. So, just as the beginning has some extra lines that are not actually part of the sadhana, here we say, *The wisdom wheel of natural experience manifests, filling space*. This refers to all the buddhas, bodhisattvas, Three Roots, and so forth, who are taken as the objects of refuge in the beginning and as the witnesses for taking the bodhisattva vow. Then, after this vow is taken, they again dissolve into us. There are also a few extra lines describing that.

Now, we have come to the torma offered to the obstructing forces, the *gektor*. First of all, understand that the *geks*, or obstructing forces, are our own thoughts; they arise out of our own mind. On the other hand, *obstructing forces* is a term given to hindrances that: first, will not relinquish command over the site of the mandala; next, steal the accomplishments; then, sneak away with the resplendence of the offerings; and, finally, create various kinds of interference. Although all these hindrances arise out of our own mind, according to the general way of practicing a sadhana, we first gently and peacefully offer them a present and ask them to leave. We do this by giving them a torma. Next, there is a commanding approach, whereby we say, "Take this torma and get out, or you will feel the heat of the herukas." Finally, we expel them wrathfully. These are also the three ways we practice here.

First, we create a torma with RAM YAM KAM..., imagining that from the state of emptiness, and so forth. The torma then appears fully endowed with the potency, fragrance, flavor, color, and texture that give rise to the five kinds of sense pleasures. By means of the mantra OM SARVA BHUTA AKAR KAYA JAH..., we then summon the *bhutas*—in Tibetan *jungpos*—which are the obstructing forces, and present the torma saying, OM MAHA BALINGTA KAYE.

Conceptual thinking is the obstructing force that arises out of our own mind. This is very significant, because the term *conceptual thinking* in Tibetan is *nampar togpa*. *Nampar* refers to the "mental objects of the five senses," while *tokpa* means "to conceptualize these objects"—apprehending an object as *that* and then forming ideas about it being attractive, repulsive, or neutral.

These three attitudes are called the "three basic evil spirits," which are male, female, and neuter. These three basic types, called the *gyalpo* spirit, *the dremo*, and *the maning*, have an entourage of followers that total 80,000 kinds of obstructing forces, demons, evil spirits, and so forth. They make all kinds of trouble, creating havoc and disasters in many different ways. Yet, they are all manifestations of our own mind. They can be condensed into the three poisons, which are basically our own conceptual thinking. We conceptualize objects as a duality of subject and object. That is the basic hindrance, or obstructor. The word *obstructor* means "that which creates a hindrance for realization of the enlightened state."

In order to get a handle on these different kinds of obstructing forces according to the general way of sadhana practice, we visualize a very beautiful torma arising out of emptiness, emanating sweet-sounding music, a lovely fragrance, a delicious flavor, a perfect texture, and so forth. We portion this out to all evil forces very liberally, saying, "Take this and go far away! Don't make any obstacles. And in case you don't go, you will be chased out, so you better leave."

Finally, with the mantra, we imagine tiny herukas arriving, like a terrific hurricane, and blowing away all obstructing forces, as though they were a pile of ashes scattered by a strong gust of wind. Powerless, they fly away to the ends of the universe. This is the meaning of these lines here.

The first line says,

> *Duality demons of ignorant confusion:*

This is exactly the Dzogchen way of understanding what obstructing forces are—they are none other than our own confusion.

> *Do not remain here; go elsewhere:*
> *Otherwise, the wrathful wisdom king of natural awareness:...*

As these lines indicate, the state of enlightened essence, rigpa itself, the absence of thought, is what overcomes conceptual thinking. When we recognize the state of nonconceptual wakefulness, we no longer have any room for conceptual thoughts. That is the meaning here, which is the Dzogchen way of expelling the obstructing forces.

After this, we create the protection circle. The idea of a protection circle is similar to chasing a thief out of our house—once he is out, we make certain to close our doors and windows. Here, in the same way, once the dualistic thinking of conceptualizing objects has been dissolved into awareness wisdom, then whatever we experience—whatever appears and exists—is none other than deity, mantra, and the state of samadhi, or original wakefulness. That's the ultimate protection circle, in which not even the name *obstructing force* can be found anywhere. There isn't even the basis for that word.

According to the general way of practicing a sadhana, to create the protection circle, we imagine a huge vajra-cross below us, a huge vajra-cross above us, and a circular wall of vajras all around us. First, there are large ones, and in between these are smaller ones; then again, between these are even smaller ones that get smaller and smaller. Finally, they are plastered with incredibly minuscule vajras, like a diamond eggshell—it's transparent but impenetrable. Not even a needle can pass through it.

On the outside, flames of fire, like those at the end of the aeon, blaze forth. This is what the line *fiery dome of wisdom vajras* means. This is the protection circle, the boundary line that cannot be crossed by any obstructing forces whatsoever. Then, we recite the mantra:

OM AH HUNG VAJRA RAKSHA RAKSHA BHRUNG॰

OM AH HUNG refers to the body, speech, and mind, meaning "deity, mantra, and samadhi." VAJRA means "indestructible;" RAKSHA means "protection;" and BHRUNG is the seed syllable for the celestial palace, but here it is also used for the protection circle.

As mentioned earlier, the preliminary practices have five points: refuge; bodhichitta; the torma to the obstructors; the protection circle, or literally "drawing the boundary line"; and the consecration of the offerings.

From the Dzogchen point of view, the offering articles are all that appears and exists. Sentient beings usually fixate on these as being concrete and solid. The moment that fixation dissolves, everything is *as it is*. The five elements are, by nature, the five female buddhas. Instead of thinking that earth is solid and material, we should understand its nature as the female buddha, Lochana; water as Mamaki, fire as Pandaravasini, and so forth. In order to combine this with the general way of practicing a sadhana, we purify the offerings, the world and all beings, and then emanate wisdom fire, wind, and water from the three syllables RAM, YAM, KHAM. This purifies all attachment to concreteness, and in this way, the world and all beings become the infinite offering cloud of the Bodhisattva Samantabhadra.

Then, within the vast *kapala* of space, the five meats dissolve into nectar-light, which is the samaya substance of the five buddha families, and so forth. The nature of amrita, rakta, and torma are the purified nature of the three poisons. Imagine them as being like a huge ocean of nectar, with an immense torma endowed with the perfect qualities of the five sense pleasures. We offer this, while saying the offering mantra that accompanies it.

In the small writing, Guru Rinpoche says,

This pacifies obstructing forces, purifies your mindstream,§
And makes you a suitable vessel for the accomplishments.§
Samaya.§

The preliminary point here—of dispelling obstructors, creating a protection circle, and so forth—pacifies troublemakers and purifies our stream-of-being, whereby we become a suitable vessel for accomplishment.

What do we mean by *a suitable vessel?* As an example, a lion's milk cannot be stored in a clay pot; it must be kept in a vessel of precious metal, such as gold or silver. If a lion's milk is poured into an ordinary ceramic cup, the cup will just shatter, because the milk is so powerful. In the same way, we become a suitable vessel for accomplishment. Furthermore, this purifies our stream-of-being, meaning that even though a vessel may be a proper container, it should not contain any poisonous substance that might contaminate whatever else is put into it. This is the purpose of the five preliminary points listed here.

The style of this sadhana gives the appearance of being just a normal type of sadhana practice, but it is, from beginning to end, actually the ultimate view. The structure conforms with the general approach to sadhana practice, while the meaning is the ultimate meaning. Isn't it? (Rinpoche laughs.) If the ultimate meaning were not included here in this sadhana, then it would be very difficult to condense full volumes of sadhanas of the peaceful and wrathful deities into just a couple of pages. At the very end of the sadhana, Padmasambhava says,

By fully condensing the Dzogchen tantras§
Into an easy method that is simple to carry out and bestows swift
*   blessings,§*
I, Padma, made this excellent composition§
As a meaningful encounter for the fortunate ones in that time.§

I have now covered the five points of the preliminaries in an most inadequate way. Next, we come to the five samadhis of the main section.

Questions and Answers

Question: What about the preliminaries for each session—how do I begin a session?

Rinpoche: It is mentioned that there are two types of ngöndro—a preliminary for the session and a preliminary for instructions. The preliminary for the session is what you practice at the outset of each session. For example, if you do three or four sessions a day, then repeat the preliminary three or four times a day, at the beginning of each session. The preliminary for the instruction is the contemplation of the "four mind-changings."

Regarding the preliminary for the session, Karma Khenpo says, *In a quiet place, sit on a comfortable seat, straighten the body posture, and leave your mind in naturalness. Exhale the stale breath three times and imagine that all your misdeeds, obscurations, moral faults, and downfalls are purified. Then, form the thought, For the sake of all sentient beings, filling the sky, I will practice this profound path.*[6] Imagine your root guru above the crown of your head and chant the six-line supplication called *Düsum Sangye* from the core of your heart as many times as you can. After that, say, *Precious root master, glorious one, essence of all buddhas of the three times, think of me! Grant my stream-of-being your blessings.* Through making this supplication, surrender totally. Doing this, the guru melts into light and dissolves into you through the crown of your head. This is the sequence to practice at the outset of each session.

Actually, this contains body, speech, and mind: the body aspect is exhaling the stale breath, the speech aspect is chanting the supplication, and the mind aspect is imagining that the guru dissolves into light and melts into you, whereby you rest indivisible from the guru.

Question: Is this preliminary for the session the same as the wake-up practice? And, if yes, how do we go about practicing that?

Rinpoche: Yes, it is a liturgy from the *Barchey Künsel.*[7] When you awaken, you should not just get up in the ordinary way. Remember that sleep is a subsidiary aspect of primordial ignorance, the unknowing that propelled us into samsaric existence to begin with—that is the main sleep. The sleep we

69

experience at night is a subsidiary branch of that state. So, when waking up, don't think you are just waking up from sleep; instead, think you are waking up from primordial ignorance—becoming totally awake.

At the same time, imagine that Padmasambhava arrives in the sky before you with a huge gathering of dakas and dakinis. They are all dressed with silk ornaments and hold damarus and bells, which they are sounding. With great splendor, they are all dancing and uttering seed syllables and symbolic words. Their minds are the state of great luminosity, the essence of self-existing wakefulness. They look directly at you. Imagine you are waking up to this. Then, sit up with a straight back and exhale the stale breath three times. Imagine the guru on the crown of your head and supplicate him—in short, say, *Düsum Sangye*, followed by "Ah, Lama Khyenno," and afterwhich, he dissolves into you. After this, check your own attitude, asking, "Am I doing this just for myself, or is it really for the benefit of countless sentient beings?" When we adopt the right motivation, whatever practice we do becomes a Mahayana practice. This is both for the wake-up practice and the preliminary for the session.

Question: What about the general preliminaries? Should we practice them as well?

Rinpoche: Of course, these are the preliminaries for the instruction, which are of two types: general and special. Here, general means what is general for both sutra and tantra—sutra means the extensive teaching, while tantra means the profound teaching. The special type is specific to Vajrayana. The first aspect, which is general for both sutra and tantra, is the four mind-changings. First, we reflect upon the support for dharma practice, called the "precious human body," which we have already obtained. Second, we reflect on the fact that we will not live forever—we will someday face death. Third, at the time of death, it is not like a candle being extinguished. Mind does not die and the ripening of karma, habitual tendencies, and so forth still occur in the mind after death. Fourth, we reflect on the negative aspects of samsaric existence, especially in the three lower realms, where there is not even a hair-tip of happiness. Even in the higher realms, there is no true happiness to be found anywhere. These four contemplations are called the "general preliminaries."

As for the specific preliminaries, first we take refuge; arouse bodhichitta; and perform prostrations, which purify karmic misdeeds and obscurations of our body. Next, we do Vajrasattva recitation and meditation, which purify the negative karma created through our voice. Then, we make outer, inner, and secret mandala offerings to purify our mindstream. Finally, we do guru yoga to purify our misdeeds accrued through the combination of body, speech, and mind. These are called the special preliminaries.

Training ourselves in virtuous actions takes effort, but engaging in evil requires no effort at all. It is spontaneous. Killing others, stealing, lying, and so forth require almost no effort at all. We need not teach insects how to kill each other. It's quite spontaneous. No sentient being needs training in the three negative karmic actions of the body, carried out on the physical plane. By nature, we engage in them. Animals need not be taught how to kill or steal.

Without having to study, we also know, quite naturally, how to carry out the four negative actions of speech: lying, using harsh words, slandering, and engaging in idle gossip. No one needs to learn how to train in the three negative actions of mind: having ill-will, craving, and holding wrong ideas. We all seem to know quite well how to carry out these activities. Sentient beings are already experts. If there were no karmic effect, we would have to train in learning how to carry out negative actions, but actually it happens quite spontaneously, due to the ripening of past karma—but we need to study the Dharma.

If we want to roll a big boulder up to the top of a mountain, we need to push it all the way up. However, to let it roll down into the valley, we needn't do much. We just let go, and it will roll down all by itself whereas, no stones roll uphill. Just nudge a stone, and it will roll downhill all by itself. In the same way, we need not learn how to engage in negative actions. Carrying out negative actions is called "being under the power of karma." But sometimes we give rise to faith in the teachings. We feel good-hearted, compassionate, devout, and so forth; yet this is very rare. That is why it is said, "Those who don't practice are as abundant as the stars at night. Those who do practice are as scarce as morning stars." This is due to karma.

For those with good karma, it is different. Many great Kagyü masters later sang, "Even in my mother's womb, my spiritual aspirations were awakened, and I had the desire to practice. At the age of eight, I remained in equanimity." That's an example of good karma ripening.

No matter where we take rebirth next time throughout the six realms, we are still like a fly trapped in a bottle. We fly around, up and down, but never outside of the container. We are trapped inside, and everywhere in the six realms is a painful state.

It is said that, although you may have a very high view, you should still have a very refined meditation. Here *refined* means we should pay close attention to and remember impermanence and mortality—even while having a high view. However, as soon as you reach the point of recognizing mind-essence and not being distracted from that, it is not so important to worry about impermanence. If something is impermanent, let it be impermanent; if it is not, then it is not. We need not think about impermanence, but this is only the case when there is no distraction whatsoever.

Here, *high view* means we should pay close attention to details about how things are, such as the impermanence of everything, at the same time that our meditation should be very fine. *Fine meditation* doesn't mean being skilled at the development stage or yogic exercises; it means facing the fact that everything is impermanent. Until we reach the point of nondistraction, this means not sleeping at night; not falling into delusion during the dream state; recognizing dreams as dreams; and maintaining one long stretch of luminosity during deep sleep. At that point, we won't need to dwell on impermanence anymore.

The Tibetan word for enlightenment, *jangchub*, means "purified perfection." In Sanskrit, it's *bodhi*. Literally, this means that the two obscurations, along with habitual tendencies, are purified; all qualities of wisdom and so forth are fully perfected, like a lotus bud, which having grown out of the mud, blooms fully. Until this occurs, we should practice as the root text for the Dzogchen commentary advises: *In a retreat, in the snow mountains, caves, or deep forests... Place yourself on your meditation seat... Supplicate one-pointedly.*[8] Inspire yourself by thinking of impermanence with compassion.

When we sit in such a place, we begin with the session preliminary, as I just explained, supplicating the guru. Chant the *Düsum Sangye*, where the first line begins: *Buddha of the Three Times, Guru Rinpoche...* The first aspect addresses the outer way of accomplishing the guru, according to *Barchey Künsel, Dispeller of All Obstacles*. *Lord of All Siddhis, Great Bliss* refers to the inner approach to sadhana, called *Sampa Lhündrub, Fulfillment of All Wishes*. *Wrathful Slayer of Mara* refers to the innermost way of accomplishing the guru, called *Guru Drakpa Tsal*.

Afterward, we should chant the supplication to the lineage masters, called *Ösel Rangshar*, which is found at the beginning of the sadhana in the

Kunzang Tuktig[9]. Every special Dzogchen teaching always contains a supplication to the masters of the lineage at the beginning. We should chant it slowly, with heart, so that it really transforms our experience and devotion blazes forth. Chant it one-pointedly. There is a nice tune that goes with it. There is also a special prayer written by Chokgyur Lingpa himself.

As is constantly taught, to realize the view of the Great Perfection, the dharmakaya itself, we must rely upon methods for purifying obscurations and gathering the accumulations and upon receiving the blessings of a realized master. Aside from this, any other method should be considered foolish. To merely learn grammar in order to understand the view of the Great Perfection, or to become skilled in arts and crafts, in debate, or in winning arguments will not lead to realization of the view.

It is sometimes good to go to the top of a hill or mountain and, with a beautiful melody, slowly chant the supplication to the lineage gurus. Afterward, stand up and slowly dance around, moving the arms and leaving awareness totally without focus. This enhances our comprehension of the view tremendously. There is a tradition that recommends practicing this way. It both dispels hindrances and brings forth enhancement, simultaneously. Hindrances for the view are dullness and drowsiness. This method dispels these hindrances, while bringing forth enhancement of the view.

Question: Do we have to visualize anything at the time of reciting refuge?

Rinpoche: It is good if you can. Imagine that the place where you are is the dharmadhatu realm of Akanishtha, which is free from all unpleasant things as well as the coarse elements of earth, water, fire, and wind. Here, in the sky before you, dwell the Buddha, Dharma, and Sangha, as well as the Three Roots and three kayas. Imagine them as stars filling the sky. The Three Precious Ones are actually present before you in the space. It is good to think like that.

In the empty essence, dharmakaya[a]: When the people in foreign countries were asked whether mind is unformed or unconditioned, they answered that it is unconditioned. That proves it is empty, right? Emptiness is unconditioned. Everyone resolved it to be unconditioned. Whatever is conditioned must have material substance. Whatever is unconditioned must be substanceless. *Substanceless* means there is nothing for the eyes to see, for the ears to hear, and for the hands to hold. As it is said, "This substancelessness is the empty essence, the dharmakaya."

If this emptiness were a total blank void, there would not be any talk of the buddhas up there, of attaining enlightenment, and of the sentient beings down here, wandering about in samsara and in the hells. Space doesn't do that, does it? Without being like that, emptiness is naturally cognizant.

In the cognizant nature, sambhogakaya: This refers to the hosts of sambhogakaya deities; the nature of dharmakaya is the cognizance, sambhogakaya. If you were to ask what sambhogakaya means, then it is something that has perfect abundance. If something is totally void, there is no way it can possess perfect abundance. The emptiness, itself, has perfect abundance; that is called sambhogakaya.

And in the manifold capacity, nirmanakaya: The *capacity* here means "union." The unity of emptiness and cognizance is called "capacity." The phrase *manifold capacity* means that the capacity is all-embracing, unconfined—not just in one or two ways; it is the inconceivable dharmata. *Manifold* means that the unobstructed wisdom of self-display manifests a manifold capacity. It does not refer to external, coarse substance, but, rather, to the unobstructed self-display. *Capacity* is the unconfined aspect of emptiness and cognizance. *Manifold* means "all-embracing."

I take refuge until enlightenment means we take refuge until we attain the level of mahabodhisattva, until we reach the state of buddhahood. There are two: bodhisattva and mahabodhisattva. The mahabodhisattva has defeated the four *maras*. Until then, the bodhisattva is not free from the dangerous path of the four maras, but the mahabodhisattva is. For the perfectly enlightened one, there is not even the name *four maras*. Therefore, it is said, *I take refuge until enlightenment.* That is the measure for refuge, the ultimate refuge. The goal is the state of perfect enlightenment: As it is said, "As long as I am not enlightened, I take refuge."

When taking refuge, first supplicate. Then rays of light stream forth from the object of refuge, purifying your evil deeds and obscurations. Imagine this. After that, imagine that the deities of the object of refuge and you have become inseparable.

Question: Do we visualize one or two protection circles?

Rinpoche: Actually, we visualize two—there are two sets. When doing retreat practice, there is one protection circle. The outer one that you visualize when you start retreat. It is supposed to remain there until you end retreat, whenever that is. It is one you never dissolve at the end of practice. The benefit of that is reducing obstacles while in retreat. It is kind of far off in the distance, because it surrounds one billion universes—you should imagine they are contained within that. The protection circle you should visualize, which is created at the beginning of practice and dissolved at the end, is the one at the summit of Mount Sumeru, and the celestial palace is within that.

Question: How should we visualize it?

Rinpoche: First, the floor, or the base, is the big vajra-cross. The four sides and the top also have a huge vajra-cross. Then, in between, there are smaller ones, and in between them there are even smaller ones, and so forth. It is also plastered with diamond vajras, so the whole thing is indestructible and so dense that not even wind can blow through. Not even a needle tip can go through. Outside that vajra dome are the emblems or implements of the five buddha families. The peaceful and wrathful ones have other emblems, which are sword, hammer, *phurba,* axe or something, and so forth.

We can visualize both the peaceful and wrathful deities or just the peaceful ones. Outside that again are the wisdom flames that burn like the fire at the end of the kalpa. There are two sets of incredible masses of flames, one that burns clockwise and the other that burns anticlockwise, swirling violently. Outside that, tiny herukas shoot out continuously in all directions, like sparks from within the huge fire, so that no obstacle whatsoever can penetrate. It's completely unassailable. That is one way of visualizing the protection circle.

The other way is recognizing the view that everything already has the nature of body, speech, and mind. So, just like it says in the *Choying Dzo,* "Whatever appears is the adornment of the dharmadhatu dharmatatu, or of space, and is the continuity of the enlightened body, and then of speech, and then of mind." Like that. So, when you recognize that everything is actually pure nature—body, speech, and mind of all the buddhas—how can there be any obstacles to catch?

Question: How do you balance the *Kunzang Tuktig* text stressing rigpa, rigpa, rigpa, but then when we ask for teachings, we get a lot of things to visualize? How do you balance that?"

Rinpoche: Since the *Kunzang Tuktig* sadhana is the Maha of Ati, there *is* something to visualize. Just simply follow the text exactly as it is, line by line, and then imagine whenever we recite. It is linking the meaning with the words, so whenever we say a word, we imagine what it means, step by step. But that doesn't mean the ultimate mandala is something we imagine. The ultimate mandala is not created by thought. It is the spontaneously present primordial mandala, as it is.

That's what it means when we have realized it, but have we? Have we already realized this, or are we not under the power of deluded thought and ignorance? If that is the case, then the important guideline for us is using visualization to remedy our confusion, because the sole meaning and purpose of development stage is to change our negative thought patterns into the right ones. As long as we have confusion and ignorance, we need to visualize in order to change that. But we don't have to visualize in a really fixed, rigid, materialistic way, thinking, "Where is the kitchen in the mandala, where is the toilet, and how big are the windows and doors?" We don't have to get that much into the details!

Question: What about the three kinds of mandalas?

Rinpoche: Within what is called the "substance mandala of signs," the best is the one made of colored sand. The second best is the one drawn on canvas. Finally, if you can't obtain the other ones, place heaps of grain upon a mandala plate for each of the peaceful and wrathful ones and use that.

Question: What is meant by the mandala of experience?

Rinpoche: The best is the experience mandala of the view; then the meditation mandala created by mind, as a visualizion. In the case of an experience mandala, you do not need to display a shrine. The supreme is the mandala of the view, the mandala beyond visualizer and something visualized. The second best has someone visualizing and something visualized, the experience mandala. The third best is the substance mandala of signs, where an actual shrine representation is arranged.

Question: What about samayas?

Rinpoche: Concerning samayas, the first-class samaya, the best, is not to be moved or steered away from the practice. This is the "nonkeeping great keeping of the samaya"—referring to when there is nothing to keep. Constantly remaining in the practice, all the samayas of body, speech, and mind are contained therein. Otherwise, there are the samayas of body, speech, and mind. The samaya of body is to practice the development stage of the deity. The samaya of speech is to utter its mantra. The samaya of mind is to train in compassion and emptiness, practicing the unity of development and completion stages. These were the second-class, or next best, samayas. The final, or lowest ones, are: The samaya of body is to not disturb or cause inconvenience to the guru's body. The samaya of speech is to not break his command or order. And the samaya of mind is to remain in the state of thinking his mind and our own mind are inseparable. These were the lowest samayas. *(Rinpoche laughs.)* The best is to remain in the practice.

There are also the Dzogchen samayas called "nonexistence" *(med pa)*, "free" *(phyal ba)*, "sole" *(gcig pu)*, and "spontaneous presence" *(lhun grub)*. The samayas of primordial purity, or *Trekchö*, are "*nonexistence*" and "*free;*" the samayas of spontaneous presence are "sole" and "spontaneous presence.*" These four—nonexistence, free, sole, and spontaneous presence—concern the view. In short, for the practice, these four together are called the "king of all samayas." If you practice these nicely, then you'll keep all samayas perfectly. If you are walking down to the Boudhanath Stupa from Nagi Gompa here, then you go step by step, and slowly you will arrive there. If you move your feet, sooner or later you will get to the Stupa. If you don't move, you will never arrive. If you just sit, you cannot arrive.

Question: How do we start a retreat on the *Leyjang* of *Kunzang Tuktig*?

Rinpoche: To start a retreat on the *Leyjang*, you need three tormas: one for the peaceful ones, one for the wrathful ones, and a torma called the Marvelous Torma. The Marvelous Torma is the torma placed among the amrita, rakta, and torma. The tormas for *Kunzang Tuktig* should not be made of clay. They should be made of flour or *tsampa*. They don't have to be very big; that is not especially useful, but smaller, nicely decorated ones are best.

Then you need two foods, one for the peaceful deities and one for the wrathful deities. The foods for the peaceful ones are different from the foods for the wrathful ones, so you need two. There is also one torma for each of the protectors Ekajati, Damchen Dorje Lekpa, and Za Rahula, each of them. You can put these three together on one plate. For the shrine mandala, you don't need a very elaborate one. You can put the heaps for the peaceful and wrathful ones together on one mandala plate.

There is nothing extremely difficult; mostly, everything here concerns mental considerations. There is nothing you should do with your hands. Mostly think about the words of the offering and nothing other than that. It is good if you know the meaning of ARGHAM PADYAM PUSHPE DHUPE, as all the Vajrayana teachings are contained within symbol, meaning, and sign. The offerings are the signs. The meaning is what we create mentally. For the symbols, you do the *mudras* with your hands. The signs are what you place on the shrine, and the meaning is the mental offering. You increase them first from ten to one hundred, from one hundred to one thousand, to ten thousand, to millions, and then offer all the billions of offerings to all the buddhas and bodhisattvas in all the buddhafields of the ten directions.

The ultimate offering is beyond the threefold conceptions of offerer, offering, and the recipient of the offering. There is only oneness in the sphere of the nature. The ultimate offering is in the space of the view.

If we don't know the meaning of the secret mantra teachings, then, from the outside, it just looks like children's play. We think, "What are they doing?" If we really know, it is extremely profound and significant. Some say, "Oh, I don't know what they are doing. They are just moving their hands around. It is merely playing around. What is the use of that?" They will wonder what the purpose is. Without an understanding of symbol, meaning, and sign, it becomes just like children's play.

When beginning a retreat, there are additional tormas required: one for the local deity and one for the spirits, which you send outside as a present for not creating any obstacles, a gift. You should give these first and then give one torma to the four great world kings. At the time of the Buddha, they promised to be, or were placed as, guardians of the Buddhist teachings. They should have one torma. At the end of the general and specific lineage prayers, a short verse is added:

> *Whoever dwells at this site, devas, nagas,*
> *Yakshas, rakshasas, or anyone else,*
> *As I request you to lend this place for the mandala,*
> *Please hand it over to me.*

Then offer the torma for the obstructing spirits, according to the text of the *Kunzang Tuktig*.

One person said, "Oh, at the monastery, they should give up all these rituals and pujas, and so on. It would be so nice if they could give up all these and only meditate. Also, at Nagi Gompa, there shouldn't be any rituals or pujas done, only meditation." The reply to that was, "It is good if they did meditation, but whether one meditates or not depends on one's merit. If one knows how to meditate, then it is good to meditate. If one does not know how to meditate and then also does not do any rituals and pujas, then one is doing nothing at all. One is just eating through the mouth, shitting through the ass, like a dog and a pig." Then the person said, "Can't they just do shamatha practice? Isn't that enough?" The reply was, "Shamatha is not enough. If shamatha were enough, then a lot of people would have been enlightened by now; it is not enough. Shamatha is making the mind still and using a lot of effort and hardship to attain that."

In Tibet, there is one small animal called *dremo*. It can hybernate for four months every year; it doesn't need to eat anything at all. There is another one called *semo*, who lives under the earth and can remain in a state of cessation, blankness, for a long time. It remains in one-pointedness. It doesn't need to drink or eat anything. It simply remains down under the earth for all this time. When it comes to the first or second month of the year, they wake up and come out. At the end of autumn, they go to sleep, hibernate. They are quite fat at that time. When the spring comes, they have become quite thin. They can sit like that, but they didn't get enlightened. The movements of the mind are the same as an ordinary person's. When the mind is still, it is the same as a meditation god, *dhyana-god*.

Question: Do we really need all the different offering objects and tormas to do this practice?

Rinpoche: First, when doing a retreat, you should gather the offerings and the tormas, as stated above. Then, when doing the daily practice, if you don't have tormas, you can create them mentally. You have the materially present and the mentally created. The materially present is like an example; it is less important. The reason for creating many mentally is that the relative should be sealed with the absolute; it is all right if the relative is not materially present, as long as there is the absolute. However, at the beginner level, one takes the materially present as the relative and the mentally created as the absolute. Concerning all relative and absolute dharmas, we need to seal. When the relative has been purified, when the delusion has been cleared, then there is no need for anything other than the absolute; there is no need for either offerings or tormas. Until then, we take support of symbolism. In the tantric teachings, there are the three I just mentioned: signs, symbols, and meaning. One should first arrange the offerings and tormas. However, in the case of the daily practice of *Shitro*, it is all right to perform the ritual even without offerings and tormas and to recite the Bodhichitta and Rulu mantras. There were many people in Kham who practiced like that.

Question: Could you please explain more about the consecration of offerings at the time of the five preliminaries? *Within the vast skull cup of space*,⁸ it says there are the five nectars, and so forth. Please explain that in more detail.

Rinpoche: It says, *within the vast skull cup of space*⁸. That means the skull cup is dharmadhatu. Within this skull cup, the vast skull cup of space, there are the five meats and the five nectars, whose natures are the five male and female buddhas. Space is the primordial purity, the nature of dharmakaya. That is the skull cup within which, in the manner of sambhogakaya, are the five aspects of male and female buddhas that should be visualized as dissolving into nectar and then being offered to the deities.

This is quite a profound terma on the ultimate view of the Great Perfection. In the development stage itself, as in Mahayoga, you won't find something like this. This is an Ati Yoga practice. Therefore, it says, *In the vast skull cup of space.* If it were Mahayoga, it would be like this: *(Rinpoche recites a long line).* Here, you merely visualize the skull cup itself. But, since this is an Ati Yoga practice, you say, *Within the vast skull cup of space,*⁸ that is the dharmadhatu, the space free from extremes. It means that from the space of primordial purity, the dharmakaya, the male and female buddhas of sambhogakaya dissolve into nectar. All the male and female deities dissolve into nectar. These are quite significant words.

According to the Sarma tradition, in the five different places are the five meats, and then the five nectars, and so on. Visualize all of these as the samaya being, into which the wisdom being is invited. Next, the OM HUNG TRAM HRIH AH dissolve into nectar. The difference is in how much or how little elaboration there is. Actually, it says that one needs the flesh of a horse, human being, dog, and so forth.

Whereas, here in this teaching, it says *in the skull cup of space,* the male and female buddhas turn into nectar. This means that from the start, one has laid out the main structure of the view. In this case, everything is within the structure of the space of primordial purity of dharmakaya. This development stage is only a simulation of development stage. It is actually the completion stage. It is the meaning of Ati Yoga.

Question: What is meant by these words: *The rakta of great bliss becomes a swirling ocean*?

Rinpoche: Rakta generally means "blood." Rakta is the Sanskrit word for blood. What is meant by blood in this case? If there weren't both the white and red essences, if there were only the red one, would a child be able to be born or not? Will a child come only from the white element? The answer to both is no. These offerings are for the purpose of emptying the causes for samsara, and the basic causes for samsara are the white and the red elements. The white element is the nectar, the amrita. The red element for samsara is the rakta, blood. We transform the whole three realms into rakta, so the attachment or passion is all gathered together. Then, we visualize the goddess Girtimamo, a red goddess without any ornaments, from whose secret place the waves of blood flow forth; the blood of existence.

There are many different types of blood; in fact, there are thirty-five kinds, thirty-five different kinds of rakta substances. All of these are rakta, but the main one is the rakta of existence, or coming, from the bhaga, the blood of existence, which is the red element of the female. Additionally, there is the blood in the aorta, the life-vein; there is the blood in the urine. In addition to these are the five kinds of bloods from plant-like trees, such as sandalwood and the rakta-tree. All these are called "substances," but, in actuality, they signify the blood for emptying the causes for samsara, which are to be offered to the deities. For this reason, we visualize the rakta.

First visualize Girtimamo, a red goddess, from whose bhaga the red rakta flows forth. The deity herself then dissolves into blood, and the passion of the whole world dissolves into the blood, the rakta; visualize it swirling with waves, a huge ocean. By offering these, all the deities experience great bliss and, specifically, the wrathful deities increase courage and bravery.

The wrathful buddhas manifest wrath out of compassion, not anger. Out of compassion, they consider: "Oh, poor beings, they cling to samsara and have entered a wrong path." They manifest wrath to guide beings from the wrong path to the right path. Their anger, or wrath, arises out of compassion. Through the rakta offering, they develop even more fierceness and ferociousness, flaming like butter poured on fire. By offering the rakta, the wrathful ones become even more wrathful. The bodies of all the savage spirits, demons, and so on are destroyed, as though struck by flashes of lightning. The rakta possesses this kind of power and potency.

The Main Practice

Tulku Urgyen Rinpoche

Now we come to the main part, which also has five points, known as the five samadhis, arranged in five sections. In the first section, we erect the framework, or basic structure, of the three samadhis: the samadhi of suchness, which is the intent of primordial purity; the samadhi of illumination, which is the intent of spontaneous presence; and the samadhi of the seed syllable, which is the nirmanakaya, the indivisibility of primordial purity and spontaneous presence. The remaining two samadhis are the samadhi of the celestial palace and the samadhi of the deities.

First, the syllable HUNG is the seed syllable of the enlightened mind of all the buddhas. As the second line states, *dharmakaya is the primordial state of emptiness*. There's a big difference between *empty* and *emptiness*. *Empty* just means "void," like space, but *emptiness* means "like space suffused with sunlight." Dharmakaya is primordial emptiness, with an all-pervading wisdom nature. Its essence, nature, and capacity have a single identity. The essence is empty, but the nature of this emptiness is *wisdom that is all-pervading*, just like sunlight. The unborn awareness, which manifests as the syllable AH, is the unity of emptiness and cognizance—the empty essence and its cognizant nature, indivisible.

The empty essence is called the samadhi of suchness, while its wisdom nature is called the samadhi of illumination. These two are also called emptiness and compassion. Their unity, which is nonarising, still manifests as the letter AH, which is called the seed samadhi. When we visualize the letter AH, or the seed samadhi, we should imagine that it radiates five-colored light that purifies the world and all beings. It sends out rays of light of the five elements, E YAM RAM LAM BAM, and then of the seed syllable SUM, for Mt. Sumeru. In this way, the five elements are purified into the lights of the five wisdoms. This is the "vast, pure space" of the five female buddhas, within which appears the celestial mansion of the five wisdoms: dharmadhatu wisdom, mirror-like wisdom, the wisdom of equality, discerning wisdom, and the all-accomplishing wisdom.

The celestial palace is literally immeasurable, meaning "beyond measurement, beyond any limits one could impose upon it by conceptual thinking." It totally defies any kind of architecture produced through normal concepts. The palace has the nature of the five wisdoms. It is two-storied, with designs and attributes that are densely arrayed decorations, a perfect manifestation of qualities.

Abundant in perfect ornaments and designs. *Ornaments and designs* means that in the densely arrayed realm of Akanishtha, the ornamentation is spontaneously present. Within our monastery and others, brocade ornamentation, such as tassels, banners, and so forth, are ornaments and designs. Here, they do not need to be arranged or put up; they are spontaneously present. The ornamentation and the decoration are inconceivable. It is not said that they can be embraced by thought, is it? They are beyond the object, the realm of thinking. *Abundant* means they are "inconceivable."

This is the two-storied palace of the peaceful and wrathful ones. First, meditate on the peaceful ones below. Then, they are lifted up, after which you visualize the wrathful ones in the place of the peaceful ones. This is a two-storied manor.

There are different ways of practicing the peaceful and wrathful deities' mandala. One is called the "two-storied style." Another is called the "group-gathering style," whereby they are all gathered together around each other. There is also a style called "the transformation," whereby the deities first manifest as peaceful, and then they become the wrathful deities. Here, the style is called "the elevated style," whereby you first visualize the mandala of the peaceful deities, and then it elevates or ascends to the second floor, thus leaving a place for the mandala of the wrathful deities to appear.

Begin with Samantabhadra in the center. The other deities are the display of Samantabhadra. All this is self-visualization; there is no mention and no need for a front visualization. Visualize yourself as Samantabhadra with consort, and from Samantabhadra, who is like the sun, comes the display of the forty-two peaceful and the flaming wrathful ones. They are like the rays from the sun of Samantabhadra. All the hundred sublime families of the peaceful and wrathful ones are contained within your body. Your body is the mandala of the victorious ones—that is what it is about.

Concerning Samantabhadra and consort, the mind, the one that acts, is Samantabhadra, and the mental object, the one acted upon, is Samantabhadri. Mind and dharmas are Samantabhadra and consort. Mind, the actor, Samantabhadra, is the cognizance aspect. The mental object, the one acted upon, Samantabhadri, is the emptiness aspect. They are empty cognizance. When explained as appearance-emptiness, then mind, the actor, Samantabhadra, is the appearance aspect. Mental object, the one acted upon, Samantabhadri, is the emptiness aspect. For this reason, mind and mental object can be called "appearance and emptiness," and also "cognizance and emptiness." That is the first condition. They are also referred to as "the doer and the deed," which I will explain later.

Then, like rays radiating from the sun, the five male tathagatas are present, since we possess the five aggregates *(skandhas)*. We have the aggregates, the gathering of many parts: forms, feelings, formations, conceptions, and consciousnesses. In the impure aspect, the situation, or status, of these five is the defiled aggregates. The five aggregates have to be transmuted. If they are not transmuted, spontaneously purified, then they will remain impure. When the aggregate of form is transmuted, it is Vairochana. The transmutation of the feeling aggregate is Ratnasambhava. The transmutation of the aggregate of conception is Amitabha. The transmutation of the aggregate of formation is Amoghasiddhi. The transmutation of the aggregate of consciousness is Akshobhya. That is the real situation.

When impurity arose in the mindstream of sentient beings, due to ignorance, immediately, its pure nature is the five buddha aspects. It is said, concerning the external world, that the five lights are the basis for the arising of objects. This means when samsara and nirvana originated in the beginning, spontaneous presence came as the expression of primordial purity. This spontaneous presence appeared as sounds, lights, and rays. At that time, there were five lights. When not recognized, they strayed into expression, and the five elements arose. The five elements, in their impure aspects, are earth, water, fire, wind, and space. The pure aspect of earth is Buddha Lochana; the pure aspect of water is Mamaki. The pure aspect of fire is Pandaravasini. The pure aspect of wind is Samaya Tara, and the pure aspect of space is Dhatvishvari. These are the five female buddhas, who represent the real situation. In the impure state, we have the aggregates and elements; in the pure aspects, they are deities. That is the reason for the buddha mandalas of deities, as we have five aggregates and five elements. These are the five male and five female tathagatas, ten altogether.

Then we have the eight gatherings of consciousnesses (perceptions), which are the eight male bodhisattvas. Then we have the eight consciousness objects, fields of perception, which are the eight female bodhisattvas. In the experience of the mind, there are eight consciousnesses and eight objects: form in the field of sight; sound in the field of hearing; smell in the field of the nose organ; taste in the field of the tongue; touch in the field of the body; and past, present, and future times, which are also objects of the consciousnesses.

After these there are the four male and four female gatekeepers. The four male gatekeepers are the four views of permanence, nothingness, self, and extremity. The four female gatekeepers are touching, the touched, the toucher, and the touch consciousness. All these are contained within our body.

We have arrogance, don't we? That is the deva muni, Indra. We have envy, don't we? That is the teacher Thaksang, in the realm of the asuras. The tamer of beings in the human realm is Shakyamuni. The muni of the animals is Senge Rabten. The muni of the pretas is Khala Mebar, and the muni of the hells is the Dharmaraja. These six nirmanakayas are our six poisons: passion, aggression, delusion, envy, arrogance, and greed. We do possess these six, and here they have turned into the munis of the six realms. All these together make up the forty-two peaceful ones.

What was first impure has now been transmuted. At the time of sentient beings, all these are impure, but here they are pure. When the peaceful ones are transformed into the wrathful ones, then Samantabhadra with consort becomes Chemchok and consort. The five male buddhas become the five *herukas* of the families of buddha, vajra, ratna, padma, and karma. The five *krodhishvaris* are the transformations of the five female buddhas. The eight *mamos* of the sacred places are the eight bodhisattvas, and the eight *tramen* of the sacred valleys are the eight female bodhisattvas. The six munis transform with Samantabhadra and consort. Next, the four male and female gatekeepers transform. There are the ones who perform the four activities: pacifying in the east, enriching in the south, magnetizing in the west, and subjugating in the north. They multiply to become six of each of the female gatekeepers, thus, seven in each of the four directions, making the twenty-eight *ishvaris*. Altogether, they make fifty-eight. The forty-two added to these fifty-eight make one hundred.

These are the hundred sublime families of peaceful and wrathful ones, which are all contained within our own body. This practice is not merely a skillful means or technique, since the peaceful and wrathful deities are the actual nature of our body and mind, the buddha-mandala of our body present as the peaceful and wrathful deities. As a totality, this is what is called the "three seats of completeness."

The first seat of completeness means that the aggregates and elements making up our body are actually the five male and female buddhas. The five aggregates are, by nature, the five male buddhas, while the five elements are, by nature, the five female buddhas. The sense faculties and their corresponding objects are, by nature, the eight male and female bodhisattvas.

With the male and female gatekeepers, the explanations sometimes differ—they are varyingly referred to as the four times; the four views of permanence, nothingness, self, and extremity; as well as touching, the toucher, the touched, and the touch consciousness. These three races are male and female tathagatas as the aggregates and elements; male and female bodhisattvas as the sense bases; and male and female gatekeepers as the karma *(las)* and power *(dbang), or power of karma.* We refer to them when saying, "the hosts of the empowerment deities of the complete three races, Vajra Samaya!" The practices of Mahayoga mention them in the invocation, but the actual meaning is the pure aspect of our present situation.

Returning to the lines of the sadhana:

> *In the middle of the four-spoked wheel,*
> *Upon a lion throne, lotus, sun, and moon,*
> *Is Guru Samantabhadra, deep blue,*
> *With the hand gesture of equanimity, embracing his consort.*

This gesture symbolizes having totally relinquished all hope and fear, attempts to accept or reject, adopt or avoid. Samantabhadra is deep blue, like the color of the sky. His hands are resting in equanimity, and his legs are crossed in vajra-posture. He is not wearing anything whatsoever, totally naked. Samantabhadra's consort is Samantabhadri. *Bhadra* means "excellent," while *bhadri* is its feminine form. *Samanta* means "in all aspects, in all ways whatsoever." There are no negative qualities at all. Together, *Samantabhadra* means "ever-excellent."

Then, in front of Samantabhadra and in the four directions are the five other buddhas. First, white Vairochana, with his consort Dhatvishvari, holds a wheel in his (right) hand. Blue Akshobhya, with consort Vajratopa, holds a vajra in his hand. Yellow Ratnasambhava, with his consort Lochana, holds a jewel in his hand. Red Amitabha, with consort Pandaravasini, holds a lotus in his hand. Finally, green Amoghasiddhi, with his consort Samaya Tara, holds a vajra-cross in his hand. The forms of these five buddhas symbolize body; the seed syllables in their heart-centers—OM HUNG TRAM HRIH AH—signify speech; and the attributes held in their hands—wheel, vajra, jewel, lotus, and vajra-cross—symbolize mind. In this way, the body, speech, and mind aspects are represented.

Next, come the eight bodhisattvas and their eight consorts, who are the eight female bodhisattvas, sometimes called the "eight offering goddesses." Here, they are depicted in two groups: four male and four female inner bodhisattvas as well as four male and four female outer bodhisattvas.

The text says,

> *In the four intermediate directions, on a lotus, sun, and moon,*
> *Are Kshiti Garbha and Lasya, white,*
> *Akasha Garbha and Mala, yellow,*
> *Mighty Avalokiteshvara and Gita, red,*
> *And Vajrapani and Nirti, green.*

Altogether, these are the two groups of four male and four female bodhisattvas, eight plus eight. Every one of them, among both the buddhas and bodhisattvas, possesses the complete thirty-two major and eighty minor marks of excellence. All are wearing silken garments and ornaments, radiating boundless rays of light.

These deities are located on the ground floor of the celestial palace. Earlier, I said that *being* is Samantabhadra; *appearance* is the five buddha families; and *manifestation* is the six buddhas of the six realms, the six munis. *Along the sides are the six nirmanakaya munis.* These buddhas are situated in the so-called in-between area, still within the palace but outside the circle of buddhas and bodhisattvas—three buddhas on the right and three on the left. These buddhas are all standing, wearing the nirmanakaya monk's garb and poised on single lotus flowers.

At the four gates in the four directions are the four great wrathful kings, endowed with the ninefold dance moods and embracing their consorts. Wearing their charnel ground ornaments, *they blaze with the fire of the kalpa.* This means they are wearing the eightfold attire of the charnel ground. Imagine that these four male and four female wrathful gatekeepers blaze with intense rays of light and fire, resembling that which blazes at the conclusion of the aeon.

Earlier, I mentioned the palace has two stories. The upper story is for the peaceful deities, while the lower story is for the wrathful deities. The ground story of the palace is a square design, with four walls in the four directions, but the upper story is spherical, like a vase. It is closed at the top, yet above it are thirteen consecutive wheels placed horizontally, like a big spire. Golden latticework surrounds it. The top ornament at the pinnacle has a vertical sun disc and a crescent moon. There are many other decorations. On the ground floor inside the celestial palace, eight pillars are connected by overhead beams, but not in the usual manner, where the beams are straight. Rather, the eight beams beside each door on the inside are connected with beams like a big circle. As you see in many temples, on the floor in the center of the room is an inlaid design of a big golden wheel. The thrones of the various deities (buddhas) are situated on the (four) spokes of this wheel. In the four intermediate directions, on the rim of this wheel, there are lotuses with sun and moon seats, not thrones. The four inner bodhisattvas and inner offering goddesses are there. A square, with corners facing in the four cardinal directions, surrounds the wheel. As the text says, *in the four corners of the square*, also upon sun and moon seats, are the four male and female outer bodhisattvas. After you develop the visualization of the entire mandala of the forty-two peaceful deities, they then ascend to the floor above.

The floor design in both the peaceful and wrathful palaces is a big wheel. The wheels are slightly different—in the peaceful palace, it is a four-spoked golden wheel, while in the wrathful palace, there is a huge raised platform of solid diamond. Upon this is the pointed, wrathful wheel composed of iron.

Now we arrive at the wrathful palace. The decor inside the wrathful palace is quite different from that of the peaceful one. From the outside, it looks like a peaceful mandala, but from the inside it appears as the wrathful mandala, now the ground floor. As seen from the outside, in the normal sense of a peaceful mandala, in the four directions there are four walls with four gates. Each wall has five consecutive walls with space in-between them, each with five different kinds of light, which manifest corresponding to the five wisdoms. The walls are covered with golden tiles. Small pillars above this allow light to enter the room. Between these, garlands and tassels hang, forming latticework of half and full nets, with many smaller ornaments suspended from them. Above this, the roof juts out, with spouts for the water to run off. The details of the celestial palace differ according to the old and new schools as well as from tantra to tantra. Various tantras of the new school offer differing explanations of how the palace should appear, but, in brief, this explanation should suffice.

When the peaceful mandala is transformed, then Samantabhadra and consort become Chemchok Heruka and consort. The transformation of Vairochana is Buddha Heruka. The transformation of Akshobhya is Vajra Heruka. Ratnasambhava transforms into Ratna Heruka and Amitabha into Padma Heruka. The transformation of Amoghasiddhi is Karma Heruka. Each of them is in union with his consort.

The text says, *in the center of the great palace of the wrathful ones,* which is actually the floor below the peaceful deities, there is a huge faceted diamond rock with eight sides. On top there is a four-pronged iron wheel, and in the center is a lotus, sun, and Rudra—Maheshawa and Umadevi, who are sprawled on their backs. The great and glorious Chemchok Heruka stands upon them, stamping them under his foot. He is dark blue with three faces. The central face is blue, the right face white, and the left face red. His three right hands hold vajras; his three left hold skulls filled with blood. He embraces the great consort Krodhishvari. Next, are the wrathful forms of the five buddhas and their five consorts.

> *Upon a huge rock, lotus, sun, and Rudra,*
> *Is the great and glorious Chemchok Heruka,*
> *Dark blue, right face white and left face red.*
> *In his three right hands are vajras; in the left ones skulls with blood.*
> *He embraces the great consort Krodhishvari.*
>
> *In the center and in the four directions, upon lotus and sun, are*
> *Maroon Buddha Heruka with consort,*
> *Blue Vajra Heruka with consort,*
> *Yellow Ratna Heruka with consort,*
> *Red Padma Heruka with consort,*
> *And green Karma Heruka with consort.*
> *Adorned with the glorious attire and charnel ground ornaments,*
> *They blaze in the twenty modes of wrath.*

We should imagine that all the wrathful deities are, in fact, the wisdom mind, or the state of realization, of all the peaceful deities. They just manifest in a wrathful mode in order to tame those who cannot be tamed through peaceful means. To understand the principle of peaceful and wrathful, we can see exactly the same approach manifest in our own countries. For example, first, there is the peaceful law of the land, whereby people discuss things with each other and adhere to the laws. Then, there are people who do not obey rules, so other measures are necessary. There are police and army as enforcers. If other countries start to invade, the populace must respond with a military defense, in order to avert or overcome the vicious attack of the enemy. Here, in the same way, those whom the buddhas cannot influence through peaceful means are tamed not through genuine anger, but through displaying an angry appearance, called "wrathful." In this way, the buddhas are able to tame all sentient beings, not merely those susceptible to peaceful means.

Moreover, we should understand that the wrathful deities are not something other, or different from, the peaceful deities, themselves. The forty-two peaceful deities are called the "state of primordial purity, itself," whereas, the wrathful deities are the transformation of the peaceful deities. They have changed form, not out of anger or hatred, but out of compassion. It is the force of compassion that changes the peaceful deities into the wrathful ones for the benefit of beings—it accelerates the effect for those who cannot be tamed by peaceful means.

The number of wrathful deities is slightly more than the peaceful, but the transformation is like this: First the main forms, Samantabhadra and Samantabhadri, are transformed into Chemchok Heruka and consort, in the center, where there is a double square with eight points. The four families are in the corners and the protruding places—eight points altogether. The five male and five female buddhas become the five male herukas and the five female krodhishvaris (on the points of the wheel). Standing on the eight points of the double square, around the wheel are the eight male bodhisattvas, who become the eight wrathful goddesses of the sacred places; they have human heads. Along the sides, outside the eight mamos but still inside the palace, are the eight female bodhisattvas, who become the eight tramen, or mamos, of the eight sacred valleys. They have heads of various animals, such as a lion, and so forth. Their bodies are different colors, and they stand upon corpses, their own corpses. The human corpse, as a seat to stand on, symbolizes nonthought, because a corpse doesn't think. When a deity stands on a corpse, it means he or she is in a state of thought-free wakefulness. Even though they have various animal heads, their form is basically human, which is terrifying. The four male and female gatekeepers become the four female gatekeepers of the wrathful mandala.

The female gatekeepers then further transform into seven each, who are outside the gates at this point. They become seven white gatekeepers, seven yellow, seven red, and seven green. Altogether, these twenty-eight beings are called the twenty-eight *ishvaris* or *wangchukmas*. They all have different animal heads. The four female gatekeepers are called the "annihilators" or "terminators," meaning they bring an end to disturbing emotions. They perform the activities of summoning, shackling, chaining, and intoxicating, which are the four acts of the four immeasurables to overcome the four types of disturbing emotions.

Outside the four gates is the outer courtyard, in which the twenty-eight ishvaris reside. So, seven exist in each of the four directions, outside the eight female bodhisattvas but not outside the palace itself. They possess the color of their direction. The seven ishvaris in the east perform the pacifying activity. Each set of seven, respectively, performs increasing, magnetizing, and subjugating activities. Each of the four female gatekeepers is holding an iron hook, lasso, shackles, and bell. We may wonder, "Why do some deities have animal heads? What is the point of that?" It is not as though they took an animal head and attached it to their own body. That's not what happened. Rather, it is symbolic. Each animal head that appears here symbolizes a particular quality possessed by that animal. It does not symbolize the stupidity of the animal realm. Some animals have incredible discriminating knowledge. Some have great courage. Some have great prowess. Each of these qualities is demonstrated or symbolized here.

Moreover, imagine that vidyadharas and victorious ones with their sons, meaning buddhas and bodhisattvas, as well as hosts of dakas, dakinis, and dharma protectors are everywhere, both inside and outside, completely filling the sky. Just as when you break open a pod of sesame seeds, you see it is totally full, in the same way the phenomenal world is utterly filled with enlightened beings.

> *Possessing the vajra body, speech, and mind,*
> *They are perfect as the essence of the five wisdoms.*
> OM AH HUNG, OM AH HUNG SVA HA

There is a mantra for this, representing body, speech, mind, qualities, and activities. At the forehead, throat, and heart of each of the one hundred peaceful and wrathful deities, imagine these syllables, OM AH HUNG, which are the nature of vajra body, speech, and mind. (White) OM is Buddha Vairochana, or vajra body; (red) AH is Buddha Amitabha, or vajra speech; and (blue) HUNG is Buddha Akshobhya, or vajra mind. Crowned with the five wisdoms, the mantra here is OM AH HUNG SVA HA, whereby SVA is Ratnasambhava and HA is Amoghasiddhi in the center and in the four directions. This shows that, in essence, everyone is Buddha Samantabhadra; however, in appearance, they are the five buddha families. Each of the deities, every one, is crowned with the five buddha families to show that all the peaceful and wrathful deities are the manifestations of the five buddha families. First, we completed the development, or visualization, stage of the samaya beings, as well as the two-storied palace of the peaceful and wrathful deities. Now, we imagine sealing the forehead, throat, and heart centers of each and every deity with these three syllables, OM AH HUNG. As a crown, they wear the five syllables OM AH HUNG SVA HA, which represent the five buddha families' empowerment.

After this, perform the invocation. Invite the wisdom deity from the dharmadhatu realm of Akanishtha. The realm of all the buddhas is called dharmadhatu. Their body is called dharmakaya. We invite the body from the place, dharmadhatu. They abide as the dharmakaya and manifest as the sambhogakaya form of rainbow light. The dharma body is a body beyond complexity, and the sambhoga body is a body made of rainbow light, adorned with the major and minor marks.

Then, there is the samaya being, which is yourself as the deity. The deity that is first visualized as looking like such and such is called the samaya being. The wisdom being is the one invited down from the dharmadhatu realm of Akanishtha.

The roots of all deities are essence, nature, and capacity. The essence beyond complexity is dharmakaya. Samantabhadra, unmoved from the essence, is naturally and spontaneously present as the five buddha aspects. Then these, without moving away, manifest as nirmanakaya forms for the sake of taming beings of the six realms. These are called deities, or wisdom beings. When invited from space, the wisdom being blends together with yourself as the samaya being, like water poured into water. For instance, if you have water in a container and pour more water in, there will be no distinction or separation between the two waters; they will have become the same.

First, we seal with OM AH HUNG. Vajra body seals body with the letter OM. Vajra speech seals speech with the letter AH. Vajra mind seals mind with the syllable HUNG. This is called sealing the deity with deity. After that comes empowering. Each of the five families—buddha, vajra, ratna, padma, and karma—empowers its respective family. Amitabha, for instance, is padma family. For the padma family, it's the padma family deity who is placed on the top of the head. After that comes the deities of the other four families in the four directions. For example, in the case of the buddha family, we start with OM on the crown of the head, then AH, and so forth in the four other places. This practice here is the general way, where first OM is on the top of the head, AH is to the east, then HUNG, SVA, and HA. On the crown of our head is Vairochana, to the east is Akshobhya, Ratnasambhava is to the south, Amitabha is to the west, and Amoghasiddhi is to the north. This is being empowered by the five buddha aspects, empowering deity with deity. Now both sealing and empowering are completed.

As to the actual invitation, first there is HUNG, the nature of the mind of all the buddhas. The HUNG from the OM AH HUNG at the time of sealing radiates blue rays of light, in the shape of countless hooks, which invite all the victorious ones with their sons from the dharmadhatu realm of Akanishtha. Light radiates from the seed syllable in your heart, which invites the deities. From the letter HUNG in your heart-center, the samaya being, light rays in the form of hooks stream forth and invite the victorious ones and their sons from the ten directions and the four times. The ten directions are east, south, west, north, southeast, southwest, northwest, northeast, above, and below. The four times are past, future, present, and unfixed time, which is the "fourth time of great equality." All the victorious ones as well as their sons and disciples are then invited. That was the meaning of the letter HUNG.

Within the unconstructed realm of dharmadhatu⁼ is the buddha realm that is free from complexity.

From the palace of sambhogakaya⁼, means for example, if the buddha realm were Nepal valley, then the palace would be Nagi Gompa, my dwelling place. *From* means all the deities dwelling at Nagi Gompa, for example.

Peaceful and wrathful buddhas with your retinues⁼, the forty-two peaceful and fifty-eight flaming blood-drinkers, who are like the sun, and their emanations, re-emanations, and re-re-emanations—countless and inconceivable retinues, who are like the rays of the sun.

By the power of your samaya, please come!⁼ SAMAYA means when buddhas attain enlightenment, they don't have any other purpose than benefiting beings. The buddhas do not have even a speck of other occupations. They only have the purpose of establishing all sentient beings in the state of liberation. That is the samaya—spiritual vow or pledge—of the buddhas. The buddhas have pledged themselves to the benefit of beings. Whereas we have our own purposes, the buddhas have no self-interest: "Be pleased to come!"

Invoking their pledge to arrive, we call upon the wisdom beings. The mantra of invitation, VAJRA SAMAYA JAH E HAYA HI, means the deities have a samaya with us.

JAH HUNG BAM HOH means the four immeasurables: immeasurable love, compassion, joy, and impartiality. With hook, lasso, chain, and bell, the deities are obliged to sit joyfully. They take their seats within the four immeasurable states, unlike opponent forces of obstructing and evil spirits, who are seized at their necks with the iron hook, tied around their limbs with the lasso, and intoxicated into oblivion with the bell. This is not used in the case of deities, who are "intoxicated" into unbiased, immeasurable impartiality. All deities are JAH HUNG BAM HOH in the nature of the four immeasurables. They are summoned, bound, chained, and intoxicated to remain in the state of the four immeasurables.

KA VA CHI indicates body, speech, and mind; it means "be pleased to take your seat in the great space of wisdom body, speech, and mind!" JNANA is wisdom; VAJRA TISHTHA ATI PU HO is our respectful greeting, while PRATICCHA HO is their response to us.

The root of all the peaceful and wrathful ones is Samantabhadra and consort, whom we have first visualized as ourself. Samantabhadra and consort are like the sun, and the rest of the peaceful and wrathful ones are the sun's rays. From the heart center of ourself as Samantabhadra with consort, sixteen offering goddesses emanate. Then they multiply into millions and billions, all making prostrations. The wisdom deities have already been invited, have become inseparable from the samaya being, and have taken their seats.

After they have taken their seats, we say something like, "Hey, Namaste!" In the same way, here we say ATI PU HO. Then all the offering goddesses prostrate to us. In response to that, we as Samantabhadra with consort say, PRATICCHA HO. As though we saluted a dignitary, he cannot avoid responding. Even when a subject says Namaste to the king or a minister, the other one will answer back. In the same way, the answer PRATICCHA HO. is given here.

Regarding the offerings, who is making them? We are. Who is receiving them? We are. We emanate countless offering goddesses carrying all different kinds of pleasurable objects. They face the mandala of deities, who are inseparable from us, and present the offerings. They are emanated by us and turn around, making offerings to us. While imagining this, we chant aloud:

OM AH HUNG, the letters of body, speech, and mind of all the sugatas.

The outer offering is a Samantabhadra offering cloud. Concerning offerings, there are outer, inner, secret, and "thatness" offerings; we make four offerings, though sometimes we make three. Samantabhadra at this time is the Bodhisattva Samantabhadra, who can emanate an inconceivable cloud-bank of offerings. That is the kind of cloud mentioned. The example is of vast and numerous clouds in the sky. *Cloud* in this context means "multitude" and "density."

The inner offering is sense pleasures and amrita medicine, nectar that includes rakta and torma. The main thing in the inner offering is the five sense pleasures of form, sound, smell, taste, and touch. If you were to ask what is meant by *medicine,* it includes the eight roots and thousand branches. Of all the earth, stones, and rocks, there is not a single thing that cannot be medicine. Everything in the elements—trees, grass, and herbs—is medicine. If you really have knowledge of this, you know everything can be medicine. The outer and inner elements are connected. There are four outer elements. The four inner elements are flesh, blood, heat, and breath. When the outer elements assist the inner ones, they become medicine.

Actually, there is medicine even in human meat and bones. There is earth elixir and plant elixir. Earth elixir comes from earth and plant elixir from herbs or trees; all of it is medicine. That was about amrita medicine.

The outer offering was ARGHAM PADYAM and so forth, eight in all, in which the five sense pleasures are included. However, they can be taken separately as inner, as well as outer, offerings. As the inner offerings, there are amrita, rakta, and torma, which, in short, are symbols of aggression, passion, and delusion. The nature of delusion, stupidity, is torma; the nature of aggression is amrita or medicine; and the nature of passion is blood, rakta. Therefore, these are the sacred substances for emptying samsara; they are very profound. When we do away with the three poisons, samsara becomes emptied. For instance, when there is no bindu of the male, no rakta of the female, and no flesh and blood in between, then there will not be any people, right? That is because the seed for people has been emptied. Likewise, these are the samaya substances for emptying samsara, and we offer them as the gesture of emptying samsara, as the symbol of cutting the root of samsara. This has very deep significance.

The innermost offering is the primordially pure space of great bliss. This refers to indivisible wisdom and space. The actual secret offering is joining and liberating. *Liberating* refers to the demon of ignorance. All enemies who harm the doctrine are the outer enemy. The inner enemy is the three poisons, and the secret enemy is ignorance. The act of doing away with them, annihilating them, is called the liberation offering. The union offering is the union of *yab* and *yum* in the space of great bliss. Externally, the *yab* and *yum* join in bliss; internally, all the dakas and dakinis dwelling in the nadis are pleased by the great bliss. The secret offering is the "emptiness endowed with all supreme aspects" and the "unchanging great bliss"—emptiness and great bliss, which primordially is the nature of tathagatagarbha. The great calm is bliss, right?

Joining and liberating are the secret offering, the primordially pure space of great bliss. The ultimate of both union and liberation is the space of primordial purity. In that way, joining and liberating are the secret offering, and the primordially pure space is the *thatness* offering.

I offer all these to the peaceful and wrathful victorious ones with their retinues. This means we are offering to the actual forty-two peaceful and fifty-eight wrathful ones and to their retinue of emanations, re-emanations, attendants, aides, and messengers. Each of them has its own emanations. An aide is like a military assistant, or guard, so it means obeying whatever is commanded.

Then, the Sanskrit mantras follow: OM VAJRA ARGHAM...HOH refers to the outer offering. MAHA PANCA...BALINGTA KHARAM KHAHI refers to the inner offering. MAHA SUKHA GANA PUJA HOH is the offering for union. MAHA DHARMADHATU TANA PUJA HOH is the offering for liberation. MAHA SHUNYATA JNANA PUJA HOH is the offering for self-existing wakefulness, the *thatness* offering. In this way, all levels of offering are complete within these lines.

Then, all the offering goddesses sing verses of praise. First, they sing four lines praising the peaceful deities:

OM

I praise your body, complete with the major and minor marks;
Your vajra speech, the natural sound of dharmata;

Your vajra mind, the unchanging wakefulness;§
And your inconceivable qualities and activities.§

The first line refers to the thirty-two major and eighty minor marks of the sambhogakaya, which are all complete within them. This was the praise of the body.

Your vajra speech is dharmata's self-sound. The self-utterance of dharmata is unceasing; that is the vajra speech.

Your vajra mind is changeless wisdom. Without any change whatsoever, your mind is the primordially pure awareness, dharmakaya.

I praise your inconceivable qualities and activities.§ The qualities and activities are impossible to conceive of, beyond conceptual mind. They are beyond thought, free from the limits of thinking. This was the praise of the forty-two peaceful deities.

HUNG, *though unmoved from the essence itself.*§ The *essence* means the primordially pure essence, where the peaceful ones are spontaneously freed. Without moving away from this essence itself, the spontaneously present nature manifests, like the rays of light from the sun.

You appear in wrathful forms before those to be tamed.§ Those to be tamed are those who are enemies of the teaching, those who have fallen under the power of conceptual thought and ignorance. To tame them, you appear in wrathful forms. The peaceful ones manifest as wrathful in order to tame the savage forces.

Sending out attendants and emanations as envoys§, first, the forty-two peaceful ones transform into the wrathful ones, and the wrathful ones turn into emanations. As mentioned, there are the so-called attendants. There are boundless emanations, re-emanations, and re-re-emanations; such a number of envoys is sent out.

First, the forty-two peaceful ones transform into the fifty-eight wrathful ones. Out of compassion and skillful means, the buddhas appear in a wrathful form in order to tame those beings who cannot be tamed by peaceful means. The peaceful deities are called the "natural purity," while the wrathful deities are called their "transformation into wrathful forms." They send out attendants and emanations as envoys, even re-emanations and re-re-emanations, in all different forms and manifestations, both male and female.

I praise the compassionate ones, who are skilled in means.⸉

They manifest in whichever way is necessary to tame whoever has need. They are skilled in the methods of benefiting beings and are endowed with great compassion. It is of no use to be skilled in methods but lacking in compassion.

Then, there are the GING, LANG KA, *and* BAR MA, attendants that are gradually emanated, sent out as envoys, helpers—actually a servant's servant. The emanation has re-emanations; the re-emanation has re-re-emanations; the re-re-emanation has inconceivable and countless numbers. Such are the emanations.

Next comes the recitation request, whereby one reminds the deity of its basic samaya, or primordial pledge, to manifest and purify during the recitation phase. Recitation traditionally has four aspects: approach, full approach, accomplishment, and great accomplishment. The first aspect is called the "moon with a garland of stars," the second is called the "firebrand," the third is called the "king's emissaries," and finally a "beehive broken open." Through this fourfold intent of approach and accomplishment, everything is accomplished, as you can see in the text, while reciting the mantra.

Here is how we go about the recitation: Visualize yourself, the samaya being, as the hundred peaceful and wrathful ones. The wisdom deities are invited from the space and dissolve like water into water. The samadhi-being in your heart center as Samantabhadra is the letter AH upon a lotus and moon seat. That is the heart samadhi-being. Surrounding this samadhi-being is the mantra chain arranged as OM BODHICHITTA MAHASUKHA JNAN-ADHATU AH⸉, and inside Chemchok is the syllable HUNG surrounded by OM RULU RULU HUNG BHYO HUNG.⸉

All sights are the body of the peaceful and wrathful ones.⸉ The external vessel of the universe and the contents of sentient beings within it are all the body of the peaceful and wrathful ones.

All that is heard is the sound of mantra.⸉ The sounds of the external elements, the voices of all the people and beings, are the tones of mantra, the Bodhichitta and Rulu mantras.

Thoughtfree awareness is the space of cognizance.⸉ This means that sights, sounds, and awareness are transformed into body, speech, and mind. It is said, "Whoever has mind has *rigpa.*" There is no one without rigpa. We just don't recognize it. Rigpa is nonconceptual, free from conceptual thought, yet it is cognizant. Without cognizance, we will not know anything. The word *space* means that space and awareness are in union. Nonconceptual awareness, which does not conceptualize, is itself the space of luminosity—space meaning empty in essence and luminous, or having a naturally cognizant quality, at the same time.

The ocean-wide realms are filled with clouds of offerings. In this way, the ocean-wide realms, the infinite worlds in all the ten directions are totally filled with cloudbanks of offerings. This upward offering is to the mandala of the victorious ones.

Innumerable activities free all beings. Downward, we perform the activities of pacifying, enriching, magnetizing, and subjugating for all sentient beings pervading the sky, all of whom have been our mothers. Liberate means to free those who have not been freed, to help those who have not crossed to cross over, to relieve those who are not relieved, and to cause those who have not gone beyond misery to go beyond misery.

This is the all-pervading mandala of the victorious ones. All sentient beings equal to space are the mandala of the victorious ones and their sons, the tathagatas' mandala.

Everything is perfect in the continuum of one taste. When we look, we can discern many different things; that is the nature of discriminating wisdom, the individually conceiving primordial knowing. All of it is, however, included within the absolute realm of dharma, dharmadhatu. *Perfect in the continuum of one taste* means "perfect within the continuum of dharmadhatu, of rigpa."

First, there is the mantra that is the nature of body, speech, and mind, the three families. It radiates rays of light upward, gathering the siddhis. Next, it radiates downward to all sentient beings of the six realms. The rays of light purify all their karmas and habitual patterns as well as their evil deeds and obscurations. Afterward, the rays of light are reabsorbed. This is called "fulfilling the two benefits." The benefit for yourself is making the upward offering and bringing back the siddhis, and the benefit for others is purifying the obscurations of sentient beings.

Actually, these are not two, up and down. Samsara and nirvana have become nondual. If you have samsara as one and nirvana as number two, dualistic fixation has still not collapsed. It is said, "As long as not becoming the single nonduality, there will be no enlightenment." When the two have been condensed into one, there is enlightenment. As long as there is duality, then it is not adequate. For this reason, *everything is perfect in the continuum of one taste.*

OM BODHICHITTA MAHASUKHA JNANADHATU AH. This is the mantra of the forty-two peaceful ones. OM RULU RULU HUNG BHYO HUNG. This is the mantra of the fifty-eight flaming blood-drinkers, herukas.

Then, Guru Rinpoche adds this note, *While maintaining the view, recite this as much as you can. Thus, you will achieve all the accomplishments and activities. Samaya.*

Reciting according to ability means we recite as many as we can. *Maintaining the view* means we should maintain the view in the continuity of rigpa. First, we cultivate the development stage, and finally—free from developer and developed—in the space free from the conceptions of the three entities, we perfect the development stage.

All siddhis and activities will be accomplished. All the siddhis of body, speech, and mind will be accomplished and all the infinite activities will thereby be fulfilled.

Samaya means this is a "pledge;" it is sworn.

The Bodhichitta mantra is the condensation of all the peaceful ones and the Rulu mantra is the condensation of the fifty-eight flaming blood-drinkers.

Here these three—approach, accomplishment, and action application—are combined into one. They are not separate.

This was the five samadhis of the main part.

Questions and Answers

Question: Can you explain again how to remain in awareness while practicing the development stage?

Rinpoche: In *Kunzang Tuktig*, it is possible to remain in unwavering awareness while meditating on the development stage. If you have grown accustomed to awareness, then remain in the continuity of awareness and let the projection and dissolution of thoughts arise as the development stage, like waves moving on the surface of water.

When the meditation manifests spontaneously within unmoving awareness, the expression of awareness arises as the development stage. In that way, the meditation is first-class; then, as a matter of fact, development and completion stages are not separated. Remaining in awareness as the completion stage and letting the awareness-expression arise as the development stage is the perfection of the development and completion stages as a unity.

If this is not possible, first cultivate emptiness, then compassion, followed by the visualization of the seed-syllable samadhi, wherein emptiness and compassion are united. Then the E YAM RAM BAM and so forth are the layers of the five elements, upon which the celestial palace rests. The syllable then descends and becomes the deity. Visualize yourself as the deity; thus, one step follows the other.

When you haven't recognized mind-nature, the completion stage is scattered and the development stage practice resembles building a house. Without completion stage, the practitioner is like a man constructing a building. Thus, solely pursuing the development stage, if you are visualizing with attachment to substance and solidity, you should dissolve the visualization methodically in the end: the palace dissolves into the deity, the deity dissolves into the seed syllable, and the syllable dissolves into the nada, and then into emptiness. Thinking, at last, "This is unborn and empty," you complete the practice with emptiness. In such a case, that process of dissolving the visualization is called the completion stage.

Actually, first cultivate the development stage, then look at who is meditating. The recognition of the nature of the meditator is itself the completion stage. You cannot practice a perfect development stage without being introduced to awareness, to rigpa. When you truly recognize awareness, the development stage practices do not interfere with awareness at all. What harm can be done to the state of awareness? All thinking is empty, empty movement. The emptiness moves. How can there be any harm to the emptiness? It is like a child at play.

Again, it is quite permissible to simply imagine the five layers of elements with the celestial palace, spontaneously manifest. You need not hold onto what you visualize. Just let go of the fixation and resolve yourself in the continuity of completion stage. Here you should resolve, and I mean resolve definitively, in the space of the three kayas.

In the Dzogchen teachings, we speak of differentiating the thinking mind *(sem)* and awareness *(rigpa)*, resolving our body, speech, and mind in the space of the three kayas. In short, this means that our body, speech, and mind are the three vajras; they are resolved to be the essence of the three vajras. When you understand this mandala of the spontaneously present nature, then all bodily appearances are the mandala of body, all resounding sounds are the mandala of speech, and all thought activity is the mandala of mind. You are not regarding something that is not and imagining it to be something that is.

The absence of complexity is body, complete within awareness. The self-utterance of primordially pure emptiness is speech. That is resolving the space of speech. Thought activity as mind is awareness, untainted by defects, empty of both grasping and fixating. Untainted by outer grasping, uncorrupted by inner fixation, it is self-contained. Thus, thought activity is the vajra mind.

To differentiate the thinking mind and awareness, you must arrive solely in awareness. The thinking mind as the expression of awareness should be abandoned. When awareness is recognized, then the thinking mind is self-abandoned. Mind is changing, and awareness is unchanging. In this way, the two are differentiated. Look at the sky, which is unchanging, and the clouds, which are changeable; clouds are like the thinking mind and the space is like rigpa, awareness. The clouds change again and again, but space never changes. Awareness is both unceasing and unchanging.

In this way, the three vajras are complete and are resolved as vajra body, vajra speech, and vajra mind. The vajra body is uncompounded; the awareness is uncompounded. That is the nature of vajra body. It is not a formation or compound. The vajra speech is the unceasing sound. The vajra mind is the unobstructed mental activity, awareness. The obstructed thinking mind is what ceases. Awareness does not cease. The mind first has one thought; when thinking of the next, the first thought has ceased. Awareness is unceasing and unlimited, beyond the conceptual mind of the three times, unmoving in the three times.

Question: What is the vajra body?

Rinpoche: Vajra body means "unconditioned." The awareness is unconditioned, unformed, right? It is not a formation. That is the nature of vajra body.

The vajra speech is the unceasing sound that is there, right? The vajra mind is the unobstructed mental activity, awareness. That which ceases, is obstructed, is mind *(sem)*. Awareness is unceasing. What do we mean by ceasing? We mean that when mind has thought one thing, then it ceases; when thinking of the next, then the first has ceased, right? When thinking of the fourth, then the third thought has ceased, right? However, awareness is actually unceasing, unlimited throughout the three times. It is beyond the conceptual mind of the three times, unmoving in the three times.

All three kayas are contained within awareness. When you have recognized that fact, you are said to have resolved. Really, nothing is impossible, once you recognize awareness. However, until recognition occurs, you will always have difficulties. No matter what you do, the perfect will not come about. Everything will remain imperfect or fake, and the development will also be unnatural. To let the awareness-expression arise as development stage and then to remain within awareness is enough. You need not examine the awareness-expression at all.

Recognize the primordially pure essence to be your face. Recognize the spontaneously present nature to be your expression. Recognize your expression to be without self-nature. This means that primordial purity *(ka dag)* and spontaneous presence *(lhun grub)*, development stage and completion stage, are ultimately a unity. That is not something that has to be cultivated; it is automatic. Right now, we cultivate a method for purifying some evil deeds, a short path, as in Mahayoga and Anu Yoga. In Ati Yoga, the development and completion are Trekchö and Tögal; they do not need to be produced. The development stage is without being developed. In the mind mandala of Ati Yoga, all the deities are complete, as there are both Trekchö and Tögal.

You cannot say there are no deities, because they appear in the Tögal display and they appear in the *bardo*. Even if you want to inhibit them, they will still appear. When somebody practices Tögal, then, without having to strive for the deities, they will spontaneously appear. They cannot be thrown away, and if they were not there at all, nothing would appear, right? *(laughs)*

Question: How do we deal with the dull state of indifference?

Rinpoche: To counteract indifference, you need to arouse sharpness, clarity. When feeling indifferent, you should invigorate awareness, sharpen it. You need clarity, wakefulness.

Question: What should we do when there is agitation?

Rinpoche: That does no harm at all. The more wild the thoughts are, the better, right? The more agitated the thought activity becomes, the sharper the awareness needs to be. Thoughts are like the bubbles in water; they arise within the water and dissolve in the water—when they are not grasped. Really, there is no harm, no matter how much the thoughts move wildly. The state without any thought movement, the indifferent state, is more of an enemy. Our greatest enemy is indifference, whereas movement is not very dangerous. In the Kagyü tradition, it is said, "Within thought, I discovered nonthought; within complexity, I discovered dharmakaya." This is found in *The Rain of Wisdom, (bka' brgyud mgur mtsho).* What is really meant by "Within thought, I discovered nonthought?" No matter how wildly the thoughts move, the awareness will arise as nonthought, which means that the awareness free from grasping and fixating is nonthought. This is not the nonthought of being unconscious, like having been hit on the head with a stick. The nonthought of awareness is free from grasping and fixating, free from concepts. It does not mean a state of cessation. "Within complexity, I discovered dharmakaya" means that the nonthought is unconstructed, and when it is free of constructs, it is dharmakaya, right? Therefore, I think there is no great danger in movement. Whereas, there is some harm in the mere abiding state.

Question: Doesn't the contrived development stage involve a lot of mental exercise?

Rinpoche: Yes, you need to generate many thoughts, to think a lot. Many thoughts, many ideas, much thinking is necessary in that kind of development stage. Mahayoga is for people with many thoughts, Anu Yoga is for people with fewer thoughts, and Ati Yoga is for people for whom thoughts are unnecessary. That is the purpose.

There are some people who have many discursive thoughts, many ideas, much thought activity, and they need development stage. It is said, "The ones with thoughts should practice development stage." Those who think a lot need to meditate on the development stage. It depends on a person's disposition *(khams)*. There are some people who have so much thought activity that only development stage is useful and completion stage is of no benefit. They think, "What is the use! There is nothing to see, nobody to see also. It would be better to have something to think of." There are many who think like that. The thoughts are quite difficult. When there are many thoughts, the disturbing emotions *(kleshas)* accumulate karma. If instead you can think of the celestial palace, the deity, and so forth, then thoughts are utilized without gathering karma and evil deeds. That is the actual purpose.

If you were to ask what the meaning or fruition is, there is the spontaneously present mandala of the victorious ones, the deities of sambhogakaya.

This spontaneously present mandala of the victorious ones, the nature of the deities, is not something nonexistent, which we make appear in the development stage. The expression of primordial purity is spontaneous presence. This spontaneous presence is the infinite purity of the sambhogakaya deities, the real development stage. The primordial purity is dharmakaya; the spontaneous presence is sambhogakaya. When you say sambhogakaya, then there will be deities also. This is the principle.

Question: Should we keep a constant visualization?

Rinpoche: It is sufficient to imagine just once, when beginning. After that, it is all right to let go and remain free from representation. When beginning, visualize the whole thing once, vividly, and after that rest in the nonconceptual state. To alternate, sometimes keeping representation and sometimes not, does no harm, but you don't need to do this. Thought occurrence is the expression of rigpa, so when it arises as the visualization it is all right, which explains why it does no harm. This is when you have attained some stability. Without stability, the expression becomes too forceful and the essence seems to get lost in that state. When the essence is "out of sight" that fault will cause development to increase discursive thoughts. On the other hand, when the essence is stabilized, the expression within the state of the essence will appear vividly (as the visualization). From the primordially pure essence, the self-existing awareness, without moving for even an instant away from this state, the unobstructed expression of awareness arises as the development stage *(laughs)*.

Question: Then what is the best approach to the visualization?

Rinpoche: You have to imagine. You imagine the phenomena of the external world to actually be the celestial palace. In the case of the completion stage with signs, you have to think somewhat in the beginning. The external world is the palace, and the inhabitants, sentient beings, have the nature of dakas and dakinis. All the sounds of the elements are the self-utterance of the Bodhichitta and Rulu mantras. The thoughts, all the hordes of the mind's thought activity, are the uncompounded dharmata, the single self-existing wakefulness. That is how you should think and visualize. At first, you should imagine all this once, and after that you can remain without thinking anything whatsoever. You do not then need to think, "This is here; that is there." It is sufficient just to have imagined it once. Otherwise, you need two after one, and three after two, and so forth. It is not necessary to give rise to such thought activity. If you did, there would be a lot of mental activity. So, just once, imagine the world to be a celestial palace; all the beings to be dakas and dakinis; all the sounds of the elements—whatever sounds are heard—to be the self-utterance of the Bodhichitta and Rulu mantras; and the thoughts of all beings, their consciousness, to be the single self-existing wakefulness. After thinking like that, you can just remain in the state of practice.

Question: What if thoughts occur?

Rinpoche: If there is a thought occurrence, then just look at the thinker. Afterward, the occurrence will simply dissolve. It is just like a ripple upon water; what can it do?

Question: Is there anything else that we need to do?

Rinpoche: There is nothing else in particular. If you needed to make something, it would not be called "self-existing wakefulness," right? *Rang byung* means "self-occurring, self-existing," and *ye shes* means "primordially known." If you had to imagine it, it would not be self-existing wakefulness.

Question: Actually, we simply have to remain in the state of Trekchö?

Rinpoche: Of course! There is nothing superior to that. But it should be a genuine Trekchö. If the Trekchö is false and the development is also false and you think, "First I should imagine such and such. Then I should look at the thinker. It does not remain. This is not quite right. Now it is right."— this kind of thinking is called the "dangerous defilement of hope and fear." In this case, the completion stage will not be very good. It is said: "At the time of meditating, it is allowed to not meditate on anything." That refers to Trekchö—at the time of meditating, it is sufficient to not meditate on anything whatsoever. That is the first-class, the top-quality way.

There are three stages, called the "relative development stage," "completion stage with signs," and "completion stage without signs." These three are called "development, completion, and Great Perfection." We say that the development is Mahayoga and completion is Anu Yoga. This is the completion stage with signs, corresponding to the six yogas of Naropa, which are Anu Yoga. The third is called the "completion stage without characteristics," the Great Perfection. The three levels of empowerments connected with these three are called "elaborate, unelaborate, and very unelaborate." To repeat, the development stage is Mahayoga, completion stage is Anu Yoga, and Great Perfection is Ati Yoga.

Question: What about pure perception?

Rinpoche: Just imagine that all phenomena are your self-display *(rang snang)*. Other people are pure because they possess the three seats of completeness. They possess the eight groups of consciousness, the aggregates, elements, and sense fields. They have the five elements and the five aggregates and the twelve sense fields. All sentient beings have these.

Question: Does a realized being truly experience the all-encompassing purity?

Rinpoche: In the future, at some stage when we possess all the qualities and have purified all the obscurations, then we will have attained the state of unsurpassable enlightenment. Other than that, sentient beings do not experience the realm of full enlightenment. If ordinary sentient beings could do that, it would be very good. That is the meaning of attaining accomplishment, attaining siddhi. When that happens, there is nothing impure in the sights, sounds, and states of mind, not even as much as a mote of dust. Such a yogi perceives nothing impure. Everything has become the continuity of pure wisdom. The whole external vessel of the world is a celestial palace. Sentient beings inhabiting it have the nature of dakas and dakinis. Why not? They do have the aggregates, elements, sense fields, and so forth. They do possess the three races, the three seats of completeness. We don't have to fabricate something that is not there. It is real. Even dogs and pigs have buddha-nature. A pig does have the aggregates and elements, and a dog does also. As sentient beings, they do have mind.

It is just that our immediate perception is not pure, but when it becomes pure, everything is seen as purity within our own perception. This is in our own perception. In the perception of others, it doesn't look like that, since they cannot experience the purity, because they are merely ordinary sentient beings. When we become a realized yogi, everything is seen as purity. This is the difference between personal perception and perception of others.

We can see other beings as pure because they are; unfortunately, due to their obscurations, they don't perceive this purity themselves. However, for a realized yogi, everything, within and without, has the purity of body, speech, mind, qualities, and activities. In the perception of a yogi, there is not even a dust mote of impurity. This is called the "great equality of samsara and nirvana." They see like that because it is like that. When all the obscurations and habitual patterns are purified, everything is seen as pure in our own perception—even though it might not appear like that for others.

Question: Isn't everything pure phenomena?

Rinpoche: If it were really so, then everybody would be buddha. Enlightenment is like awakening from sleep; all daytime perceptions and phenomena are made by the grasping mind, and all that is experienced at night is made by sleep. When awakening from sleep, there is nothing left of the dream. When the perceptions and experiences of the deluded, grasping mind have been completely purified, there is nothing left of these present confused experiences. Then, all phenomena are the display of rainbow light, major and minor bindus. That is when manifestation occurs. If there is no manifestation, it is simply the space of primordial purity.

The worldly experience of phenomena is called impure perceptions. These are the confused perceptions of sentient beings. Whereas, in the experience of somebody who has only pure perceptions, the house will be a celestial palace of rainbow light, major and minor bindus. How amazing would that be! You cannot say "nonexistent," because there are manifest qualities. You cannot say "existent," because there is no sense of concrete earth, fire, water, and wind. This proves they are primordially nonexistent.

At the time of death, there are the sounds, colors, and light rays as well as the lights of the five wisdoms, such as mirror-like wisdom, discerning wisdom, and so forth. This is the origin, the source. But when these are misunderstood, they become the nirmanakaya phenomena: houses, earth, water, fire, wind, and so forth. All the phenomena of the worldly realms—such as the aggregates, elements, sense fields, flesh, blood, warmth, breath, and so on—are not bad. They are excellent, because the virtue of being human enables us to attain enlightenment. In the form and formless realms, we don't have this material body of flesh and blood. It is merely like a cloud in the sky; therefore, the three seats of completeness are incomplete. The human body is called the "vajra body possessing the six elements," which are flesh, blood, warmth, breath, space, and consciousness. The formless realm lacks these, which makes it impossible to practice the perfect Dharma and have the force and power to maintain or remain in rigpa. Lacking sufficient strength, we cannot attain siddhi, and, in such a case, it is very difficult to recognize rigpa. So, in fact, we have to rely on this physical body of the aggregates and elements; therefore, we have now attained the best, the most supreme. The human body in the desire realm is the actual body in which to attain enlightenment.

Question: Can beings in the formless realms recognize awareness?

Rinpoche: In the four formless realms—endless space, endless consciousness, neither this nor that, and nothing whatsoever—there is no recognition of rigpa, and then one again falls down.

Question: Aren't the Dzogchen teachings all-pervading?

Rinpoche: They are not all-pervading. First, they were in the realm of Akan-ishtha, then in Tushita, and then on the summit of Mt. Sumeru, where they spread. All the beings there were fortunate ones who had the right karmic connection. Hundreds and hundreds of thousands attained enlightenment, but not all of them. Has anybody said that the god realms have been emp-tied? *(Rinpoche laughs.)*

Question: Can you please go more into detail about the offerings?

Rinpoche: There are two kinds of offerings, the actual ones and the mentally created ones. Concerning the mentally created ones, first we imagine the offering goddesses being sent out. There are both male and female offering devas; for example, the female offering devas present offerings to the male deities and the males offer to the female deities. We mentally imagine all this. When it comes to the actual offering, then the male and female yogis have to perform the actual deed themselves, making the offering. Without the actual offerings, we emanate male and female offering devas as dakas and dakinis. It is like this in the case of Vajra Varahi, where we emanate a daka as being the nature of her consort Chakrasamvara, making the union offering to her.

This kind of offering is not a conditioned offering. Passion, aggression, and delusion have been destroyed here. As in the four joys, there are joy, supreme joy, transcendent joy, and innate joy. Supreme joy is when our phys-ical bliss has been transcended, gone beyond. Then the joy is unconditioned; we should realize this and offer it to the deity. At this point, the usual joy from the union of male and female has been transcended. When joy is tran-scended, there is innate joy, which means "coemergent great bliss," where rigpa itself is the unchanging and naturally great peace. When grasping and fixating are transcended, rigpa is emptiness endowed with all the supreme aspects and unchanging great bliss. These are very important terms in secret mantra. When within rigpa the conditioned bliss is transcended, the uncon-ditioned and changeless bliss is called "innate joy." We should imagine that we are offering that. All the mentally created offerings are something we imagine, whereas we should really offer the actual ones.

Question: What is the offering of the perfect view?

Rinpoche: The offering of the perfect view means we should recognize our mind-essence and maintain its continuity.

Question: Does that refer to the absence of offering and offerer?

Rinpoche: Yes, it is the threefold purity beyond offerer and what is being offered. *Threefold* means "the act of offering, the one who makes the offering, ourself, and the offering given." All of these are empty, possessing not even as much as a hair-tip of existence in the primordially pure space of self-existing awareness, where everything is, ultimately, devoid of existence. Recognizing this nonexistence and then resting *(rigpa)* in that itself is the most perfect of all kinds of offerings. It is the great ultimate offering, the best.

Question: Where can we find more details about the deities?

Rinpoche: You can look them up in the *Karling Shitro*; everything is in there. Chokgyur Lingpa's *Ocean of Amrita* is a *Maha Shitro*. Many details are there, such as all the peaceful deities having three faces and six arms.

Question: What about the wrathful deities?

Rinpoche: As is said in the *Sangtik Phurba* of Chokgyur Lingpa, the peaceful and wrathful ones are holding all the different articles, such as clubs, skull cups, staffs, tridents, and so forth.

The transformations of the eight male and female bodhisattvas are from male into female and female into female. The emanations are not restricted to a certain sex, as the eight mamos of the sacred places are emanations of the eight male bodhisattvas. The eight female bodhisattvas and the eight tramen are both female. These are the transformations described.

Question: What about the four male and female wrathful gatekeepers?

Rinpoche: The female gatekeepers are transformed into seven each. To the east, the seven who perform the pacifying activity are the emanations of the pacifying gatekeeper. Likewise, the southern one, who increases, becomes seven. The western one, who overpowers, also becomes seven as does the northern one, who performs the subjugating activity. The twenty-eight ishvaris should, therefore, be regarded as the four female gatekeepers, six for each direction plus the four gatekeepers placed outside.

Question: Can you explain further about this?

Rinpoche: When described in detail, there are the fanged ones, the winged ones, the clawed ones, and the horned ones. Each of them has a particular virtue. Based on the symbolism of each animal's virtue, they appear as having different heads.

Question: Is it good to know the significance of each?

Rinpoche: Yes, it is good to know all the details. For instance, the meaning of having the hawk head is that the hawk is clever; the owl head indicates the ability to see at nighttime. The virtue of each of them is from the analogy of its head. It is not the case that they are reborn with an animal head due to their bad karma *(laughs).*

The significance of the fanged ones is that they can destroy all the evil and negative forces; they have the head of a tiger, a lion, and so forth. The clawed one can right away kill enemies, without any weapons. The winged ones can fly through the sky. This is the kind of symbolism. Even if we cannot have the pure recollection of each and every one of them, it is alright to have a general or overall idea. However, if we have to explain them to others, then we need to know exactly who is who and how they are. That is if we need to answer questions concerning them. Otherwise, it is enough to have the pure recollection that they are enlightened aspects.

Question: What is meant by "our body as the buddha-mandala"?

Rinpoche: The aggregates, elements, actions, and sense bases, which are within us, are all a mandala. They are complete in one mandala; the qualities are complete. When the qualities are not complete, they are incomplete. As I said earlier, *gdan* means "complete."

Question: How many mantras should be recited?

Rinpoche: You should recite 100,000 for each syllable *('bru 'bum)*. This is the short version. The expanded version is that amount multiplied by four, so four times 100,000 for each syllable. This depends on our diligence. Right now is not the Age of Fruition, the Age of Lung, or the Age of Accomplishment. We have reached the Age of Holding Mere Signs (*rtags tsam 'dzin pa*). For this reason, we need to multiply by four. To recite 400,000 for each syllable is the best. You should then continue until the number has been completed. *Time recitation (dus kyi bsnyen pa)* means to count the months and years. *Sign recitation (rtags kyi bsnyen pa)* is where one has to practice until having a vision of the deity. These were the three: number, time, and sign.

Question: Before you said that everything is pervaded by Samantrabhadra. Is that so?

Rinpoche: Why not? Everything is the expression of Samantabhadra. All of samsara and nirvana is the space of Samantabhadra. All the tamers, the buddhas, and the ones to be tamed, the beings, all are the expression of Samantabhadra. You may ask why is it that all sentient beings are the expression of Samantabhadra, according to Dzogchen. It is because all beings have tathagatagarbha (*de gshegs snying po*), which is the expression of Samantabhadra. Not recognizing this, one becomes a sentient being. However, we do have the enlightened essence. Also we have the five major elements: earth, water, fire, wind, and space; which are the five female buddhas. They are the expression of Samantabhadra as well. This is the meaning of "all samsara and nirvana is the expression of Samantabhadra." That is why he is called the "general ground of the whole of samsara and nirvana." It is never said that he is only the main, general ground of nirvana and not of samsara. He is the general ground of all of samsara and nirvana.

When practicing the development stage, we need to first begin with the suchness samadhi. That is Samantabhadra. The all-illuminating samadhi is the five buddhas, and the seed samadhi is nirmanakaya. When practicing these, again, we expand the samadhi by sending out the seed syllables of E YAM RAM LAM BAM, and so forth. We have to unfold the four elements. All these come out, expanded from Samantabhadra. There is no practice of development stage without the suchness samadhi. If there were no space, could the four elements of earth, water, fire, and wind be created or not?

Could they be destroyed? No, they couldn't. It is like that. In this way, Samantabhadra is like the foundation. It is not the case that we say Samantabhadra is the foundation for the pure and not for the impure.

It is only because of not recognizing that there is impurity. In actuality, there is not even a sesame seed of impurity. It is our own perceptions that are deluded, none other than that. In the great continuity of wisdom self-display (*rang snang ye shes kyi 'khor lo chen po*), where all the universe and the beings appear from the space of primordial purity, there is not any impurity. In the beginning, there was neither pure nirvana nor impure samsara. But samsara and nirvana, or that which appear like that, is just a momentarily impure, obscured experience. That is how the impurity arose. Whereas Samantabhadra, since the beginning, is primordially purified, primordially perfected.

Question: How do we go about elevating the forty-two peaceful deities from below up to the first story, to make a place for the wrathful ones?

Rinpoche: You emanate all these. You are Samantabhadra, and from you, like rays from the sun, you visualize, or develop, all the hundred peaceful and wrathful deities. When the peaceful ones are visualized, then you elevate them upstairs.

Question: How do we do that?

Rinpoche: You just think that they move upstairs. It is not that you have to move them by hand. There is no difficulty involved there.

Question: Are we also Chemchok Heruka?

Rinpoche: Of course. It is like the sun and its rays. And why is this? Because you are Chemchok Heruka as Samantabhadra, who changed into that form. You can think that these appear like rays from the sun and rays from the rays of the sun.

Question: In what directions do the different deities face?

Rinpoche: You should meditate like this: You are Samantabhadra, like the sun, and the hundred peaceful and wrathful deities are like the rays of the sun. They are emanations of Samantabhadra. First, the five buddhas appear from Samantabhadra, and the eight male and female bodhisattvas appear from the five buddhas. Their emanations, re-emanations, and re-re-emanations appear. The forty-two deities are called naturally pure. The root of the peaceful and wrathful ones is the forty-two peaceful ones. Like rays from the sun and rays from the rays spreading out, Samantabhadra turns into Chemchok Heruka. It is just a transformation; it is not like two people. One Samantabhadra stays and one emanation becomes Chemchok Heruka. Then, the emanations of Chemchok Heruka are the five classes of herukas, who are the emanations of the five buddhas; thus, the five buddhas are transformed into the five herukas. The five buddha consorts become the five krotishvaris. They face in the direction of the main figure. They can face toward the main figure. The wrathful ones can face to the main figure or outward, away from you. Facing outward means that the obstacles should not enter from outside. Why do the female wrathful ones look inward? It is to prevent the siddhis from disappearing outwardly, or outside. Actually, all deities face that way.

Either the deities, the peaceful ones, all face Samantabhadra, or the deities to the north face north, the ones to the east face east, the ones to the south face south, and the ones to the west face west. That way is also all right. There is no difference between these two ways. You can practice whichever of these is most comfortable.

The eight male bodhisattvas are transformed into the eight mamos of the sacred places (*gnas kyi ma mo brgyad*). Their names are *Puga, Siga*, and so forth. They have Sanskrit names. The eight male bodhisattvas become the eight wrathful ones *(khro mo brgyad)*. The female ones have become the eight tramen (*phra men ma*). These tramen goddesses have animal heads, such as dog, pig, and so forth. All are animals. There are eight for the sacred places and eight for the countries or valleys. Sacred places are like Swayambhu, Namo Buddha, Boudhanath, and so forth; whereas, the countries or valleys are like the whole valley of Kathmandu. The eight mamos of the sacred places are the transformation of the eight male bodhisattvas, and the eight *tramen of* the sacred countries or valleys are the transformation of the eight female bodhisattvas. Finally, there are the eight male and female gatekeepers. The gatekeepers are wrathful, like *lokapalas* or worldly protectors. The six buddhas of the six realms look like nirmanakaya, in monk's dress. They don't look like sambhogakaya, although all the deities are sambhogakaya. The six types of tamers of beings, the six munis, are standing up, which signifies benefiting beings. They are standing on single lotuses. They don't need thrones. The six munis of the six realms are standing on single lotuses.

Question: What is meant by natural purity *(gnas su dag pa)?*

Rinpoche: To say that the peaceful deities are naturally pure *(gnas dag)* means that, primordially, as emanations of Samantabhadra, they are pure. They are not momentarily pure or temporarily pure. They are primordially pure. It is said, "Mind is Samantabhadra and mental objects are Samantabhadri." Mind and mental objects are the cognizance and emptiness. These are merely the male and female names being given to cognizance and emptiness. Cognizance and emptiness, since the very beginning, are the mind of the buddhas, the tathagatagarbha, the oneness. This is what is meant by the peaceful ones are naturally pure, primordially pure, without any impurity. Momentarily, they manifest or transform into wrathful forms. The peaceful ones, primordially or naturally pure, are the expression, and they naturally transform into the wrathful ones. For example, if Erik is usually peaceful, if he gets a stick and gets angry, then momentarily or temporarily he is transformed into wrathful. This is an example of how it is. There are not two people, one who is peaceful and one who is wrathful.

You may ask what is meant by the expression "the peaceful ones are primordially, naturally pure." It means that the empty-essence dharmakaya, the cognizant-nature sambhogakaya, and the all-embracing-capacity nirmanakaya, the three kayas, are pure; they are not something impure. That is what is meant by primordially pure, because there is no delusion in the ground. The primordial purity is originally, or primordially, pure. It is said that, although there is no confusion in the ground, at the time of the ground, the confusion seems to arise. An example of this is a multi-colored piece of rope. It is not a snake; it is merely a rope, but when we see the multi-colored rope, the confusion of thinking it is a snake can arise. Therefore, it can happen that we see a rope as a snake and become afraid. Likewise, in the primordial purity, there is no confusion. At the time of the ground, seeming confusion arose and sentient beings appeared. The primordially pure ground possesses the qualities of essence, nature, and capacity. If we have to give it a name, then it is called the "naturally pure, peaceful one." *Naturally pure* and *primordially pure* are synonyms.

The naturally transformed wrathful ones means that the wrathful deities are transformations. All of them are the display of Samantabhadra, since the very beginning. According to the *Ocean of Amrita* of Chokgyur Lingpa, Samantabhadra and Samantabhadri are in the east and west. It says to visualize Samantabhadra with consort in the east and west. The emanations, re-emanations, and re-re-emanations—as well as the forty-two peaceful, victorious ones and the fifty-eight herukas—all issue forth from him. You may ask why are there differences in number in this transformation: forty-two of one kind and fifty-eight of another kind. It is because each of the four female gatekeepers turns into seven emanations: seven ones performing the pacifying activities to the east, seven ones performing the increasing activity to the south, seven ones performing the magnifying activities to the west, and seven ones performing the subjugating activities to the north. Seven times four is twenty-eight, right? In short, they come from the four female gatekeepers. With the two male gatekeepers, it becomes fifty-eight.

Actually there is nothing difficult here in visualizing. You merely think they are like such and such. You don't have to put stone and mud on top of each other, like building a wall. When you become a little proficient in this, you will have no difficulty whatsoever. Otherwise, some people say it is impossible to visualize the field of accumulation in front of oneself or above one's head and to receive the empowerments, as they cannot come down from above, and so forth. Many people say these things, because of clinging to substantial reality. You should only visualize like vivid flashes, in entirety. Otherwise, if you think of the head, then the bottom has disappeared and so forth. Simply think that the whole entire body from the top of the head to the bottom of the feet appears completely and vividly all at once.

That is how we should practice to have a perfect development stage. If we cannot do like that, then there is something called "developing the feeling of the deity being there," and this is also sufficient. If we want to do the perfectly correct development stage, then we have to perfect three fields: *dbang yul, shes yul,* and *snang yul.* To be able to visualize, or develop, these three fields—the field of sense perception *(dbang yul),* the field of consciousness *(shes yul),* and the field of experience *(snang yul)*—we visualize until it becomes completely manifest and we can see it with our eyes. If we have to practice like that, it becomes quite difficult, right?

It is said that subject and object are Samantabhadra and Samantabhadri. Actually, they are cognizance and emptiness; it is also all right to say appearance and emptiness. It's said that appearance is the male and emptiness the female. These are Samantabhadra and consort, and their emanations are the five buddhas. When we purify our aggregates, their pure aspect is the five buddhas. The natural purity of the five elements is the five female buddhas. This is the meaning of *gnas dag:* they are pure from the very beginning. You should visualize all these as well as the male and female bodhisattvas, who are the children of the victorious ones, the buddhas. These are the emanations and re-emanations. The re-emanations are the six munis who tamed the beings of the six realms. All this should be visualized within the palace. When all of these are visualized, they move up to the first story. Then the lower part changes into the wrathful palace, with the blood lakes, corpses of fully grown humans and babies, and various other things, such as banners of human skin, and so forth. It should be a very frightening, or terrifying, kind of place. You were Samantrabhadra, right. From the awareness expression, visualize Chemchok Heruka. The naturally peaceful ones are visualized first. Then, from their expression, they transform into the wrathful ones. Chemchok is Kuntuzangpo, yourself, becoming wrathful. The five buddhas become the five herukas. The five female buddhas become the five krodhishvari. The groups of consciousnesses are the eight male bodhisattvas. The eight consciousnesses objects are the eight female bodhisattvas. Then there are the different views, such as permanence, eternalism, nihilism, of self, and so forth. Those are the four gatekeepers. The four times of past, present, future, and unfixed time are the four female gatekeepers. Each of the four female gatekeepers makes seven emanations for each of the four gates. Actually, there are just six emanations plus the four who are already there, making seven.

When the sun is reflected on the surface of water it is not that the sun has disappeared from the sky and is only reflected in the water, right? There is both the sun in the sky and the one on the surface of water. If there are a hundred bodies of water, there will be a hundred suns. This is an example for Samantabhadra and the hundred peaceful and wrathful buddhas. Samantabhadra is like the sun. If you have one hundred containers of water, then one hundred reflections of the sun can appear, right? That is an example for the emanations from the emanation base. After having visualized the deities, there is the empowerment of the five syllables.

Question: Do we visualize the syllables or the deities at that time, for the OM AH HUNG SVA HA?

Rinpoche: In the detailed tradition, it is said that the deity should empower the deity *(lha yis lha la dbang bskur).* The tradition in the human realm means that when a prince is crowned as a king, he is being empowered. When it concerns the deities, there is not a single deity that is not included within the five buddha families. The meaning of the deity empowering the deity comes from the habitual pattern we have as human beings. We have the habit of eating food, so that is why we make offerings in the development stage, to purify that fixation. We like to be praised and wear nice cloth, so that is why we praise the deities and offer cloth, and so forth. We like to wear ornaments, so we offer jewel ornaments to the deities. As we are crowned and empowered, the deities are crowned and empowered. Depending on what buddha family we are meditating on—if, for example, we are doing the buddha family, then above our heads should be Vairochana, to the east Akshobhya, and so forth. When empowering, the five buddhas should be with the buddha of that particular family in the center, above our heads. The places meant for these five buddhas are not as in the traditional ornament; they should be in the five places.

Question: Can you go over once more where the deities are?

Rinpoche: If you were to ask where the deities are to be visualized, then concerning the peaceful ones they should be visualized within a chest or small shrine made of a precious substance with a jewel at the top. The wrathful ones should be visualized within a skull cup, a human skull cup. Within this skull cup, visualize the five aspects of the buddhas. At the top of the skull cup, there should be one jewel. The drawings are flat, but in the visualization, the peaceful ones should actually be in a chest. If you are doing an extensive version of practice, start out with the nature of mind in the form of a seed syllable, a hand emblem, and a bodily form. These are body, speech, and mind. The hand emblem is what deities usually hold in their hands. It is a symbol of mind. The seed syllable is the symbol of speech, and the bodily form is the sign of body itself. When beginning a visualization of a deity, you should start out with the hand emblem. In that way, the vajra, jewel, lotus, cross-vajra, and wheel are the hand emblems to be visualized as the five buddhas. Then, in one instant, they become the speech, which are the seed syllables OM HUNG TRAM HRIH AH. These letters OM HUNG TRAM HRIH AH become the five bodily forms. It is not the case that one starts out with body, then speech, and then mind. As in the case when a child is conceived, first the consciousness is attached to the sperm and the blood, and then slowly the child develops and is born, right? It is never the case that first the child is born and then the mind comes later. Therefore, first is the sign of the nature of mind, which is the hand emblem.

What the deities hold in their hands is called a hand emblem. For example, in the case of Guru Rinpoche, first visualize a golden vajra. After that, the letter HRIH, and then Guru Rinpoche appears in the bodily form. This is in the case of an extensive or detailed practice. In an abridged version, start with the letters OM HUNG TRAM HRIH AH, which then become the bodily forms of the five buddhas.

First, the five buddhas grant empowerment at the top of your head. Then also our body, speech, and mind are sealed by the body, speech, and mind of the buddhas, in that the body is Vairochana, the speech is Amitabha, and the mind is Akshobhya. These two are called "empowerment" *(dbang bskur)* and "sealing" *(rgyas gdab)*.

Question: Should only the main deity be empowered or all the deities in the retinue too?

Rinpoche: By empowering the main deity, all the retinue is simultaneously empowered. How is this? If the sun in the sky is empowered and sealed, then the thousand reflections of the sun in ponds of water will also simultaneously receive the signs of empowerment and sealing. Yes, it is like that example. You do not need to empower each single deity. Also if the sun is sealed with OM AH HUNG, then the thousand reflections of the sun in water will also have the OM AH HUNG. Therefore, if the main figure is empowered and sealed, the retinue is automatically empowered and sealed too. You do not need to visualize the procedure for each and every one of them. In this way, the five buddhas have been empowered and sealed and the five herukas have been empowered and sealed, all of them.

Question: How do we arrange amrita, rakta, and torma?

Rinpoche: First, when beginning the retreat, you should gather amrita, rakta, and torma. You need two skulls: the amrita is poured in the right and the rakta in the left. The amrita is sacred medicine of eight roots and one thousand branches, and the rakta is tea. The substances of amrita and rakta that I have should be added to these. There are thirty-five aspects of rakta. The amrita medicine has eight roots and one thousand branches. You can use either wine or liqueur. In the left skull cup, you should pour blood, but as it will start to smell, you can use tea instead. Tea is actually the rakta of plants. Sandal is also rakta, the rakta of wood. The blood of wood is sandal. The blood of plants is tea. The blood of existence is the womb-blood of women, the bhaga-blood of a female and the heart-blood of a daka, the blood from the heart of a male. Just any blood is not useful; it needs to come from a wisdom dakini. Our rakta comes from a wisdom dakini.

Question: Could you explain more about the amrita medicine?

Rinpoche: Amrita medicine is mainly the white bodhichitta. As I said, it has eight roots and one thousand branches. If you ask where they come from, then on the northern part of Mt. Sumeru, there is the sandalwood tree. Also there is the one called *Sandal Koshika.* There are two kinds. It has one trunk and eight major medicines, and the thousand different leaves are called the thousand branches, subsidiary aspects. All of these were scattered into the world of *Jambu* continent. This didn't just happen by accident, but through the blessing of the Buddha. Everything we now call medicine is from different kinds of stones, herbs, and so forth. It is prepared and given to people to cure sicknesses.

First of all, our body is composed of the five elements, and when we say the eight roots and thousand branches, they are also composed of the five elements. Therefore, they can cure sicknesses and help. The main source of medicine is the sandalwood tree, with the eight root medicines and the thousand branch medicines. That is the meaning when you say the amrita with the eight roots and thousand branch ingredients *(bdud rtsi rtsa brgyad stong sbyar).* However, it is not only these; there are also the different kinds of mineral stones, different kind of plants, bones, and meats. Through the blessing of the buddhas, all of the world and beings, what appears and exists, are different kinds of medicine. In this case, the root of medicine is the white bodhichitta; in addition, there are the eight root medicines and the thousand branch medicines. Through this amrita offering and by the blessing of the five buddha families dissolving into the secret medicine *(sman sgrub),* the whole of the universe and the beings' phenomenal realm become blessed as nectar. This nectar fulfills the wishes of all the deities and pacifies all the enemies and hostile forces and spirits. That is the meaning of "consecrating the phenomenal realms as being nectar" *(snang srid bdud rtsir byin gyis brlabs)*. This is quite incredible, and the basis of that is the amrita medicine. These are the purposes of the amrita, rakta, and torma.

The torma is for delusion, rakta is for passion, and the amrita is of the nature of aggression. In this way, they have the nature of the three poisons. When the blessings of all the buddhas' body, speech, and mind have dissolved into these three, they become like beer when it ferments, which means, "consecrated by the blessings." Through the offering of these, the yidams and the gurus are all pleased and their wishes are fulfilled. All the dharma protectors fulfill the activities and all the eight classes of gods and demons are pacified. All the beings in the lower realms are established in liberation. Whoever is touched by the amrita receives the blessings. This is the incredible basis of Vajrayana.

Among the three—symbol, meaning, and sign—these are the symbols; whereas, the real meaning is the appearance and emptiness, emptiness and cognizance, as previously mentioned. The entire phenomenal realm—whatever appears and exists, universe and beings—has been consecrated as self-existing wakefulness, the unity of cognizance and emptiness. In the Nyingmapa tradition, when we perform a ritual, we always say, "wisdom fire, wisdom wind, wisdom water." There is always something with wisdom. This is the basic principle here. For example, it is said, "emanating the wisdom fire, wind, and water." It always says wisdom. Accumulating the wisdom accumulations, offering the wisdom offerings. *Yeshe* is a Tibetan word; in Sanskrit, they say JNANA. Everything is blessed through wisdom, JNANA. The same is true when you say RAM YAM KAM OM AH HUNG. In fact, there is no section without JNANA, wisdom. Also, JNANA DAKINI SAPHARIVARA, and so forth and MAHA PANCA AMRITA RAKTA, and so forth are all blessed through wisdom. If you do an extensive version, then, for each of the rakta, there are details like visualizing Girtimamo, the red goddess for the rakta. For the amrita, there are the sixteen vowels and thirty-two consonants that are all to be visualized. Also, there are the five meats and the five nectars in the different directions: horse flesh, human flesh, dog flesh, cow flesh, and so forth. You visualize all these, and above these are the syllables OM HUNG TRAM HRIH AH. Then, just like wine fermenting, they all turn into amrita. The detailed development stage of amrita and rakta has many parts, details, but it is alright without these. If you have to think of all these, it becomes endless, innumerable parts. You have to produce many virtues or white thoughts. You should be free from conceptual thoughts, but here you have to produce many. *(Rinpoche laughs.)* The development stage involves producing a lot of thoughts and, of course, they are white or virtuous. It is said that one practices development stage, the white thoughts, in order to annihilate the black thoughts; whereas in completion stage, there is no need for either white or black thoughts. *(Rinpoche laughs.)*

Question: Where are these amrita and rakta from?

Rinpoche: They were acquired by the siddhas of the past and have been passed down uninterrupted until today. For the amrita, you need the bodhichitta of Guru Rinpoche, which we have. We have the rakta of Yeshe Tsogyal.

Question: What about the torma?

Rinpoche: For the torma, there is torma substance that should be mixed into it. If you cannot get it, you can use *mendrub* instead. In this way, arrange the amrita, rakta, and torma, placing them together with the ARGHAM PADYAM, and so forth. You also need an image or a photo, whichever is easier. For the daily practice, you can do without these offerings and simply offer the mentally created. Visualize the celestial palace. The five outer sense objects are the offerings. The five sense organs have five objects; these are the offerings.

You do need the torma substance; merely having the five nectars and five meats is not sufficient. We have it from *terma,* and it has been transmitted ever since from there. For the five meats, there is human flesh, cow meat, dog meat—five in all. We have these from the termas of Ratna Lingpa and Guru Chöwang. Ratna Lingpa had the meat from one of his former lives as a white horse, who could fly through the sky. We still have the continuation of meat from this horse.

Another *tertön* had the meat of a dog that was a very high incarnation. In this way, there are stories for these things. The meat is the continuation of them. It's not just as if we were to bring in any kind of horse or dog meat— they will be of no use. They need to be from a nirmanakaya.

Question: How do we get these special kinds of meat?

Rinpoche: I have the handed-down substances. I possess the unbroken continuation of them from the termas of Chokgyur Lingpa and Jamyang Khyentse. Most Nyingma lamas have them. As in the case of the five meats, the five nectars should only be from great vajra-holders possessing the three vows. They should be from a great learned and accomplished master—such as his urine, feces, flesh, and blood. It is that kind of nectar that we should use; just to bring any kind of piss and shit along is of no benefit.

Question: How do we offer the two offerings of TANA and GANA, union and liberation?

Rinpoche: Nowadays, both of these are imitations, because the application has died out, whereas in ancient times they were to be actually applied. Those to be liberated are the savage, demonic forces, the ego-clinging. The purpose of the liberation activity is to cure the great demon of conceptual thought.

What is the meaning of the union activity really? Since primordial time, the two, emptiness and great bliss—the emptiness endowed with all the supreme aspects and the unchanging great bliss—are within awareness. The reason why we take the support of a female is to use skillful means. We perform the action as an application of skillful means. We perform the action application as an aid in realizing what is already within ourselves. If you are unable to do the actual act, then you can do what is called "mental creation." That is where all the mandala deities emanate the sixteen offering goddesses, who then offer the union to the deities of the mandala. You should imagine that the offering of union is made. Concerning the liberation, imagine that all the hostile spirits of ego-clinging are liberated into the primordial pure space of nonego. These were the two offerings.

Question: Are both the union and liberation offerings contained within the recognition of awareness?

Rinpoche: Of course, while remaining in the state of the recognition of rigpa, awareness, from there the awareness-expression takes place. First, visualize yourself as Samantabhadra with consort, from whom the offering goddesses are emanated. Then these offering goddesses present the offering of union to you.

After this, emanate the liberator *(ging)* from your heart center, who destroys, or kills, all the savage demons within, which are ego-clinging and conceptual thoughts. They present the offering of primordial purity. When thoughts are liberated, there is primordial purity. After this, they all dissolve into your heart-center again. These are the purposes for all the offering goddesses and the *(ging)*, and so forth. First, they are sent out from your heart center, and after having performed the activities, they dissolve back again.

Question: What is the meaning of the "seat of the wrathful male and female, power of karma *(las dbang khro ba khro mo gdan)* in the three seats"?

Rinpoche: The power of karma or action *(las dbang)* refers to the four times and the four views, which are: the view of permanence, the view of nothingness, the view of self, and the view of conception, sign. The four times are past, present, future, and unfixed time. We call this the seat of the male and female, power of karma or action; for example, the four times are the power of karma. Of the four views, the view of permanence means that all the world and everything lasts. The view of nothingness means there is nothing at all. The view of self means "thinking, I." The view of conceptions means that earth is earth, water is water, and so forth. All these, the earth, water, wind, and so on, are the deities of the three seats. The earth is Buddha Lochana, water is Buddha Mamaki, fire is Pandara Vasini, wind is Samayatara, and space is Dhatvishvari. However, if you think earth is earth, water is water, and fire is fire, and so on, then that is the power of karma, *(las dbang)*. When we say, "The *power of karma* is the seat of the male and female wrathful ones," then the wrathful ones refer to the four gatekeepers. The male wrathful ones are the four male gatekeepers, and the females are the female gatekeepers.

The four male gatekeepers are Vijaya, Achala, Hayagriva, and Amritakundali, in this order. The four female gatekeepers are the past, present, future, and the unfixed time. There are other interpretations of this. For example, for the sensation of touch, there is touching, the toucher, touched, and the sensation of touch or the touch perception *(reg shes)*. That means we have an object, sense organ, and perception; these are also called the four female gatekeepers. You can find the details of this in the *Guhyagarbha Tantra*, which is very extensive and takes a long time. All this is the intent, the contents of the *Guhyagarbha Tantra*. Concerning the object, sense organ, and sense perception, then, for example, there is form as the object. The sense organ is the eye, and the perception is the mind. The fourth is when the three, the object, sense organ, and perception are conjoined, or in contact. There is the touched, the touching, the toucher, and the sensation of touch, the perception of touch. In the case of the sensation of sight, then there is the object seen, and the seer, or the eyes. When these two meet, there is seeing, the perception. Then there is the sight consciousness, by which we see whether this is nice or not nice, and so forth.

However, in general, it is said that the four times are the four male gatekeepers and the four views of permanence, nothingness, self, and conception are the four female gatekeepers. According to one tradition, object and time are meeting and that is the union of the male and female wrathful gatekeepers. In some traditions, they are combined with the four immeasurables. These can be combined in different ways; the intent of the tantras is very vast. So, in short, *the seat of the wrathful male and female power of karma (las dbang khro ba khro mo gdan)* means the "four male and four female gatekeepers."

Question: Can you explain further what the three seats are, in totality?

Rinpoche: Primarily, we must understand the correct meaning of the "complete mandala of the three seats of completeness," (*gdan gsum tshang ba'i dkyil 'khor*). Then you can practice the ritual. The first of the three seats is the aggregates and elements, as the seat of the male and female tathagatas. The male tathagatas are the five male victorious ones, and the female tathagatas are the five consorts. The root of the aggregates and elements is mind *(yid)* and mental object *(chos)*, which basically means appearance-emptiness. Appearance is the lord, and emptiness is his consort. Mind and mental object, as appearance and emptiness, are, first of all, Samantabhadra and his consort. Likewise, the pure aspects of the five aggregates are the five buddha principles (*rgyal ba rigs lnga*). The purified five elements of earth, water, and so forth are the five consorts. This is what you should understand by "aggregates and elements as the male and female tathagatas."

Seat means "having complete," the qualities are completely contained, spontaneously present. When one possesses the aggregates and elements, the male and female tathagatas are complete. That is the meaning of the "three seats of completeness." The aggregates and elements are the completeness of the male and female tathagatas. The actions and senses are the completeness of the male and female wrathful gatekeepers. The sense bases are the completeness of the male and female bodhisattvas. If you really want this in detail, it can be found in the *Guhyagarbha Tantra,* as Orgyen Tobgyal Rinpoche says.

The other various texts and commentaries are simply elaborations on the three seats of completeness; the whole *Shitro* is contained within these three completenesses.

The peaceful ones turn into the wrathful ones. The eight male and female bodhisattvas turn into the eight ladies of the sacred places (*gnas ma brgyad*) and the eight ladies of the sacred valleys (*yul ma brgyad*); the eight ladies of the sacred places are the transformation of the eight male bodhisattvas into female ones, and the eight ladies of the sacred valleys were first the eight female bodhisattvas.

In the development stage of *Kunzang Tuktig,* as I noted previously, you can remain unmoved from awareness, while meditating on the development stage. If you have grown accustomed to awareness, then remain in the continuity of awareness and let the projection and dissolution of thoughts arise as the development stage, like waves moving on the surface of water. The aggregates and elements arise as the tathagatas; the actions and senses arise as the wrathful gatekeepers. In short, the mandala of deities is first of all the forty-two peaceful ones. They are in the palace that has four corners, four gates; the upper part has the round shape of a vase, and the lower part is like a square celestial palace. To begin with, visualize the peaceful mandala below; then it ascends to the upper story and visualize the wrathful mandala below. In this way, the *Shitro* is two-storied: the peaceful ones are above and the wrathful ones are underneath. This is alike in both *Kunzang Tuktig* and the *Karling Shitro.*

Question: Could you explain the two mantras?

Rinpoche: For the peaceful ones, the Bodhichitta mantra is the essence of the peaceful ones. Bodhichitta is Sanskrit for compassion. Concerning compassion, there are two, the relative and absolute. The relative one involves the four immeasurables and the six paramitas, through which we develop bodhichitta. The absolute is beyond the complexity of the four extremes, the essence of views, the realization of the ultimate *Madhyamika.* The essence of these two kinds is bodhichitta.

The essence mantra of all the peaceful ones is Bodhichitta: OM BODHI-CHITTA MAHASUKHA JNANADHATU AH. MAHA means "great;" SUKHA means "bliss." JNANA means that everything since the beginning is primordial knowing *(yeshe)*. Therefore, it is primordially known—the aspect of non-confusion is called JNANA. In JNANADHATU AH, DHATU means "dharma-dhatu." This is the deity of space; the root of everything is space. Absence of complexity is dharmadhatu; there is nothing whatsoever that is not included within dharmadhatu, just like the space of sky. The root of all dharmas is called "dharmakaya;" the *kaya* here refers to "manifesting as dharmakaya from dharmadhatu." Dharmadhatu is like the buddha realm, and dharma-kaya is like the master abiding in that realm. So, DHATU means space. AH means nonarising.

OM is the body. RULU RULU is the wrathful ones, the herukas. Actually it means "drinking blood from the skull," the same as the term blood-drinker. HUNG is the essence of the male wrathful ones. BHYO is the essence of the female wrathful ones. This mantra is the combined mantra of all herukas' minds. In particular, it is the mantra of Yangdag Heruka, in which case OM RULU RULU HUNG BHYO HUNG is for Yangdag, and OM VAJRA SATTVA AH is for Vajrasattva as the peaceful. When Vajrasattva becomes wrathful, the mantra is the Rulu mantra, the essence mantra of Yangdag. But, in general, it is the main mantra of all the wrathful ones.

Question: In one single recitation of the *Shitro* mantra, are all the aspects of approach, accomplishment, and activity complete or not? What is the intent, or the visualization, for each of them?

Rinpoche: At first, there is the "moon with a garland of stars." Here in the heart-center of Samantabhadra, the syllable AH is surrounded by a garland of mantric syllables, which refers to the moon with a garland of stars. Then, as the mantra starts to revolve, it becomes the second visualization, which is called the "firebrand." These two refer to *"approach* and *close approach,"* which, in this practice, are completed at once. It is generally said that the moon with the garland of stars is the intent of the approach. The firebrand is the intent of the close approach. The third is the "messenger of a king." This is when light rays are emanated out from the mantra chain. We offer upward to the mandala of the victorious ones and downward as generosity, purifying all the obscurations and karmas of sentient beings. This radiating upward and downward, making offerings and purifying sentient beings, is called the messenger of the king intent, and this belongs to the accomplishment. The fourth is the "beehive breaking open," the great accomplishment. These are called the "four types of recitation intents."

The two first ones, approach and close approach, are contained here as approach. The fourth, the great accomplishment, includes all four. At the time of making a *drubchen,* we need the same amount of people as each of the deities practiced. For example, if we are going to make a gathering for the peaceful and wrathful deities of the *Kunzang Tuktig,* then we would need one hundred people. Otherwise, in the general context, we call it "approach, accomplishment, and actions." All are then contained in three aspects, in which case approach and close approach are contained in approach, accomplishment and great accomplishment are included in action. The application of the activities are, for example, in the Guru Rinpoche practice, the Harinisa mantra fulfilling the pacifying, enriching, magnetizing, and subjugating activities, by means of the four gatekeepers. Here, *action* means "fulfilling whatever act we find necessary," either through pacifying, enriching, and so forth. If we need magnetizing, there is a magnetizing activity. If we need to subjugate, there is a subjugating activity. Through the supreme activity, we can accomplish the supreme action.

In this case, there are five activities, which are pacifying, enriching, magnetizing, subjugating, and the supreme—which is the spontaneously accomplished activity. This is the "samadhi action of self-existing wakefulness," which is the supreme activity. In general, for example in the Guru Rinpoche practice of *Tukdrub Barchey Künsel,* there is a recitation first for Amitayus, which is *the approach.* Next, the recitation for Avalokiteshvara is the close approach. The one for Guru Rinpoche is the *accomplishment, and* the Tötreng Tsal mantra is the intent of the great accomplishment. Finally, the Harinisa mantra fulfills the activities, the application of the activities.

In the *Kunzang Tuktig* practice, all of these are contained in one single recitation. *(Rinpoche recites the lines for the recitation part):*

> *All sights are the body of the peaceful and wrathful ones.*§
> *All that is heard is the sound of mantra.*§
> *Thoughtfree awareness is the space of luminosity.*§
> *The ocean-wide realms are filled with clouds of offerings.*§
> *Innumerable activities free all beings.*§

This is the all-pervading mandala of the victorious ones;§
Everything is perfect in the continuity of one taste.§

Is there anything not included in that? Here the approach, *accomplishment, and actions* are all contained in one mantra recitation. *All sights are the body of the peaceful and wrathful ones*§, *All that is heard is the sound of mantra*§, there are no exceptions; nothing is left out. This is not merely the four intents of recitation; everything is included. *Thoughtfree awareness is the space of luminosity*§ refers to our thoughts. These words are really incredible, inconceivable. Now even an ocean of offering clouds fills the buddhafields. *Innumerable activities free all beings*§ is the line that indicates fulfilling the two purposes, or benefits. *Innumerable* means the "five activities, including the supreme activity." These refer to the application of activities *(las 'byor)*. *This is the all-pervading mandala of the victorious ones*§ refers to the sights, sounds, and awareness. *Everything is perfect in the continuum of one taste*§, means that everything is completed in the space of rigpa, primordial purity. That is the supreme activity, where everything is contained. Nothing is lacking, is there?

Everything is perfect in the continuum of one taste.§ The *one taste*, here, refers to "dharmakaya or dharmadhatu." Everything in the world, the beings, what appears and exists, are completely embraced in the primordially pure space—completely embraced by the primordially pure space that is uncompounded and unconstructed. In the single expanse, all dharmas of samsara and nirvana are included.

It is said that in the past, in India, it was forbidden to say the term *the single sphere of dharmakaya (chos sku thig le nyag gcig)* aloud. This term was too profound and too important. Also, the *Dzogchen protectors* were listening very carefully. As well, all the spirits in the sky would faint, because the words were so profound. They could not be contained in their minds. For this reason, the gurus taught their disciples through a copper pipe. These teachings are now contained in *The Three Sections of Dzogchen, (rdzogs chen sde gsum)* and in *The Oral Transmission of the Old School, (rnying ma bka' ma)*. The oral instruction from teacher to student is directed through a copper pipe, because nonhumans—the spirits, demons, and so on—flying around in the sky should not be able to hear it. It would be too much for them. If they heard that, they would completely faint, like when a person falls unconscious.

Actually, one hundred recitation intents are included here, not only four. *(Rinpoche is laughing.)* Even if there were one hundred different kinds of recitation intents, they would still be included. There is nothing incomplete here. The awareness is nonconceptual cognizant space, not the conceptual awareness without cognizance. *(Rinpoche says, laughing.)* Awareness is nonconceptual wisdom, free from conceptual thought. It is not an absent-minded or thoughtless state that is blanked-out or like being hit on the head with a stick. That is the nonthought state of mind *(rtog med)*, the ordinary mind's absent-minded state, where thoughts have ceased. That is the seed of stupidity. Here, concerning awareness *(rigpa)*, the cessation of ordinary thoughts means that it is the functioning of nonconceptual wisdom, cognizant space.

Question: At the time of recitation, how does one recognize whatever arises as dharmakaya, and what is the method for nondistraction?

Rinpoche: The method for nondistraction is mindfulness. But in the beginning, mindfulness is called "deliberately applied mindfulness." Following training, we don't need mindfulness with effort any more; effortless mindfulness occurs naturally. The dharmata mindfulness follows this. In all, there are six kinds of mindfulness. This, itself, is the method for nondistraction. When you have your cattle grazing on the mountainside, you look after them and watch whether they have been eaten or not by wild animals or whether they themselves are eating grass or not. This is called the "watchman." It is keeping an eye on something. To keep an eye on whether *rigpa* is distracted or not, first of all, you need mindfulness with effort. When you slowly, slowly become practiced, or accustomed to it, then it becomes effortless. Finally, you reach dharmata mindfulness and wisdom mindfulness. In the scriptures, there are mentioned six different kinds of mindfulness. When reaching the stage of exhaustion of dharmas beyond concepts, recollection occurs as wisdom, which means mindfulness has turned into wisdom *(yeshe)*. When that takes place, you don't need to be mindful, because there is neither distraction nor confusion, day and night. It is then said that mindfulness has become wisdom. There is another quote, "When rigpa has reached the natural space, analytical meditation naturally ceases. The watcher, the mindfulness, disperses and vanishes into emptiness. How delightfully free and easy it is in the space of nondual awareness." That's how it becomes in Dzogchen.

Well, if you ask what you need in the meantime, there is no way around being mindful. The main thing here is effortless mindfulness. When mindfulness with effort has become self-sustained, there is vivid, wakeful, effortless mindfulness, without any need for force or struggle, without any tenseness, just naturally alert. When you have become accustomed to that, there is only undistracted rigpa. At present, rigpa is totally without any strength; it is completely wild, or untamed, just like *a spoiled child*. That is how mind is right now. Even though dharmakaya permeates all of samsara and nirvana, what appears and exists, if we don't recognize it, we continue in this wild habit we have fallen into since beginningless time up until now. That is why it is necessary to apply mindfulness, whether it's according to Madhyamika, Mahamudra, or Dzogchen. According to Dzogchen, it's called "awakeness or wakefulness" *(dran rig)*. *Awakeness* means that *mindfulness* and *rigpa* are mixed. In Mahamudra, it is called "watchfulness" *(dran rtsis)*. According to Madhyamika, it is called *dran shes*, which is a combination of mindfulness and alertness *(shes bzhin)* and carefulness *(bag yod)*. If you ask for an example for this, it is like a newly wedded bride. When a newly wedded bride has been taken to the home of her husband, she is very careful. It is said, "One should be like a newly wedded bride. She has no anger whatsoever. She speaks very softly. She moves in a very gentle way and does everything very nicely and carefully." That is the example of carefulness. This is conscientiousness and *carefulness*, according to the path of Madhyamika. On this path, it is said that one needs mindfulness, conscientiousness, and carefulness. Definitely one should not be mindless, thoughtless, and careless. One should have presence of mind, conscientiousness, and carefulness. These things are necessary.

In short, when practicing the *Kunzang Tuktig* in the recitation practice, first you visualize the buddha-mandala of your body. Then practice the approach, accomplishment, and application of the activities simultaneously, like the bees swarming from the beehive. Visualize your body as the deity, meditate on speech as mantra, and rest the mind as samadhi. All appearances of form are the nature of the deity's body. All sounds are the nature of the deity's speech. All thoughts are the nature of the deity's mind. These are called the "three things to carry concerning sights, sounds, and awareness" *(khyer so gsum)*. According to the secret mantra tradition of Nyingmapa, sights have the nature of body, sounds the nature of speech, and thoughts the nature of mind. These are called the "three things to do." *To carry* means "to bring onto the path;" it means "to not abandon." There are three things you should bring onto the path. In this state, you should be the watchman of mindfulness.

In the beginning, it is necessary to have mindfulness with effort and clear wakefulness with effort. Even though it takes a little effort, slowly it will be spontaneous, like the constant flow of a river. A river flows slowly sometimes and quickly at other times. The placid flow of a river means that it is constant, peacefully flowing on without stopping; in such a way, one remains in a state of nondistraction. In this, there should be nonmeditation. There are some people who say they are meditating without being distracted. That is fine, if they do so without thinking that. Be without distraction, but also without meditating. Meditation can be called "cultivation." It is not said, "With meditating and distraction," right? It is said, "Without being distracted, without wandering, and without cultivating, meditating." There is a nondistraction that is cultivated, where one merely sits and holds on to the idea of being undistracted. There is a certain kind of Tibetan medicine against stomach disorder, which if it is not digested becomes poison in the stomach. This is like the idea of sitting and thinking, "I am not distracted. I am not distracted." It is simply a thought.

Actually, when you say "self-existing wakefulness" *(rang byung ye shes)* that means it is not manufactured; it is *wisdom*, undeluded, undistracted. In *rang byung yeshe, yeshe* means "primordial knowing." We are not aware of and don't know what we have had since the very beginning. To know *what is* since the beginning is called "primordial knowing." *Rangjung* means "that which is in one's being already, is not forced or produced through effort, neither accepted nor rejected," and *yeshe* means "primordial knowing." We do not say, "primordial not knowing." It is primordially known. If this self-existing wakefulness is mixed with even a hair-tip of meditator and meditated—where the meditated is the self-existing wakefulness and the meditator is thinking, "Oh, I am completely undistracted"—that is dualistic fixation. That will tie us down. If there weren't this defect, all sentient beings would be buddhas. Why not? All beings possess the buddha-mind. From dharmakaya, the self-existing wakefulness is primordially permeating from Samantabhadra down to the smallest insect. It does not say temporarily permeating, it says primordially permeating. If it were merely a temporary permeation, we wouldn't have known about it. We could think, "Oh, it is probably not from the beginning. Maybe it is only some temporary thing.

I don't know." If it were temporarily permeating for some time, it would be difficult to know. However, that is not said. It is said, "primordially pervading." It has been permeating sentient beings since the very beginning.

If you ask what causes disaster, or brings us down, it is the idea of meditator and meditated. That is like taking self-existing wakefulness as something to meditate on and our conceptual mind as the meditator. We gain the intellectual knowledge of this being an empty and cognizant state and hold it in mind. "Ah, the Lama has said there is something empty and cognizant; this must be it. Oh yeah. Now I must not lose it through distraction." In this case, the whole thing is a fabrication. Without that, it is said to be unfettered and freed. There was nothing to tie down the self-existing wakefulness since the very first. If something were tied again, it would have to be untied. But it is untied without fetter. That which is never fettered does not need to be untied; it is free. Untied, free, naked, fresh—this is not something we need to make. This is where we all have to arrive.

Most people make what is self-existing into temporarily existing. They try to make what is primordially known *(yeshe)* into something that has to be newly understood, or re-known. What does not need to be contrived, they make artificial. What does not need to be held, they try to catch. That is called "conceptual delusion, being deluded by thoughts." This is what has happened life after life, lifetime after lifetime. It is said, "It is free from being fettered and beyond being freed also." This is very significant. If something were fettered, we would have to untie it. There would be a job to do, but as it is primordially unfettered, we don't need to free it again. If it were tied or bound at first, then we would need to free it again. This is concerning what is true. However, right now as sentient beings, we are fettered. We are fettered by dualistic fixation, and this needs to be freed. Nevertheless, what is to be freed and the freer are the same here.

It is like this smart-mouth, in the teachings down in Boudha, who said, "Oh the knife cannot cut itself. How can it see itself?" He said that. He was just shooting off his mouth. Actually though, it is like that. The knife cannot cut itself. There is no cutter and nothing to cut. Even if there were something to be cut, it couldn't be cut. Similarly, one should simply remain freely. If there were something to cut and something that cuts, then it would be like the knife that cannot cut itself. *Free (lhug pa)* is very significant. It doesn't say, "cut." Simply remain freely. What else do you have to ask? Now I have said all these things.

Question: Are the twenty-eight ishvaris all mixed together, or are they in four groups of seven?

Rinpoche: According to tradition, the seven white ones are to the east, the seven yellow ones to the south, the seven red ones to the west, and the seven green ones to the north. They should be in each of the four directions, seven white to the east, seven yellow to the south, and so forth.

Question: Are the seven with the fangs and seven with the wings in one of the four directions?

Rinpoche: No, it doesn't mean that all seven white ones have fangs. Of the twenty-eight, there are seven with fangs, seven with wings, seven with claws, and so forth. They are mixed together. You will understand this when you read the detailed *sadhana*. It only says there are seven with fangs, seven with wings, seven with claws, and so forth. It doesn't say there are seven of these to the south, seven to the west, and so forth.

Tersar Peaceful Deities Torma

Conclusion and the *Zurgyen*

Tulku Urgyen Rinpoche

CONCLUSION

We have reached the end of the five sections of the main part. Now we have arrived at the five concluding stages. We can dissolve the mandala, or we can add in a traditional aspect of sadhana practice called the *Kangshag,* the mending and apology. I will come back to this later.

At the conclusion of the sadhana itself, again there is the dissolution and re-emergence section. Just as everything evolved out of the three kayas, again it dissolves back into the sphere of the three kayas. The mandala dissolves into the palace, into the deities, into the central figure, into the seed syllable, and finally remains as unconstructed emptiness. To eliminate the tendency toward eternalism, the permanence of all things, as well as the tendency toward nihilism, the idea that nothing exists, we again manifest as the single form of the deity and then carry out daily activities.

First, we recite the amendment mantras, repeat the offerings and praises, and recite the Vajrasattva mantra three times. Dissolving takes place with HUNG HUNG HUNG, whereby we imagine that everything we have visualized as the forms of the deities, the palace, the buddhafield, and so forth, which have been visible yet empty of any self-nature, dissolves from the outside inward. The palace dissolves into the deities, the surrounding retinue of deities dissolves into the central figure of Samantabhadra, Samantabhadra dissolves into the seed syllable in his heart-center, the letter AH, and that letter, itself, dissolves until nothing whatsoever is kept in mind. This covers the body aspect.

All sounds that have been heard are empty, yet resounding. Now, they also vanish like thunder, which resounds throughout the sky and then totally vanishes. This covers the speech aspect.

For the mind aspect, leave the nonarising empty essence of awareness without any fabrication whatsoever. In this way, all aspects of manifestation of body, speech, and mind remain as the innate state of dharmadhatu, the unimpeded state of Samantabhadra's mind.

With AH AH AH, re-emerge again as the body, speech, and mind of the peaceful and wrathful ones. Whatever appears is the body of the peaceful and wrathful ones, whatever is heard is their speech, and all states of mind—unfabricated awareness—are the mind of the peaceful and wrathful ones. Inseparable, they appear from the expression of Samantabhadra. This is called dissolving and emerging.

Next is the verse for bringing onto the path, followed by the dedication of merit and the formation of aspirations. Finally, there are the four lines for auspiciousness of dharmakaya, sambhogakaya, and nirmanakaya, again ending up with the reminder of the sphere of the three kayas. So, from beginning to end, this practice is about the sphere of the three kayas.

In the aspiration and dedication, the first four lines are called the "ultimate aspiration," whereby it says,

> OM AH HUNG༔
> *The external universe, the nature of space, is the realm of*
> *five-colored light.༔*
> *The inner contents of sentient beings are the five male and female*
> *families.༔*
> *Everything in the nature of the five wisdoms,༔*
> *Is spontaneously present as the display of Samantabhadra.༔*

All the five elements and so forth are the realm of five-colored light, while the inner contents, sentient beings are the five families of the male and female buddhas. That is the ultimate aspiration.

Next is the dedication:

> HOH༔
> *This practice of Samantabhadra and the peaceful and wrathful*
> *victorious ones,༔*
> *And all the virtue gathered throughout the three times,༔*
> *I add together and dedicate to unexcelled great enlightenment.༔*
> *May I and all the infinite sentient beings༔*
> *Exhaust the two obscurations, perfect all qualities,༔*
> *And awaken as the unified state of Vajradhara.༔*

Next, the verses of auspicious are here combined with the ultimate meaning:

OM࿐

May there be the auspiciousness of the empty essence, dharmakaya.࿐
May there be the auspiciousness of the cognizant nature,
    sambhogakaya.࿐
May there be the auspiciousness of the manifold capacity, nirmanakaya.࿐
May there be the auspiciousness of their inseparability,
    Samantabhadra.࿐

In the small writing, which is not said aloud, Guru Rinpoche says,

This activity practice, The Manifest Essence,࿐
Which benefits whoever encounters it,࿐
Will spread the heart-teaching of Samantabhadra,࿐
From the conclusion of the Dark Age until the end of this aeon.࿐

By fully condensing the Dzogchen tantras࿐
Into an easy method that is simple to carry out and bestows swift
    blessings,࿐
I, Padma, made this excellent composition,࿐
As a meaningful encounter for the fortunate ones in that time.࿐

In order to make this meaningful for anyone who encounters it, Yeshe Tsogyal wrote this down with devotion and concealed it as a profound terma treasure.

Tsogyal respectfully recorded it࿐
And concealed it as a profound treasure.࿐
May my fortunate son discover it.࿐
Through his discovery, may this teaching flourish!࿐
Samaya. Seal of treasure, seal of concealment, seal of profundity.࿐

I, Chokgyur Dechen Lingpa, extracted this from the Turquoise Cave on the southern slope of Namkhadzö in Dokham and translated it from the yellow parchment

in Orgyen Samten Ling at Rudam Snow Range. May it be virtuous! May all be auspicious!

I have now explained the terma root text, which is called *The General Practice of the Peaceful and Wrathful Ones According to The Heart-Essence of Samantabhadra, The Kunzang Tuktig.*

Tersar Wrathful Deities Torma

THE ZURGYEN

In Chokgyur Lingpa's time, the mending and confession practice, *(kang-shag)* was done in a more extensive way, using his terma *Tukje Da-ö, Moon-light of Compassion,* which contains the complete chants for the fourfold apology and fourfold mending. The fourfold apology is for body, speech, mind, and their combination—all are in the *Moonlight of Compassion.* Later on, Karma Khenpo wrote a mending and confession practice particularly for the *Kunzang Tuktig.*

One or two generations later, Samten Gyatso, my uncle and guru, said, "Karma Khenpo is surely a great emanation, but since the *Kunzang Tuktig* is a terma, it would be better to have a mending and confession practice using actual words of Padmasambhava that are also a terma teaching. There is nothing wrong with Karma Khenpo's composition; it's just that terma should go together with terma." So, he asked Tersey Tulku, his younger brother, who was the reincarnation of one of Chokgyur Lingpa's two sons, to arrange a concise version of the mending and confession practice—one that would complement the condensed style of *Kunzang Tuktig* itself. The earlier ones were quite lengthy, and there is no need to have one that is one hundred times longer.

As you can see in the authors' colophon at the end of the *Zurgyen* text, Tersey Tulku wrote that he got both the order and the permission to do this from his older brother and guru, Samten Gyatso. He arranged this and wrote it out at Radza Dzong-Go—Majestic Fortress Peak—a retreat place where I lived when I was young. That is the text we have today. We usually refer to it as the *Zurgyen, the Side-Ornament.* It can be added in after the recitation, or speech aspect, in the sadhana practice. When we do that, the speech aspect is not finished, since part of the *Zurgyen* still involves mantra recitation. Recitation usually has three aspects called "approach, accomplishment, and activity-enactment." The Bodhichitta Rulu mantra in the *Leyjang* completes the first two aspects, approach and accomplishment, *nyenpa* and *drubpa.* The activity recitation is in the *Zurgyen.*

The *Zurgyen* contains several topics. The vital point of *Kangshag*—mending-apology—is to provide the means to continually reconnect and make amends with the peaceful and wrathful deities. The purpose of the *shagpa,* "apology," is to purify breaches and damages of samaya, while the *kangwa,* "mending," is to exhaust the causes of samsara by offering amrita, rakta, torma, and butter lamps. These two sections are very profound and essential in connection with the practice of the peaceful and wrathful deities.

Activity Recitation

The *Zurgyen* begins by stating that all the peaceful and wrathful deities send out light-rays to the "object to be benefited." In our case, the object to be benefited is simply all sentient beings. It's not just one person in particular. If a master uses the *Zurgyen* to confer empowerment on disciples or to perform the name-burning ceremony for the dead, then they would be the beneficiaries in those cases.

Generally speaking, there are the four activities of pacifying, increasing, magnetizing, and subjugating, but here there is also an activity known as "overturning the depths of the lower realms," by means of Vajrasattva's mantra. We visualize Vajrasattva, as the text explains, and chant his mantra in combination with the mantras of the peaceful and wrathful deities. There is then an appendage for purifying the three lower realms—first for the hells, then for the hungry ghosts, and lastly for the animals. At the end, add in OM DAHA DAHA NARAKA and so forth for the hells, PRETAKA for the hungry ghosts, and TIRYAKA for the animals. Afterward, imagine that Vajrasattva absorbs into you while saying, "By reciting the one hundred syllables, the quintessence of all the tathagatas, you have purified all breaches and so forth." The lower realms are thus purified.

After that, there is an optional section. If the master consecrates the vase, which is only necessary for the sake of empowerment or for the name-burning ceremony[10], there is a self-initiation during the consecration of the vase. At the very beginning of the consecration of the vase, the text says, "When acting for the welfare of others, either in the context of empowerment or the name-burning ceremony, there is a consecration of the vase." According to the Nyingma system, there is a way whereby, through the magic of one's state of samadhi, the self-visualization, the front visualization, and the vase visualization—all three—are perfected in a single instant, as automatically as a reflection appearing in a clear mirror. But, if you don't possess this power of samadhi, here is how to go about it: Use the liturgy to imagine that in the heart-center of the chief deity—in this case it is yourself—there is the letter AH standing on a moon disc and lotus flower. The flower has one hundred petals, and upon each petal is one syllable of the

Hundred Syllable mantra. Each syllable resounds with its own sound. The letter AH has emanated all these surrounding one hundred syllables. Then they are transformed into the bodily forms of the one hundred peaceful and wrathful deities, each sitting on one petal. They all radiate light.

At this point, we take the vajra with its dharani-cord and hold it to our heart. The other end of the dharani-cord is attached to the *namgyal bumpa*, the victorious vase. On top of the vase is a small conch shell, where the cord is attached. During the recitation, we imagine that the mantra leaves our mouth, swirls around the dharani-cord to the tiny vajra on top of the conch, and dissolves into the nectar within the conch. From the conch, it flows down into the victorious vase that contains the mandala of the peaceful and wrathful deities. There is also a section for a second vase called *lekyi bumpa*, activity vase, into which the nectar of Vajrasattva dissolves. This is used for purification. You can skip this if you are not using the activity vase, since it is not part of the mending and confession practice. The vase recitation involves the complete three kayas, since the vajra on top of the conch symbolizes dharmakaya, the reflection of the conch in the vase water symbolizes sambhogakaya, and the water itself, where the reflection then dissolves, symbolizes nirmanakaya.

Conclude the recitation—meaning before the apology begins—with the amendment-mantras as well as the offerings and praise. There is a short verse for offering and praise added in here, which is also a *kangwa*. It starts out HUNG, *yeshe lhatsok* .... Then recite the Vajrasattva mantra. This completes the speech section.

The Yeshe Kuchok

Yeshe Kuchok—the Supreme Wisdom Body—which in fact is a complete sadhana practice in itself, follows next. It originates from an important tantra, and, in intent, it is equal to the *Kunzang Döngyi Trinley*, the *Ultimate Activity of Samantabhadra*. It includes the meaning of all the peaceful and wrathful deities. *Activity* here means "sadhana," because it contains all the essential ingredients needed for the ultimate sadhana. Not only a terma, it is also included within the scriptures of the Nyingma Kama tradition, the oral transmission of the old school. The *Yeshe Kuchok* is extremely precious.

The Four Aspects of Apology and Mending

The *Zurgyen's* main part begins with the four aspects of apology, which are the body, speech, mind, and their combination. The first is to pay homage to all the peaceful and wrathful deities. The second is to recite the Vajrasattva mantra and to apologize for and purify the misdeeds of speech. Recite the *Lamenting Apology* to purify your voice. *The Apology of the Expanse of the View* is to purify your mind. Finally, there is an apology for purifying the combination of body, speech, and mind. This completes the fourfold apology.

The four aspects of mending are the offering of amrita, rakta, torma, and butter lamp. Their purpose is to deplete the sources of samsara. The amrita symbolizes aggression, rakta symbolizes desire, torma symbolizes stupidity, and the butter lamp represents self-existing wakefulness *(rangjung yeshes)*. Amrita, rakta, and torma also refer to the white and red element, as well as flesh. The flesh of the body is represented by a torma, which symbolizes stupidity.

After the outer offerings, the inner offerings begin with *the five elements and the five wisdoms.* The words in the next line—*Possessing the five desirable qualities of form, sound, smell, taste, and touch*—mean that these phenomena are not arranged by anyone; they are self-existing offerings. The liturgy text has clear headings for each section, so it's easy to see what's what—for amrita, for rakta, for the feast, for the union and liberation, and for the lamp offering. Then there is an apology involving the meaning of the four empowerments. This is the basic intent of the *Ocean of Amrita*, which is essentially contained here.

Regarding the fourfold mending, the first is for the natural purity of the peaceful and wrathful deities, and the next is for the transformed purity of the wrathful deities. Finally, there is the *Ultimate Mending of Dharmata.* Here, primordial union means that perceptions and their emptiness are primordially indivisible. Primordial liberation or deliverance refers to the fact that the ignorance causing our attention to roam through samsara is liberated, "killed" actually, at the moment of recognizing the state of *rigpa. Marigpa,* "ignorance," dies. That's the primordial or basic liberation.

All the sections included within the extensive sadhanas of the peaceful and wrathful deities are also included here in the *Zurgyen.* Just as an elephant has a head, legs, and main torso, a louse also has a head, legs, and torso. This is the louse-sized sadhana. *(Rinpoche laughs.)* It is good to practice the main sadhana in the morning and the *Kangshag* in the late afternoon. Together, these two form a complete daily practice of the peaceful and wrathful deities. After one year, you will have practiced the totality of the peaceful and wrathful deities, on a daily basis, three hundred and sixty times. An excellent target!

Next, there is the lamp aspiration. The lamp is the symbol for rigpa, while darkness is marigpa, unknowing. When you light a lamp in darkness, everything is perceived very clearly. This is the analogy. Through the support of a butter lamp, you chant this very profound aspiration.

The Feast Offering

Tsok, or feast, literally means "gathering," the gathering of a great heap of merit. You must gather the basic articles of means and knowledge: the edibles, such as biscuits and other substances, represent "means," while the beverages, juice or tea or whatever, symbolize "knowledge." The offerings are then consecrated by means of a chant. Another chant invites the guests. An apology and the offering of the feast follow.

During the deliverance offering, you "deliver" the general enemies of the Dharma and the specific enemies of the yogis and yoginis. There are many details to learn regarding who and exactly what is being delivered, but, in short, it is also contained in just these few lines. Likewise, there are many details about who the recipients of the residual offering are, the seven of this, the eight of that, the ten of this, and so on.

After the pure aspiration, we insert the *Inexhaustible Garland of Lightning,* the petition to the dharma protectors, since they uphold the Buddhadharma. This protector prayer is also called *Maza Damsum*—the torma-ritual for Ekajati, Rahula, and Vajrasadhu. Finally, there is a short verse of offering and praise, and receiving the siddhis.

Conclusion

Afterward, jump back into the *Leyjang* sadhana, dissolve, and re-emerge as taught above.

Wondrous Torma

Questions and Answers

Question: After dissolving the visualization and emerging, when entering the path of action in between sessions, what should we imagine at that time?

Rinpoche: First, in the visualization practice, you have meditated on the celestial palace, the thrones, and the deities seated upon them. In this context, the visualization you have created in yourself is called the samaya being. The deities invited from dharmadhatu are the jnanasattvas, wisdom beings. The seed syllable in the heart-center is called the samadhi-being, due to the way you visualize the seed syllable in the heart-center. These are called the "threefold beings, or sattvas." You visualize the deities for the purpose of body and recite the mantra for the purpose of speech. When you complete this, again make offerings and praises. When all this is finished, you come to the completion stage, which is for the sake of accomplishing the mind. The accomplishment of body and speech are finished, completed. The completion stage for accomplishing mind is after the repetition of the offerings and praises. Then the celestial palace and everything else around dissolves into the retinue of deities. The whole retinue dissolves into the central male and female deity. The female dissolves into the male, who then dissolves into the letter in the heart-center, the seed syllable in the heart-center. From the bottom of the seed syllable, it dissolves into the head, which finally becomes emptiness. This is called the dissolving.

In the non-Buddhist beliefs, there are the beliefs in permanence and nothingness. Permanence means that there is somebody who has made the whole thing, everything is made or created by a god. Nothingness means there is nothing, there is no cause and effect at all. Basically, they have these two beliefs. In order to clear away the view of permanence, you dissolve the visualization, the development stage. But, if you just remained in mere emptiness, you would fall into the view of nothingness, nihilism. To combat the wrong view of nothingness, you re-emerge in the form of the deity. Whichever deity you are practicing, for example Guru Rinpoche, you dissolve and then emerge as Guru Rinpoche. In the case of the peaceful and wrathful deities, you dissolve and then emerge in the form of Samantabhadra with consort. Everything has dissolved into emptiness. The ultimate emptiness is called "primordial emptiness *that* is rootless." It is the nature of the tathagatagarbha. Your own awareness rests in that state. Then a thought will arise, and in the very moment it occurs, you should think, "I am Samantabhadra." In all paths of action, you should regard yourself as Samantabhadra. Also, when dedicating the merit and making aspirations, you are Samantabhadra, and in whatever activities you do, you are Samantabhadra. It is Samantabhadra eating; it is Samantabhadra doing pee-pee. Then Samantabhadra goes to sleep. *(Rinpoche laughs.)* Then, again the next morning, there is, first, the samadhi of suchness, the emptiness of dharmakaya. The all-illuminating samadhi is sambhogakaya. Through the nirmanakaya, you again visualize yourself as a deity, and in everyday action you should imagine yourself as Samantabhadra.

Question: How can we actually structure the practice from morning to evening if we have to work?

Rinpoche: There is one way of structuring that I feel is very practical. In the morning, you begin a sadhana and practice up until the recitation. You recite as much as you feel like at that point. Immediately, without leaving the sadhana behind, go and start doing your daily work. At the end of the day, sit down again and recite the vowels and consonants, repeat the offerings, praises, and the purification mantra. After that, bring the sadhana to a conclusion. In this way, your entire day is part of the sadhana. This is extremely important. You shouldn't think that the practice is happening only when you're sitting down at the puja table; rather, consider that practice is happening as often as you can remind yourself. That is what really counts.

Practice is not only the mantra and visualization; it is recognizing mind-essence. You shouldn't think that recognizing mind-essence is only limited to sitting down on a meditation seat. It can take place while walking, talking, eating, working, and so on. Whether these activities become practice or not depends on whether you remind yourself to recognize mind-essence. That is what you should put effort into, because that is what really counts. Try as much as you can to recognize the state of rigpa during the daytime, from the time you wake up in the morning, and continue throughout the day. In between, during free moments, you can recite the mantra. If there is no chance to do so, if something has to be done, then take care of it. However, while doing it, again and again remind yourself to recognize and simply allow the natural state to be sustained repeatedly. This is what is really necessary. I encourage you to practice in that way.

Question: How do we make offerings to the buddhas and the protectors of the Dzogchen teachings and the Dharma in general? How should we do this, who are they, and where do they come from?

Rinpoche: The quality of these *Kunzang Tuktig* teachings belongs to the Great Perfection, which is the penultimate summit of all vehicles. It is the teaching that grants enlightenment in a single lifetime. It is also guarded by the particular protectors of the vajradhatu, Ekajati, Vajrasadhu, and Rahula. They guard the authenticity of the teachings. The chief protector of the Dzogchen teachings is the female Ekajati. Her emanations, re-emanations, and so forth are first the six sisters and then hundreds of thousands of dakinis, who oversee and supervise the transmission. When the transmission is not taking place in the right way, they give punishment. In that, various types of inauspicious events happen in this life, and there is no happiness in the future lives. that's one thing.

These three main protectors, Ekajati, Rahula, and Damchen Dorje Lekpa, also called Vajrasadhu, actually dwell within our own body. The main support of this vajra body, which is the mandala of the peaceful and wrathful deities, is structured around three main channels, the central channel and the left and right ones. The essence of these three channels is, in fact, these three protectors. In that, the central channel is Ekajati and the right and left are Rahula and Vajrasadhu. They are also the essence of the three kayas as well as essence, nature, and capacity—empty essence, cognizant nature, and manifold capacity. They differ from the ordinary dharma protectors and guardians of the teachings in that ordinary protectors can dispel obstacles; they can bring some level of achievement. But only the dharmadhatu protectors, meaning those of the essential nature, can clear the obstacles for complete enlightenment and carry us onward to the omniscient state of buddhahood. So it's a very good idea if everyday, without break, you can make a short torma offering or give a small drink, an oblation, to the three main protectors. There are long texts that can be chanted for this. If we are able to do so, it is excellent; but otherwise, there is a short one that is six lines or eight lines, starting with HUNG *Mahakala*[11]. The first line is for all the male protectors. The second one is for Ekajati and all the female protectors. The third one is for the neutral protectors, meaning the union of both male and female. In this way, all dharma protectors are included in just a very short chant. It would be excellent both for our practice and for our progress, if we can make a short dharma protector offering on a daily basis. That will clear obstacles. That will bring a great help as well. We should understand that these Ekajati protectors are innate to ourselves.

Additionally, there are different ways to make offerings, depending on who the guests are. We usually speak of four types of guests. The first is the respected guests, the Three Jewels. Below them are the qualified guests, the protectors and guardians of the Dharma. Below them are the pitiful guests, all sentient beings. The lowest ones are the obstructing guests, the spirits who make obstacles and our karmic creditors.

These four types are treated in different ways. When, for instance, giving a drink to the Three Jewels and the dharma protectors, you imagine that what you raise up in your hand is an immense ocean of sense pleasures. You don't throw it on the ground; it is given in a respectful way, because they are the guests possessing great qualities. When giving to sentient beings or to karmic creditors, you do not pay great respect. To the sentient beings, you give straightforwardly, at an even level, but the offering to obstructors and creditors is thrown down on the ground. There is also a particular way to hold what is being given. When the offering is being given to ones higher than yourself, hold the bottom of the vessel. If it is to someone equal, hold it in the middle. The offerings to those below you are held at the top, even putting one finger in the vessel and then throwing it outside.

Where are these beings? Wisdom beings dwell indivisible from the Akanishtha realm of dharmadhatu: in other words, they are immaterial, unmanifest. When they manifest, they appear by the mere thought of the one who calls upon them, in an instant. You don't have to think they are in a particular place and need to travel from a certain direction to arrive before you to receive the offering. They simply appear by your mere thought. You don't have to imagine all the details of what they look like. It's the same as when you invite somebody over. You don't have to imagine that they have clothes on; they just come wearing their particular dress. It is like that.

There are different ways to invite beings as well. For the wisdom beings, you say, "Please approach." For protectors or beings on the same level, you say, "Assemble here." And to the low ones, you say, "Come right here and take this!" There are different attitudes also. For instance, in the Vajra Kilaya petition to the protectors, you say, "From the Akanishtha palace of dharmadhatu, Vajra Kilaya with your retinue of boundless protectors, please approach." Where are these deities, the wisdom protectors? They are dwelling in the dharmakaya buddhafield, at a level that is totally unmanifest.

Of course, there are different details in the different invocations to protectors. Sometimes a liturgy may say, "From the eastern direction of the dharmakaya buddhafield, or from the western direction of Akanishtha, please approach!" Thus, they are summoned from different directions. Occasionally, there are references to actual places. For example, Rahula and Ekajati are sometimes invoked from a certain geographical place or sometimes simply "From your natural abode." That natural abode actually refers to the cognizant nature indivisible from the empty essence. We always invoke the wisdom protectors from the cognizant nature.

Sometimes protectors have many names and different titles that have to be mentioned, and all these are read like a roll call, a long list of who they are. *The Great Slayer of Tsang, the Great Dralha of such-and-such*—you may repeat a lot of epithets and titles. You often find this in the rituals for protectors.

Question: Is it necessary to offer the *torma to the obstructors* every day?

Rinpoche: If you cannot do it every day, it is all right. Instead, you dispell the obstructing forces without a torma, *(bgegs bskrad)*. If you want to offer the torma every day, you cannot do it without making a torma every time; that would be improper. For example, if you say to a person, "Please eat this nice food and go away," then you didn't give any food. The person will have to say, "Oh I didn't get any food, and I will have to go without any food." However, in the case of dispelling the obstructing forces without a torma, *(bgegs bskrad)* there is no mention of eating food. You say, "Go away; get away!" For dispelling the obstructing forces without a torma, you don't need a torma.

Question: What about the *Kunzang Tuktig Leyjang*?

Rinpoche: In the *Kunzang Tuktig,* there is no mention of a torma for the obstructors. It says, *Duality demons of ignorant confusion,* Do not remain here, *go elsewhere,* which means, "Don't stay here, go away!" If you want to give a torma, then first you should say the appropriate mantras, with the RAM YAM

KAM, and so forth. Sprinkle the torma and recite SUMBHANE SUMBHANE, and so forth. It has to be inserted at this point, if you want to, because the root text itself is simply dispelling the obstructing forces without a torma. When you first start a sadhana, you should send out the torma for the obstructors, but for daily practice it is not necessary.

Question: Is it necessary to offer a torma together with *The Inexhaustible Garland of Lightning and Lama Yidam (bla ma yi dam)*?

Rinpoche: It is good if you can. But you should do it together with the *apologizing and mending practice, with the* OM YE SHES SKU MCHOG. If you don't say that one, you should give it after finishing the recitation. This is called the "dharmapala petition" *(gsol kha)*.

Question: At the end of *The Inexhaustible Garland of Lightning (ma gza' dam gsum)*, should we offer torma or tea *(gser skyems)*?

Rinpoche: You can offer *either*. If you don't have a torma, there is another thing called "container for offering tea," which you can use for the short way and the torma for a more extensive form. If you don't have torma, you can make a small triangular shape of barley flour and then put it in the tea offering container. Also, if you have different kinds of grains—such as rice, barley, wheat, and a mixture of these—you can put them in the tea offering container *instead* of a torma. These are a substitute for torma. It is okay without them. You should not offer mere tea. Either add some grain or scratch a multi-metal plate, made for this, which is first-class.

Question: What should we do?

Rinpoche: You can do what you like. It is good to offer.

Question: When should it be offered?

Rinpoche: Just at the end of the recitation. Immediately at the end of the recitation, you say the A A I I U U, and so forth. Then you chant the offering and the praises. When that is finished, you say the *Lama Yidam*[12] and at the end of that *The Inexhaustible Garland of Lightning (ma gza' dam gsum)*.

Question: Why is that?

Rinpoche: Because *Lama Yidam* is in a higher position, since it has all three of the Three Roots.

Question: Should we make a tea offering for both of these together?

Rinpoche: Yes, no need to have separate ones: "On the torma plate of the external world, I arrange the torma of the inhabitants of sentient beings." This is what you should have understood. It is not only a torma and a plate that you offer. On the torma plate of space, you offer the torma of rigpa, you arrange the torma of rigpa. That is the real torma offering.

TEXTS

Ekajati

The Brilliant Concise Meaning

A Profound Instruction on Kunzang Tuktig
The Heart Essence of Samantabhadra
A Terma of Chokgyur Lingpa

Karmey Khenpo Rinchen Dargye

NAMO GURU MAHANIDHI SAMANTABHADRAYA⁞

Like completely refined gold, this is the heart-essence of all tantras, scriptures, and instructions; the source of all the supreme and ordinary siddhis; the single supreme path traversed by all the victorious ones throughout the three times; the entrance door for all the fortunate ones who aspire towards liberation; and the short path for attaining enlightenment in this very life. It is the terma of Chokgyur Lingpa called *Kunzang Tukkyi Tigle, the Heart Essence of Samantabhadra*.

In this practice, there are three topics: the preliminaries, the main part, and the concluding section.

THE PRELIMINARIES

The first section has two parts: the general common preliminaries and the special preliminaries for becoming a suitable vessel for the path.

The General Common Preliminaries

In the terma text, it is said,

> *In order to put this path into practice,⁞*
> *The fortunate person who wishes⁞*

To attain complete enlightenment for the sake of countless beings,
Quickly, and in this very life,
Should carefully search for a true master,
Do everything that pleases him,
And abandon all offensive actions.
Then, having fully ripened your being through empowerments,
Keep your mindstream pure by keeping the precepts
And endeavor in the steps that purify obscurations and gather the
accumulations.

As stated, it is extremely important to do the following: correctly and carefully attend an authentic master and spiritual guide, who is the foundation of all the paths; develop the mind that is set on supreme enlightenment, which is the core of the path; receive the profound empowerments, the entrance to the Secret Mantra Vajrayana, which is the ultimate part of the path; and purify your mindstream, by means of keeping the three sets of precepts completely and without conflict.

The *Lotus Essence Root Tantra* (*Tsagyü Pema Nyingpo*) says,

Enter through the successive empowerments,
And, as an aid, keep the samayas pure.

The general common preliminaries have two parts: the preliminaries for the session and the preliminaries for instruction.

The Preliminaries for the Session

In a quiet place, upon a comfortable seat, straighten your body posture and leave your mind in naturalness. Exhale the stale breath three times and imagine that misdeeds, faults, and failings are thereby purified. Then form the thought, "For the sake of all the infinite number of sentient beings, I will practice this profound path!" And, while visualizing the root guru at the crown of your head, repeatedly make wholehearted supplications, such as *Düsum Sangye Guru Rinpoche* and others.

At the end, supplicate with total surrender, saying, "Essence of all buddhas of the three times, glorious and precious root guru, please think of me! Kindly bless my stream-of-being!" Imagine that the guru then melts into light and is absorbed through the crown of your head. This practice should precede all sessions.

The Preliminaries for Instruction

First, there are the preliminaries, which are common to both sutra and tantra, namely taking to heart the difficulty of finding the freedoms and favorable conditions, impermanence and death, the effects of ripening karma, and the inherent faults of samsara.

Then there are the particular preliminaries of refuge, bodhichitta, Vajrasattva, mandala offering, and guru yoga, which can be done according to *Vima Tukdrub*. Genuinely practice these in full before continuing with the following.

The Special Preliminaries for Becoming a Suitable Vessel for the Path

About the preliminaries for this particular path, the root text says,

> *Retreat to snow mountains, caves, or forests,*
> *And, in solitude, sit on a comfortable seat,*
> *Supplicate your master one-pointedly,*
> *And motivate yourself with compassion and the thought of impermanence.*

In a retreat in the snow mountains, caves, or deep forests, and so on, in a location that has been blessed by the victorious ones of the past, place yourself on your meditation seat. Then, with intense devotion, to transform your attitude, supplicate one-pointedly by chanting the *Düsum Sangye* from the preliminaries for the session, followed by the supplication to the lineage masters, entitled *Self-Manifest Luminosity.*

Za Rahula

The Mind Ornament of Samantabhadra

The Stages of Instruction in the Entire Path of *The Heart Essence of Samantabhadra*, the Pure Gold Luminous Great Perfection, Composed as Concise Key Points

Dilgo Khyentse Rinpoche

NAMO VIDYADHARA HERUKA SHRIYE

The expanse of the space of primordial purity, endowed with the
*   supreme of all aspects,*
Manifests as a smile of the four visions of spontaneously present
*   luminosity.*
Through these infinite kayas and wisdoms of great bliss,
May the sanctuary of spontaneity, where dualistic fixation goes beyond
*   reference point, be victorious.*[13]

The beauty of the blooming white lotus grove of ripening and freeing,
On the muddy lake of the karmas and kleshas of my being,
I string together and spread out with the fingers of devotion,
As necklaces for the fortunate ones.

Orgyen Chokgyur Dechen Lingpa, the natural form of ultimate wisdom, the utterly pure fruition of all buddhas beyond learning, manifested for the disciples of this dark age in the form of a vidyadhara realized in the unity of the great all-pervading and self-existing capacity. His *Kunzang Tuktig* is the essence of his ocean-like profound termas, the quintessence of the Instruction Section of Dzogchen. It is like pure, refined gold. The arrangement of oral instructions for practicing the *Döntri Yishin Norbu Nyingpo* of *Kunzang Tuktig* has three parts: the preliminary, main, and concluding sections.

The first of these is composed of general, special, and extraordinary preliminary practices.

THE GENERAL PRELIMINARY PRACTICES

The Minchey Dönwang Yishin Norbu says,

> *First, the guru Samantabhadra, the great lord of sky-yogis, should accept disciples who, with exceedingly deep devotion and unwavering trust, yearn to quickly attain complete enlightenment.*

As so stated, here and elsewhere, a qualified sublime master, a glorious protector, should, when accepting worthy disciples who yearn for liberation, first ripen them through empowerment as a preparation for the path, so they can practice the most profound meaning of Dzogchen, which is the ultimate, quick path among all means to attain the state of the lasting happiness of complete liberation, the essence of the 84,000 divisions of the Dharma, the summit of the nine gradual vehicles, and the heart of the oral instructions of the vajra vehicle of Secret Mantra.

As the *Döntri* says,

> *Then, having fully ripened your being through empowerments,*

In this way, prior to beginning the preliminary practices, the following empowerments should be performed in accordance with the tradition. As the general, within the mandala of the peaceful and wrathful ones, there are the benefiting empowerments to accept the devoted ones and the enabling empowerments for the diligent ones. As the extraordinary, there are the ground empowerments of primordial purity and spontaneous presence, the path empowerments of entering Trekchö, and the fruition empowerments of Tögal, should be given following the *Dönwang Yishin Norbu*, the *Ultimate Empowerment Wishfulfilling Jewel*, which are, respectively, divided into four: elaborate, unelaborate, very unelaborate, and extremely unelaborate empowerments.

After the ripening empowerments, the preliminaries for the liberating instructions follow. The precepts of Secret Mantra are obtained through empowerment, the mere receiving of which empowers you to hear, read, and practice the profound meaning. However, it is the samayas that sustain the life-force of the empowerment in your stream-of-being. As the root text says,

Keep your mindstream pure by keeping the precepts,⸓

In this way, it is crucial to protect the vows of Individual Liberation, Bodhichitta, and Secret Mantra in general. In particular, guard the roots and branches of the general, special, and supreme samayas, like protecting your eyes, and keep your stream-of-being pure. Immediately upon receiving the vase empowerment, all three vows are born in your stream-of-being. So, in order to develop them further, protect them through being mindful, alert, and careful. Then the qualities of the paths and bhumis will quickly arise without difficulty.

Next, the general preliminaries for the path include generating an attitude of renunciation, taking refuge, arousing bodhichitta, reciting Vajrasattva, and offering the mandala and the Seven Branches, which are part of the guru yoga.

And endeavor in the steps that purify obscurations and gather the
  accumulations.⸓
Retreat to snow mountains, caves, or forests,⸓
And, in solitude, sit on a comfortable seat,⸓
Supplicate your master one-pointedly,⸓
And motivate yourself with compassion and the thought of
  impermanence.⸓

As was just stated, contemplate as follows: "I will train and familiarize myself with the fact that nothing lasts forever, neither the world nor the beings within it. I have no doubt that samsara is futile and am resolved to the fact that all samsaric activities have nothing but evil deeds as their cause and misery as their effect.

"Therefore, I recognize that this body with its freedoms and riches is the perfect condition facilitating dharma practice, a support superior to that of a god. I recognize that it is difficult to find, so, without squandering it on the pointless activities of this present life, I will concentrate on the essential Dharma. With renunciation as the basis for dharma practice and with trust in the consequence of karma as its main pillar, I will exert myself to the utmost, applying all thoughts, words, and deeds to virtuous actions. Since death comes without warning and its circumstances are not certain, I won't plan far into the future.

"That which is meaningful is the excellent path of increasing happiness, the precious state of liberation. Therefore, I will apply myself exclusively to that which attains it, namely virtuous thoughts, words, and deeds. Following a qualified master for the means and instructions on how to accomplish this, and for all the essential points on what to adopt and what to abandon, I will enter the path of liberation without error or mistake—doing exactly as he says."

Thinking this, in the space before you, as the single wisdom display of the glorious protector root guru, Samantabhadra, the assembly of the peaceful and wrathful deities along with a retinue of the Three Roots and guardians, are manifest, filling the sky. In their presence, you and all other beings act in unison with body, speech, and mind. To take refuge from now until enlightenment, completely surrendering with single-minded trust and devotion, is the relative, causal refuge. To maintain the continuity of the nondual view, by recognizing that all of them are primordially indivisible from self-existing awareness, the wisdom comprised of essence, nature, and capacity, is the ultimate, resultant refuge. With these two as a unity, say,

NAMO༔

In the empty essence, dharmakaya,༔
In the luminous nature, sambhogakaya,༔
And in the manifold capacity, nirmanakaya,༔
I take refuge until enlightenment.༔

Accumulate the set number.

To open the gate to all paths, contemplate as follows: "Although we are all primordially enlightened within the single state of nondual dharmata, through a compassionate attitude, I will bring those sentient beings, who do not realize the natural state as it is and who are tormented by delusion and karmic consequences, to the unmistaken ultimate state." Reflect on this while chanting,

HOH༔

In order to establish all beings equal to the sky༔

In the state of buddhahood,⸝
I will realize the dharmakaya of self-existing awareness,⸝
Through the teachings of the Great Perfection. ⸝

Thus, as the life force of the path, firmly keep the resolve toward enlightenment, which is emptiness suffused with compassion.

If the momentary conceptual obscurations are not purified, you will not behold the natural face of self-existing wakefulness. Therefore, while possessing all the vital points of the four powers, visualize Vajrasattva inseparable from the guru, above your head, and with one-pointed concentration on the downpour and purification of the nectar, say,

This ordinary body of momentary delusion,⸝
Is a primordially pure body of light.⸝
In a state of brightness, I visualize, distinct and perfect,⸝
The naturally present Vajrasattva.⸝
OM VAJRA SATTVA AH⸝[14]

Having said that, recite the Hundred Syllables and the Six Syllables as many times as you can. At the end, to practice the ultimate repentance of the great primordial purity of dharmakaya, which is beyond confessor and confessed, is the royal purifier of all obscurations, and is single-handedly sufficient to remove obstacles on the path.

With the attitude of offering the spontaneously perfect universe of billionfold Mt. Sumeru realms—an ocean of undefiled riches, the natural forms of the luminous dharmadhatu wisdom—to the field of accumulation, the all-encompassing buddha-mandalas of peaceful and wrathful ones of the three kayas, accumulate the set number of mandala offerings. That is the mandala practice, a simple and effective enhancement to the path, the chant for which is:

Within the space of emptiness,⸝
I place as heaps, awareness resting freely.⸝
This mandala of undivided space and awareness,⸝
I offer to the sugatas of primordial purity.⸝
GURU MANDALA PUJA HO⸝

In particular, the authentic experience of true, original wakefulness within your stream-of-being depends on nothing other than your guru's blessings. So, in the sky before you, visualize your guru as Samantabhadra with consort, a brilliant deep blue, unadorned, naked, and sitting resplendently with crossed legs upon a lotus and moon within a sphere of rays of rainbow light. Full of trust and devotion, make the following supplication, totally surrendering your entire being:

OM AH HUNG⁞

To the capacity, the nirmanakaya guru,⁞
I supplicate longingly with elaboration.⁞
Conferring the vase empowerment upon my body,⁞
Bless me to realize empty experience.⁞

To the nature, the sambhogakaya guru,⁞
I supplicate from the unelaborate state.⁞
Conferring the secret empowerment upon my speech,⁞
Bless me to realize empty cognizance.⁞

To the essence, the dharmakaya guru,⁞
I supplicate from the very unelaborate state.⁞
Conferring the knowledge empowerment upon my mind,⁞
Bless me to realize empty bliss.⁞

To their unity, the essence-kaya guru,⁞
I supplicate from the completely unelaborate state.⁞
Conferring the fourth empowerment upon my three doors,⁞
Bless me to realize empty awareness.⁞

Although the accumulation of merit is primordially perfected within the innate nature, accumulating and purifying are important methods that fully actualize it. So, in the presence of the visualized supports for the accumulations, together with the one-pointed attitudes for the Seven Branches, repeat this suitable chant:

To the sky-like sugatas,⁞
I prostrate as great luminosity;⁞
In the state of awareness, I present offerings;⁞

In the unceasing expanse, I apologize and,⁞
As it is permanent and never obscured, I rejoice.⁞
Turn the dharma wheel beyond being and nonbeing.⁞
Remain as something to be experienced.⁞
May the supreme certainty be attained.⁞

It is exceedingly good if you can complete 100,000 prostrations combined with the Seven Branches, the essence of accumulating and purifying. At the end, with the great bliss wisdom of the guru's three vajras indivisible from your own three innate doors, in this primordially pure state, receive the four empowerments, mingle your mind with his, and rest in evenness. This is the meditation practice of guru yoga, the essence of the path, taking effect. So, to exert yourself until the resultant signs manifest is to bring the training to perfection as a prelude to the path. Then the experiences and realization of the main part will occur without any hardship. Therefore, resolve the oral instructions and apply them correctly. In order to do that, abide in secluded places, such as retreats in snow mountains, caves, or forests, which are free from distractions and bustle and where the conditions for meditation training are complete. Thus, establish an abode of one-pointed practice.

THE SPECIAL PRELIMINARIES

Since there are many average disciples who proceed gradually along the path these days, it is essential to first accomplish the concentration of mind, by means of the development stage based on the *Tünmong Shitro Leyjang, The General Practice Manual of the Peaceful and Wrathful Ones,* completing the full number of recitations.

In an elaborate way, you can use a mandala or heaps, amrita, rakta, and tormas; or in an unelaborate way, imagination alone is sufficient. Either way, the basis for accomplishment is the totally pure Ultimate Being Samantabhadra, unconstructed primordial purity, who appears in the form of the peaceful wisdom (mandala) of vajradhatu—and the spontaneously present display of luminosity, appearing in the forms of the sporting wrathful herukas, who destroy the origin of samsara, namely confused, grasping thoughts. Taking this as the basis for accomplishment, the method to accomplish is the unity of development and completion, perfected in an instant's recollection, in which samaya- and wisdom-being are nondual, and all that appears and exists is the display of the ground. Through this, you will ultimately realize the state of dharmakaya, primordially pure space, and of rupakaya, the unity of luminous awareness. Thus, while understanding that this method is vital for realizing the level of the never-ending adornment wheels of body, speech, mind, qualities, and activities of the three kayas of enlightenment, correctly follow the practice manual (sadhana) of the peaceful and wrathful ones and cultivate the clear forms, stable pride, and pure recollection of the visualizations of the development stage.

As enhancement, do as many recitations of the peaceful and wrathful ones as you can, such as 400,000 for each syllable. Perform the feast offering occasionally, such as on the tenth day of the waxing and waning moon, and at the beginning and end of a recitation retreat. Without missing a day, chant the petition-offering to the guardians of this teaching, composed by Tersey Rinpoche. All these details should be known from the general system of approach and accomplishment practice. If you have sadhana articles physically present, you should receive the siddhis when completing the practice. Furthermore, going through this practice of the development state, and combining it with the exclusive practice of the view, meditation, and conduct of Trekchö, will then be a self-sufficient path of development and completion. Therefore, for those who do not immediately engage in the path of effortless Tögal, it is fine to practice in such a manner. Understand that this is the unmistaken tradition of the forefather gurus.

THE MAIN PRACTICE

Next, the explanation on how to practice the path of the main part is stated in brief like this:

In the manner of ground, path, and fruition.

Accordingly, here is an explanation of how to resolve the ground through the view, practice the path by training, and attain the fruition, the state of ultimate freedom.

This is the general procedure of empowerments for accepting the
devoted ones, according to the Pure Gold Great Perfection,
the Heart Essence of Samantabhadra, entitled:

The Destroyer of All Evil Deeds and Obscurations

Padmasambhava, revealed by Chokgyur Lingpa

ཀྵཿ

Homage to Guru Samantabhadra!༔

In order to accept the devoted ones,༔
The general procedure of empowerment is taught.༔
As to the preparatory, main, and concluding rituals,༔
First, carefully arrange the mandala༔
And lay out the vase with articles and essences.༔
The representations of body, speech, and mind༔
And the offering materials༔
Should be gathered without lacking any.༔

Then, perform a full empowerment recitation.༔
The vajra master should enter, himself,༔
And relieve the disciples of hindrances and mishap.༔
Having bathed, and wearing clean clothing,༔
Prostrate, offer a gift, and respectfully say,༔

HO༔
Guru, glorious Vajrasattva,༔
Please regard me with loving-kindness.༔
Lead us out of the place of samsara༔
And let us enter the citadel of liberation.༔

Supplicate like that. Then, take refuge, arouse bodhichitta, and say,༔

HO⁞

Sugatas, peaceful and wrathful victorious ones, please consider
me.⁞
From today until the essence of enlightenment,⁞
I will not abandon the samayas of body, speech, and mind,⁞
Even at the cost of my life.⁞

Consecrate the samaya water with OM AH HUM.⁞

HO⁞

In the continuity of body, speech, and mind,⁞
By this you will accomplish all the siddhis.⁞
If you do not guard it, you will be born in the hells.⁞
Therefore, keep the samayas.⁞

OM AH HUM VAJRA KA VA CI SAMAYA RAKSHA TISHTHA⁞

The disciples take the oath one-pointedly, and say,⁞

SAMAYA IDAN NARAKAN⁞

Above the head, in the throat, and in the heart-center,⁞
In the navel, in the secret place, and in the soles of the feet,⁞
Are A SU NRI TRI PRE and DU, upon which⁞
The actual forms of the body, speech, and mind of the victorious
ones,⁞
The syllables RAM YAM and KAM force downward.⁞
Imagine that the surging forth of wisdom fire, wind, and water⁞
Burns, scatters, and washes, after which they are purified.⁞

RAM SPHARANA PHAT. YAM SPHARANA PHAT. KAM SPHARANA
PHAT.⁞
OM DAHA DAHA SARVA NARAKA GATE HETUM HUM PHAT.⁞
OM PACA PACA SARVA PRETAKA GATE HETUM HUM PHAT.⁞
OM MATHA MATHA SARVA TIRYAKA GATE HETUM HUM PHAT.⁞
OM CACHINDHA CACHINDHA SARVA NRI GATE HETUM HUM PHAT.⁞
OM TRATA TRATA SARVA ASURA GATE HETUM HUM PHAT.⁞
OM PHRITA PHRITA SARVA SURA GATE HETUM HUM PHAT.⁞

Also, visualize the body to be a mass of light.⁞

From the state of emptiness, upon a lotus and moon,
Is the white bhagavan Vajrasattva,
Holding vajra and bell, seated in half-vajra posture,
And visualized as ornamented with silks and jewels.
The three places are marked with OM, AH, and HUM.
The inconceivable wisdom gatherings of body, speech, and mind
Of all the assemblies of mandala deities
Are emanated and absorbed.

OM AH HUM JNANA KAYA VAKA CITTA ABESHAYA A AH.

Dissolving again and again, play the musical instruments.
When the signs of the descent of great blessings occur,
Stabilize the wisdom with:
OM SUPRATISHTHA VAJRAYE SVA HA.

By saying that, wisdom becomes firmly established.
OM RATNA PUSHPE PRATICCHA HO.

Cast the awareness flower.
Give the secret name that accords with the family,
Such as Vajrasattva and the others.
First is the Crown Empowerment,
Fully adorned with the marks of the five families.
OM RATNA PUSHPE MALE ABHISHINCA HUM.
CAKSHU PRABESHAYA PHAT.

Open the eye of ignorance,
And explain the introduction to the mandala.
Purifying all obscurations, liberation will be attained.
SAMAYA.

Second, the main part is conferring the empowerments.
Perform the meditation of the mandala deities,
And imagine that Vajrasattva confers the empowerments.

HUM
Within the space palace of the vase,
Awareness, the assemblies of peaceful and wrathful victorious ones,
Melts into light. With this wisdom nectar

Empowering the fortunate child,ᦞ
May all impure perceptions be purifiedᦞ
And all the natures of vessel and its contents be pure.ᦞ
AKSHOBHYA KALASHA ABHISHINCA HUM.ᦞ

The water fills your body and purifies stains.ᦞ
Imagine that the aggregate of consciousness is transmuted,ᦞ
The mirror-like wisdom is realized,ᦞ
And the seed of accomplishing Vajra Akshobhyaᦞ
Is planted in your being.ᦞ

The residual of the water overflows.ᦞ
Crowned with the victorious ones of the five families,ᦞ
Imagine that you, thereby, obtain the wisdom crown.ᦞ

SVAᦞ
From the nature of the five wisdoms,ᦞ
By adorning the noble child withᦞ
The head ornament of the five families of jinas,ᦞ
May the wealth of wisdom be fully completed.ᦞ
RATNASAMBHAVA MUKUTA ABHISHINCA TRAM.ᦞ

Imagine that the aggregate of sensation is transmuted,ᦞ
The wisdom of equality is realized,ᦞ
And the seed of accomplishing Ratnasambhavaᦞ
Is planted in your being.ᦞ

Give the empowerment symbols, the vajra and bell.ᦞ

HUMᦞ
The unchanging vajra wisdomᦞ
Conquers all disturbing emotions and thoughts.ᦞ
The very nature of discrimination,ᦞ
The vajra empowerment, I give to you.ᦞ
PADMA DHARA VAJRA ABHISHINCA HRIH.ᦞ

Imagine that the aggregate of concept is transmuted,ᦞ
The discriminating wisdom is realized,ᦞ
And the seed of accomplishing Amitabhaᦞ
Is planted in your being.ᦞ

HUM༔
Within the state of emptiness,༔
The various sounds of the phenomenal realm༔
Accomplish the two meanings of dharma.༔
This bell empowerment, I give to you.༔
KARMA AMOGHASIDDHI ABHISHINCA AH.༔

Imagine that the aggregate of formation is transmuted,༔
The all-accomplishing wisdom is realized,༔
And the seed of accomplishing Amoghasiddhi༔
Is planted in your being.༔

Empower with the vajra name.༔

HUM༔
By conferring this supreme vajra empowerment,༔
This son of the victorious one is Vajrasattva.༔
The vajra name is proclaimed as the body.༔
May empowerment for buddhahood be obtained.༔
OM VAJRASATTVA ABHISHINCA OM.༔

Imagine that the aggregate of form is transmuted,༔
The dharmadhatu wisdom is realized,༔
And the seed of accomplishing Vairochana༔
Is planted in your being.༔

In this way, giving the disciples the empowerments of benefit༔
Makes them a suitable vessel for secrets.༔
Then, for the body empowerment:༔
Imagine that the assembly of peaceful deities abides in your heart,༔
The wrathful assembly in your bone mansion,༔
The assembly of the vidyadharas in your throat,༔
And that the assembly of dakinis abides in your navel.༔

HUM༔
By conferring the empowerment of the nondual lord and lady,༔
And the chief of the mandala, Samantabhadra,༔
May the transmuted mind and object, doer and deed,༔
Be realized as inseparable space and awareness.༔
A A ABHISHINCA HUM.༔

HUM

By conferring the empowerment of the lords and ladies of the five
    families,

May the transmuted five poisons and five elements

Be spontaneously present as the five wisdoms

And realized as the nature of the five lights.

OM HUM SVA AM HA. MAM LAM MAM PAM TAM. ABHISHINCA
    HUM.

HUM

By conferring the empowerment of the eight bodhisattvas,

May the eight gatherings be naturally purified.

By conferring the empowerment of the eight female bodhisattvas,

May the eight objects be transmuted.

BODHICHITTA ABHISHINCA HUM.

HUM

By conferring the empowerment of the six munis,

May the six disturbing emotions be transmuted,

The six paramitas be perfected,

And the benefits to beings be unceasing.

MAHA MUNE ABHISHINCA HUM.

HUM

By conferring the empowerments of the four gatekeepers,

May the four extremes, permanence, and nothingness, be purified.

By conferring the empowerments of the four female gatekeepers,

May the four places of rebirth be purified.

KRODHA KRODHI ABHISHINCA HUM.

HUM

By conferring the empowerment of Chemchok, lord and lady,

Supreme sovereign of all the wrathful ones,

May all thoughts of grasping and fixating be liberated

And the nondual wisdom be realized.

HUM HUM ABHISHINCA HUM.

HUM

By conferring the empowerment of the five herukas,

May the five poisons of disturbing emotions be liberated.
By conferring the empowerment of the five lady herukas,
May the fixation on the five elements as concrete be liberated.
HUM HUM ABHISHINCA HUM.

HUM
By conferring the empowerment of the eight ladies of the places,
May the thoughts of the eight gatherings be liberated.
By conferring the empowerment of the eight ladies of the valleys,
May the eight impure objects be liberated.
HA HE ABHISHINCA HUM.

HUM
By conferring the empowerment of the four female gatekeepers,
May the four extremes, permanence and nothingness, be liberated.
JAH HUM BAM HO. ABHISHINCA HUM.

HUM
By conferring the empowerment of the twenty-eight ishvaris,
May disturbing emotions, grasping, and fixating be liberated.
BHYO ABHISHINCA HUM.

HUM
May the vidyadhara gurus of the three lineages
Bless all the fortunate ones.
May all impure perception be purified
And pure perception dawn.
MAHA GURU ABHISHINCA HUM.

HUM
By conferring the empowerment of the dakas and dakinis,
May everything be purified as male and female deities.
May all the stains of the disturbing emotions be purified
And dawn as wisdom.
DHEVA DHEVI DHAKI ABHISHINCA HUM.

Imagine that the obscurations of your body are purified,
You are empowered to meditate on the deity,
And the seed of appearance dawning as deities
Is planted in your being.

From the throat centers of all the assemblies of deities,⁘
Mantra garlands and seed syllables descend like rainfall.⁘
Imagine that they dissolve into the nadis of the disciples,⁘
And the supreme empowerment of speech is obtained.⁘
Perform the recitation transmission, the mantra list,⁘
And give the blessed mala.⁘

HUM⁘
The supreme speech of all the victorious ones,⁘
Is the continuity of resounding emptiness, beyond arising and
   ceasing.⁘
By conferring the empowerment of all the dharani mantras,⁘
May sounds heard be realized as mantra.⁘
VAJRA VAKA ABHISHINCA HUM.⁘

Imagine that all the obscurations of speech are purified,⁘
And the seed of realizing sound as mantra⁘
Is planted in your being.⁘

From the hearts of the assembled deities of peaceful and wrathful
   victorious ones⁘
Countless attributes are emanated.⁘
The instant they dissolve into your heart-center,⁘
Remain in the state of nonthought⁘
And rest evenly in the continuity⁘
Of the self-occurring, self-liberation of thoughts.⁘

HUM⁘
The vajra mind of all the victorious ones⁘
Is aware emptiness, beyond arising, dwelling, and ceasing.⁘
By conferring the empowerment of the vajra of mind,⁘
May luminosity dawn as wisdom.⁘
VAJRA CITTA ABHISHINCA HUM.

All the obscurations of mind are purified,⁘
And the seed of realizing luminosity as wisdom⁘
Is planted in your being.⁘

Imagine that by these enabling empowerments, which accomplish
   the benefit of oneself,⁘

Such as meditating on the form of the deities,°
Reciting mantra, and resting in evenness,°
Are conferred to the diligent ones.°

Third, the concluding actions:°
The guru should explain the samayas in detail.°
Together, the disciples should promise.°
And, after giving thanks and themselves as servants,°
Perform the concluding ritual of the mandala,°
Dedicate the virtue, and make aspirations.°
All actions perfected, it will be meaningful.°
SAMAYA.°

This procedure of empowerments,°
If it is conferred on a person possessing devotion,°
Will grant the attainment of liberation.°
By conferring the empowerment of meditation and recitation,°
It will grant the subsequent attainment°
Of all the siddhis of body, speech, and mind.°

Therefore, this text, meaningful to encounter,°
Was taught by me, Padmakara.°
Tsogyal respectfully wrote it down°
And buried it as a treasure for the sake of the future.°
When it meets the destined son,°
May it make the secret doctrine flourish°
And benefit whoever encounters it.°

SAMAYA. SEAL.°

I, Chokgyur Dechen Lingpa took this out from the Cave of Glowing Turquoise on the southern slope of Yegyal Namkhadzö at Lawa Kangchik in Kham, and translated it from the yellow parchment in Orgyen Samten Ling at Rudam Snow Range.

Damchen Dorje Lekpa

Kunzang Tuktig Ngondro
The Excellent Path to True Goodness

The Liturgy for the Preliminary Practices
According to the Pure Gold Great Perfection

Karmey Khenpo Rinchen Dargye

NAMO GURU MAHANIDHI VAJRASATTVAYA፧

The Pure Gold Great Perfection is the heart essence of Padmasambhava, the Great Lake-Born Master, and its preliminary practices have two parts, the general and the special.

THE GENERAL PRELIMINARIES

This first part has three sections: changing one's attitude through renunciation; going for refuge, the foundation for all the vehicles; and generating bodhichitta, the root of Mahayana.

Changing One's Attitude Through Renunciation

The terma root text of *Tukdrub* says,

> *Having obtained the supreme freedoms and favorable conditions, and*
> *being weary of impermanence,*፧
> *Through intense renunciation, endeavor in accepting and rejecting what*
> *concerns cause and effect.*፧

As stated, these are the reflections on the four mind-changings, namely: on the difficulty of finding the freedoms and riches, on death and impermanence, on the cause and effect of karma, and on the defects of samsara.

Vividly imagining the meaning of the words, say,

Ema
Dalgye jorchu gyenpey tenzang chog
Shintu nyeka legpar nyedü dir
Namkün sangchen zabmö kyedzog kyi
Drubla zhölney nyingpo langwar ja-o

EMA
This excellent body, adorned with the eight freedoms and ten
    riches,
Is extremely difficult to find. Now, having fully obtained it,
I will continually engage in the practice of the great secret,
The profound development and completion, and so make my life
    meaningful.

Chinö mitag nangchü drokün kyang
Kyeta chi ngey namchi cha yang mey
Chidü penpa chöley zhenmey chir
Longmey tsechig drubla tsönpar ja-o

The external world is impermanent, as are the beings contained
    within it.
Death inevitably follows birth,
Though exactly when remains uncertain.
But when death does arrive, only the Dharma can help me.
Therefore, without wasting time, I will endeavor in practice
    one-pointedly.

Gewey gyuley dreybu dewa dang
Migey waley dug ngel kyetsül la
Ngeshey kyeney tarpey gyurgyur pey
Gela beyching digley dogpar ja-o

Developing conviction as to how the fruit of happiness is produced
    from the seed of virtue
And how suffering is produced from nonvirtue,
I will be diligent in virtuous actions, the cause of liberation,
And will turn away from evil deeds.

Ngensong neysum dezhin tori tey
Rigdrug tomen garkye zöka wey
Dug ngel sumgyi gyaley madey chir
Kündön dzogpey jangchub drubpar ja-o

In the three evil states, as well as in the higher realms,
Wherever I am born, high or low, among the six classes,
I can never transcend the trap of the three unbearable sufferings.
Therefore, for the sake of everybody, I will accomplish perfect
    enlightenment.

Assimilate the meaning in your mind and train in it until you gain
certainty.

Going for Refuge, Which Is the Foundation for All the Vehicles

The terma root text of *Tukdrub* says,

> *The person possessing faith and compassion,*
> *Who wishes to attain supreme and common siddhis in this very*
>   *lifetime,*
> *Should mature his mind through empowerments, maintain pure*
>   *samaya,*
> *Go for refuge, the root of the path, and*
> *Develop the essence of the path—the two types of bodhichitta.*

As stated, taking refuge avoids errant paths and is the general foundation for all the vehicles. Visualize the object of refuge while saying,

> Rangney sachog dagzhing salwey khar
> Sengtri pema nyidai den ngai ü
> Tsawey lama guru pema la
> Gongda nyen-gyü rigdzin gyamtsö kor

> Visualizing my dwelling and surroundings as a pure land, in the
>   sky above,
> On the central of five seats, each comprised of lion throne, lotus,
>   sun, and moon,

Is the root teacher as Guru Padma
Surrounded by an ocean-like group of vidyadharas of the mind,
  sign, and hearing lineages.

Yeysu chomden shakya tubpa la
Chokchu düsum sangye namkyi kor
Gyabtu tegpa rimgü dampey chö
Veydur zhunmar seryig rangdra chey

On his right is Bhagavan Shakyamuni,
Surrounded by the buddhas of the ten directions and the three
  times.
Behind him are the sacred teachings of the nine gradual vehicles,
Written in self-resounding golden letters on refined lapis lazuli
  parchment.

Yöndu jampal lasog nyesey tar
Gyalsey jangsem nyenrang pagtsog kor
Dündu yidam dorje sempa la
Sang ngag chinang gyüdey lhatsog kor

On his left are his close sons, Manjushri, and all the others,
Surrounded by buddha sons, bodhisattvas, and the noble assembly
  of shravakas and pratyekabuddhas.
In front is the yidam, Vajrasattva,
Surrounded by the assembly of deities of the inner and outer tantra
  section of the secret mantra.

Bartsam khandro damchen trintar tib
Tugjey tu nga jinlab zi ö bar
Deyi dündu dagdang pamey tsö
Dranyen barmey rigdrug semchen kün
Shemey deyney nyenpor kyabpa zhin
Khorwey tsön ney tardö tsechig pey
Güpey chagtsal kyabsu drowar gyur

In between, gathered like cloudbanks, are dakinis and loyal
  guardians.
All are endowed with the power of compassion and blaze with
  blessings and majestic brilliance.

In front of these, headed by myself and my parents,
Are all the six kinds of beings, whether enemies, friends, or
neutrals.
Like seeking clemency when dragged before the executioner,
We respectfully bow down and go for refuge,
With one-pointed yearning to be set free from the prison of
samsara.

Preceded by whichever extensive refuge formula is suitable, say the
following:

Namo:
Ngowo tongpa chökyi ku:
Rangshin selwa longchö dzog:
Tukje natsok tulku la:
Jangchub bardu kyabsu chi:

NAMO:
In the empty essence, dharmakaya,:
In the cognizant nature, sambhogakaya,:
And in the manifold capacity, nirmanakaya,:
I take refuge until enlightenment.:

After completing any set number of recitations, imagine that light rays
from the object of refuge purify all the evil deeds and obscurations of yourself and others.

Generating Bodhichitta, the Root of Mahayana

Turning away from the lower paths, develop the Mahayana path, the root of
which is developing bodhichitta.

Hoh:
Khanyam drowa malü pa:
Sangye sala köpey chir:
Dzogpa chenpoi man ngag gi:
Rangrig chöku tokpar ja:

185

HOH༔
In order to establish all beings equal to the sky༔
In the state of buddhahood,༔
I will realize the dharmakaya of self-existing awareness༔
Through the teachings of the Great Perfection.༔

After reciting this as many times as you can, rest in equanimity and then dedicate the merit.

THE SPECIAL PRELIMINARIES

The special preliminaries have three parts:

The visualization and recitation of Vajrasattva to purify evil deeds and obscurations.
The mandala offering to gather the accumulations.
The meditation on guru yoga, the root of blessings.

The Visualization and Recitation of Vajrasattva

First is the power of object, which is visualizing the deity.

Ah༔
Dag gi chiwor peydey teng༔
Sangye kün-gyi yeshe ku༔
Dorje sempa dewachey༔
Drimey tönkey dawey dang༔

AH༔
Above my head, on lotus and moon,༔
Is the wisdom form of all buddhas,༔
Vajrasattva of great bliss,༔
Stainless as the glow of the autumn moon.༔

Chagnyi dorje drilbu nam༔
Rang ö nyemma gyepar tril༔

186

Dardang rinchen gyen-gyi dzey§
Zhabsung dorje kyiltrung gi§
Jaser tigley longna zhug§

His two hands, holding vajra and bell,§
Joyfully embrace Atopa, his own light.§
Adorned with silks and jewel ornaments,§
And with his two legs in vajra-posture,§
He sits in a sphere of bindus and rainbow light.§

While visualizing in this way, and with the "power of remorse"—the intense feeling of regret and sorrow for all evil deeds and failings—practice the antidote, which is the "power of application," the visualization for reciting the mantra.

Tugkar dawey kyilkhor ü§
Desheg kün-gyi tugsog hung§
Yigey gyapey ngagkyi kor§
Depey ötrö dönnyi jey§
Tsurdü dütsi chugyün bab§
Rangi tsangpey goney zhug§
Digdrib nyamchag künjang ney§
Dagching drima meypar gyur§

In the center of the moon disc in his heart,§
Is HUNG, the heart-life of all the sugatas,§
Encircled by the Hundred Syllable mantra.§
By chanting, light shines forth fulfilling the two goals.§
Upon its return, a stream of nectar flows down,§
Entering through the crown of my head,§
It purifies evil deeds, obscurations, damaged and broken vows,§
Making me pure and immaculate.§

Visualizing this one-pointedly, recite the Hundred Syllable mantra:

OM VAJRA SATTVA SAMAYA, MANU PALAYA, VAJRA SATTVA TENOPA, TISHTHA DRIDHO MEBHAVA, SUTOSHYO MEBHAVA,

SUPOSHYO MEBHAVA, ANU RAKTO MEBHAVA, SARVA SIDDHIM
ME PRAYACCHA, SARVA KARMA SUCHAME, CHITTAM SHRE YAM
KURU HUNG, HA HA HA HA HOH, BHAGAVAN SARVA TATHAGATA
VAJRA MAME MUNCHA VAJRI BHAVA MAHA SAMAYA SATTVA AH⁞

Recite this as many times as you can, as well as the quintessence mantra (OM BENDZA SATO AH OR OM VAJRA SATTVA AH). In the end, chant the *Lamenting Apology of Rudra,* or say the following, whichever is suitable:

Gönpo dagni mishey mongpa yi⁞
Damtsig leyni galshing nyam⁞
Lama gönpö kyabdzö chig⁞
Tsowo dorje dzinpa ni⁞
Tugje chenpö dagnyi chen⁞
Drowey tsola dagkyab chi⁞

Protector, due to my ignorance and delusion,⁞
I have gone against and broken the samayas.⁞
Guru, protector, please grant refuge.⁞
Supreme vajra-holder⁞
With the nature of great compassion,⁞
To you, the leader of beings, I go for refuge.⁞

Then say:

Kusung tug tsawa dang yanlag gi damtsig nyamchag tamchey
tölshing shagso. Digdrib nyetung drimey tsog tamchey
jangshing dagpar dseydu sol

I openly admit all damaged and broken samayas, both the root and branch samayas of body, speech, and mind. Please cleanse and purify all the negative actions, obscurations, failings, and stains I have gathered.

Shey solwa tabpey lama dorje sempa gyeshing dzumpa dang
cheypey rigkyi bu khyenam kyi digdrib dagpa yinno shey
nangwa jinney rangla timpey gyü jingyi labpar gyur

Guru Vajrasattva is delighted by this prayer, and with a smiling face he says, "Son of noble family, all your actions, obscurations, and failings are purified." Thus absolving me, he melts into me, and blesses my nature.

The Mandala Offering To Gather The Accumulations

In the sky before you, visualize the mandala of the field of accumulation, as when you were taking refuge. Make the preparations, such as the perfumed water and the materials for the heaps. As a preliminary, offer the extensive mandala of the thirty-seven heaps, which corresponds to the arrangement of your physical parts:

> Om bendza bhumi ah hung
> Zhi yongsu dagpa wangchen sergyi sazhi
> Om bendza rekhe ah hung
> Chi chagri khoryug gi korwey üsu hung

OM VAJRA BHUMI AH HUNG
The completely pure basis is the broad and vast golden ground.
OM VAJRA REKHE AH HUNG
In its center is the HUNG, encircled by a ring of iron mountains.

> Ri gyalpo rirab, Shar lüpag po
> Lho dzambu ling, Nub balang chö
> Jang drami nyen, Lüdang lüpag
> Ngayab dang ngayab shen
> Yoden dang lamchog dro
> Drami nyen dang drami nyen gyi dra

The king of mountains, Mount Sumeru.
East Videha. South Jambudvipa.
West Godaniya. North Uttara-Kuru.
Deha and Videha. Chamara and Upachamara.
Shatha and Uttara-mantrina. Kurava and Kaurava.

> Rinpochei riwo, Pagsam gyishing
> Döjoi ba, Mamö pey lotog
> Khorlo rinpoche, Norbu rinpoche
> Tsünmo rinpoche, Lönpo rinpoche

Langpo rinpoche, Tachog rinpoche
Magpön rinpoche, Terchen pöi bumpa

The mountain of jewels. The wishfulfilling tree.
The wishfulfilling cow. The effortless harvest.
The precious wheel. The precious gem.
The precious queen. The precious minister.
The precious elephant. The precious, excellent steed.
The precious general. The great treasure vase.

Gekpama, trengwama, luma, garma
Metogma, dugpöma, nangsalma, drichabma
Nyima dawa, rinpochei dug, chogley nampar gyalwey gyaltsen

Grace goddess. Garland goddess.
Music goddess. Dance goddess.
Flower goddess. Incense goddess.
Lamp goddess. Perfume goddess.
The sun and the moon.
The precious parasol.
The banner of victory, victorious over all opponents.

Üsu lhadang mi yi paljor pünsum tsogpa matsangwa meypa
Rabjam gyamtso dülgyi drangley deypa ngönpar ködey

Vividly displayed in the middle of these is all the wealth of gods and men, complete and perfect, surpassing the number of drops in the infinite ocean.

Denyi tsawa dang gyüpar cheypey
Palden lama dampa namdang
Yidam kyilkhor gyi lhatsog
Sangye dang jangchub sempa
Pawo khandro chökyong
Norlha terdag tsogdang cheypa,
Namla bülwar gyio
Tugje drowey döndu zheysu sol,
Zheyney jin-gyi labtu sol

This I present to the sublime and glorious root and lineage gurus, to the deity assembly of the yidam mandala, to the hosts of buddhas, bodhisattvas, dakas, dakinis, dharma protectors, wealth gods, and terma guardians. Out of compassion, please accept it for the sake of all beings and upon accepting it, please grant your blessings.

> Sazhi pöchü jugshing metog tram
> Rirab lingzhi nyidey gyenpa di
> Sangye zhingdu migtey bülwa yi
> Drokün namdag zhingla chöpar shog
> Idam ratna mandala kang nirya tayami

> The earth is perfumed with scented water and strewn with flowers,
> Adorned with Mount Sumeru, the four continents, the sun, and the
>   moon,
> Imagining this as the buddha-realm, I offer it,
> So that all beings may enjoy that pure realm.
> IDAM RATNA MANDALA KAM NIRYATAYAMI

> Om ah hung⁈
> Dagdang taye semchen gyi⁈
> Lüdang longchö getsog kün⁈
> Lingzhi rirab nyidar chey⁈
> Lhami longchö sammi khyab⁈
> Künzang chöpey trinpung che⁈
> Gyünmi cheypar trül jeytey⁈
> Könchog rinchen tsawa sum⁈
> Chösung norlha gyamtso la⁈
> Güpey tagtu bülwar gyi⁈
> Sönam tsogchen rabdzog ney⁈
> Yeshe nangwa gyepar shog⁈
> Om guru dhewa dhakini sarva ratna mandala pudza megha ah
>   hung⁈

> OM AH HUNG⁈
> I and all the infinite beings,⁈
> Offer our bodies, luxuries, and all our virtue,⁈
> The four continents, Mount Sumeru, the sun, and the moon,⁈

And the inconceivable riches of gods and men.§
This vast offering cloud of Samantabhadra,§
Unceasingly displayed,§
I offer continuously, and with veneration,§
To the rare and sublime Three Jewels and Roots,§
As well as to the ocean of dharma protectors and wealth gods.§
Having totally perfected the accumulation of merit,§
May the illumination of wisdom spread.§
OM GURU DHEVA DHAKINI SARVA RATNA MANDALA PUJA MEGHA
AH HUNG§

Now comes the actual practice where you keep count:

Om ah hung§
Khamsum nöchü paljor dang§
Daglü longchö getsog kün§
Tugje dagnyi namla bül§
Sheyney jin-gyi labtu sol§
Om sarva tathagata ratna mandala pudza hoh§

OM AH HUNG§
The three realms, vessel and contents, glory and riches,§
My body, luxuries, and all virtues,§
I offer to the lords of compassion.§
Accepting them, please bestow your blessings.§
OM SARVA TATHAGATA RATNA MANDALA PUJA HOH§

At the end of offering innumerable outer, inner, and secret mandalas, dissolve the field of accumulation into yourself and seal by dedication.

Meditation On Guru Yoga,
The Root Of Blessings

Dün-gyi namkhar sengtri peydey teng§
Tsawey lama rigdü dorje sem§
Karsal zhalchig chagnyi dordril dzin§
Dardang rinchen gyenden röltab zhug§

In the sky before me, on a lion throne, lotus, and moon,⁞
Is my root guru as Vajrasattva, the embodiment of all families.⁞
He is white and radiant, with one face and two hands holding vajra
    and bell.⁞
Dressed in silks and jewel ornaments, he is seated in the playful
    posture.⁞

Tugkar chöku küntu zangpo la⁞
Desheg zhiwey lhatsog namgyi kor⁞
Drinpar pema gargyi wangchug la⁞
Pawo khandro rigdzin tsogkyi kor⁞

In his heart center is dharmakaya Samantabhadra,⁞
Surrounded by the assemblies of the peaceful sugata deities.⁞
In his throat is Padma Gargyi Wangchuk,⁞
Surrounded by the retinues of dakas, dakinis, and vidyadharas.⁞

Dungkhang nangdu palchen heruka⁞
Tragtung trowö lhatsog namkyi kor⁞
Utsug guru pema jungney la⁞
Dzogchen gyüpey lama namkyi kor⁞

In his bone palace is Palchen Heruka,⁞
Surrounded by the assemblies of wrathful heruka deities.⁞
Above his head is Guru Padmakara,⁞
Surrounded by the gurus of the Dzogchen lineage.⁞

Düsum sangye jangsem trin tartrik⁞
Choktsam gyedu drubpa kagye lha⁞
Ogtu kasung damchen gyamtsö tsog⁞
Nangtong gyutrül drawey rölpar shar⁞

The buddhas and bodhisattvas of the three times are assembled
    like cloudbanks.⁞
In the eight directions are the deities of the Eight Sadhana
    Teachings.⁞
Below is an ocean-like gathering of loyal protectors and guardians
    of the teachings.⁞
All are manifest as the appearing, yet empty, display of the
    Magical Net.⁞

Imagining the field of accumulation, say,

> Lama dorsem shitrö lha:
> Chogsum gyalwa seychey la:
> Namkün tüdey chagtsal zhing:
> Chinang sangsum chöpey bül:

> To Guru Vajrasattva and the peaceful and wrathful deities,:
> To the Three Jewels and the victorious ones with their sons,:
> I constantly pay homage, make prostrations,:
> And present outer, inner, and secret offerings.:

> Nyamchag digdrib tölzhing shag:
> Sönam künla jeyi rang:
> Tagtu chökhor korwa dang:
> Droney bardu zhugley du:
> Dagni güpey solwa deb:
> Sönam gangdey khanyam dro:
> Lamey jangchub neytob shog:

> I deeply apologize for damaged and broken vows, evil deeds, and
>   obscurations:
> And rejoice in all merits.:
> I respectfully supplicate you:
> To always turn the wheel of dharma and:
> To remain as long as sentient beings exist.:
> By this merit, may all beings, as infinite as space,:
> Attain the abode of unsurpassable enlightenment.:

Say this as many times as you can.

> Namo:
> Dagdang drokün semchen nam:
> Yeney sangye yinpa la:
> Yinpar sheypey dagnyi kyi:
> Jangchub chogtu semkye do:

NAMOᐟ

I and the six classes of beings, all living things,ᐟ
Are buddhas from the very beginning.ᐟ
By the nature of knowing this to be as it is,ᐟ
I form the resolve towards supreme enlightenment.ᐟ

Thus aspire towards the ultimate enlightenment. Then say,

Chöku küntu zangpo la solwa debᐟ
Drugpa dorje changchen la solwa debᐟ
Tönpa dorje sempa la solwa debᐟ
Rigdzin garab dorje la solwa debᐟ

I supplicate dharmakaya Samantabhadra.ᐟ
I supplicate the sixth, the great Vajradhara.ᐟ
I supplicate the teacher Vajrasattva.ᐟ
I supplicate the vidyadhara Garab Dorje.ᐟ

Lobpön jampal shenyen la solwa debᐟ
Guru shiri singha la solwa debᐟ
Chimey pema jungney la solwa debᐟ
Lhacham mandarava la solwa debᐟ

I supplicate the master Manjushrimitra.ᐟ
I supplicate the guru Shri Singha.ᐟ
I supplicate the immortal Padmakara.ᐟ
I supplicate the princess Mandarava.ᐟ

Khandro yeshe tsogyal la solwa debᐟ
Semlong kheypa nyerchig la solwa debᐟ
Jebang nyishu tsa nga la solwa debᐟ
Damdzin chökyi lodrö la solwa debᐟ

I supplicate the dakini Yeshe Tsogyal.ᐟ
I supplicate the twenty-one learned ones of the Mind and Space
    Sections.ᐟ
I supplicate the king and the twenty-five disciples.ᐟ
I supplicate Damdzin Chökyi Lodrö.ᐟ

Chokgyur dechen lingpa la solwa deb༔
Tertön gyadang tsagyey la solwa deb༔
Drinchen tsawey lama la solwa deb༔
Zhiwa zhibchu tsanyi la solwa deb༔

I supplicate Chokgyur Dechen Lingpa.༔
I supplicate the one hundred and eight treasure revealers.༔
I supplicate the gracious root guru.༔
I supplicate the forty-two peaceful ones.༔

Barwa tragtung ngabchu la solwa deb༔
Dagpa rigdzin lhatsog la solwa deb༔
Kasung damchen gyamtso la solwa deb༔

I supplicate the fifty flaming herukas.༔
I supplicate the pure assembly of vidyadhara deities.༔
I supplicate the ocean of guardians and loyal protectors of the
    teachings.༔

Chönyi ngönsum tongwar jin-gyi lob༔
Nyamnang gongdu pelwar jin-gyi lob༔
Rigpa tseyley pebpar jin-gyi lob༔
Chönyi zeysar kyölwar jin-gyi lob༔
Jalü khachö drubpar jin-gyi lob༔

Grant the blessing to see the manifest dharmata.༔
Grant the blessing to increase experience.༔
Grant the blessing to reach the culmination of awareness.༔
Grant the blessing to arrive at the exhaustion in dharmata.༔
Grant the blessing to accomplish the celestial rainbow body.༔

In this way, supplicate one-pointedly, reciting as many times as you can.
Then say,

Gyalwa gong-gyü rigdzin dayi gyü༔
Gangzag nyen-gyü zabmo tergyü sog༔
Dzogchen gyüpey lama la solwa deb༔
Nangzhi taru chinpar jin-gyi lob༔
Jalü khachö drubpar jin-gyi lob༔

Buddha mind lineage, vidyadhara sign lineage,⚬
Noble beings hearing lineage, profound treasure lineage, and so
    forth,⚬
I supplicate all Dzogchen lineage masters.⚬
Grant the blessing to arrive at the end of the four visions.⚬
Grant the blessing to accomplish the celestial rainbow body.⚬

Count this short supplication.

Detar solwa tabpey lhatsog namkyi neysum ney ja ö tigley
tigtren kuzuk yigdru chagtsen gyi nampar char babpa tar jönney
rangla timpey wangdang jinlab ngödrub malüpa tobpar gyur⚬

By supplicating in this way, from the three places of the entire assembly
of deities, rainbow lights and bindus, both large and small, appear in the
form of bodies, letters, and attributes, falling like rain and dissolving into
me, so that I obtain all the empowerments, blessings, and siddhis.⚬

Recite as many times as you can the Hundred Syllables, the quintessence, and the general mantra for the peaceful and wrathful ones. Then take
the following mantra as the main body of the recitation:

OM AH HUNG GURU SHRI VAJRA SATTVA HUNG⚬

At the end of the session, dissolve the entire retinue into the main
figure. Next, receive the four empowerments.

Palden lamey kuyi ney zhi ney⚬
Özer jungwa dag gi neyzhir tim⚬
Kusung tugdang yeshe dorje yi⚬
Jin-gyi labney wangzhi tobpar gyur⚬

From the four places of the body of the glorious guru,⚬
Rays of light stream forth and dissolve into my four places.⚬
Blessed by the vajra body, speech, mind, and wisdom⚬
I obtain the four empowerments.⚬

Now comes the ultimate guru yoga of simplicity.

Kyabney kündü lama nyi༔
Gyepa chenpö rangla tim༔
Ran-gyang künshi machö pey༔
Ngangla yini dzinpa dral༔
Namdag trödrel chökyi ku༔

The master who embodies all objects of refuge༔
With great joy dissolves into me.༔
In the state of unfabricated all-ground,༔
My mind, free from fixation,༔
Is the pure dharmakaya devoid of constructs.༔

Saying and thinking this, watch the innate face of awareness and emptiness, which is free from the constructs of the three times. Finish the session with that and enter the detailed or abridged development stage, or else endeavor in the main practice, Trekchö and Tögal. When the time to enter the path of action has come, say,

Hoh༔
Künzang gyalwa shitro drubpa dang༔
Düsum sagpey gewa jinye pa༔
Domtey lamey jangchub chenpor ngo༔
Dagdang tayey semchen malü pa༔
Dribnyi künzey yönten kündzog ney༔
Zungjug dorje changdu sangye shog༔

HOH༔
This practice of Samantabhadra and the peaceful and wrathful
    victorious ones,༔
And all the virtue gathered throughout the three times,༔
I add together and dedicate to unexcelled great enlightenment.༔
May I and all the infinite sentient beings༔
Exhaust the two obscurations, perfect all qualities,༔
And awaken as the unified state of Vajradhara.༔

Om༔
Ngowo tongpa chökü tashi shog༔
Rangshin salwa longkü tashi shog༔

Tugje natsok tulkü tashi shog^a
Yermey küntu zangpö tashi shog^a

OM^a

May there be the auspiciousness of the empty essence,
    dharmakaya.^a
May there be the auspiciousness of the cognizant nature,
    sambhogakaya.^a
May there be the auspiciousness of the manifold capacity,
    nirmanakaya.^a
May there be the auspiciousness of their indivisibility,
    Samantabhadra.^a

Thus, dedicate the root of virtue towards the essence of enlightenment, seal with perfect aspiration, and make the final adornment by uttering the verse of auspiciousness. Train in passing the time during all breaks with activities that are in accord with the Dharma.

Based on the inconceivable aspirations and activities of the great tertön dharma king and his sons, and through the timely ripening of the perfect coincidence of place and time, at the monastic seat of Chishor Lhünpo, the supreme refuge, Jedrung Rinpoche bestowed upon me the auspicious gift of a crown for the gurus, the lords of all families, to always remain above my head, and for the essence teaching of the Dakpo Kagyü to spread throughout the land.

Following his command, this old monk and disciple of the great tertön with the name Khenpo (Rinchen Dargye) composed this text between sessions, while staying at the Dharma Wheel of that monastic seat (Riwoche Monastery) and completed it in a small encampment at Gomshung Dayib. For lasting benefit and peace, may it become a cause for the activity of these profound teachings to satisfy all beings' needs everywhere, according to their wishes.

Self-Manifest Luminosity

The Supplication to the Lineage Gurus According to the Great Perfection Heart Essence of Samantabhadra

Chokgyur Lingpa

Emaho
Khordey künla khabpa chökyi ying
Ogmin tugpo köpey zhingkham su
Künzang dorje changla solwa deb
Zhigyü tenla phebpar jingyi lob

EMAHO
In dharmadhatu, pervading the whole of samsara and nirvana,
The densely arrayed realm of Akanishtha,
I supplicate Samantabhadra Vajradhara.
Grant your blessings to establish certainty in the continuity of
    ground.

Rangzhin salwa yeshe lhündrub pey
Ngepa ngaden longkü zhingkham su
Rig nga shitrö tsogla solwa deb
Lamgyü taru chinpar jingyi lob

In the luminous nature with spontaneously present wisdoms,
The sambhogakaya realm of the five certainties,
I supplicate the assemblies of the five peaceful and wrathful
    families.
Grant your blessings to reach perfection in the continuity of path.

Tugje natsok gangla gangdül wey
Ma ngey natsok trulkü zhingkham su
Dzogpey sangye namla solwa deb
Dreygyü ngöndu gyurwar jingyi lob

In the diverse and unlimited realms of nirmanakaya,
The manifold capacity that trains beings according to their needs,
I supplicate all perfectly awakened ones.
Grant your blessings to realize the continuity of fruition.

Kyepar ngönpar gawey zhingkham su
Yeshe rölpey zhalyey khangpa ru
Palden dorje sempa la solwa deb
Trekchö tawa togpar jingyi lob

Especially in the realm of True Joy,
In the celestial palace of wisdom displays,
I supplicate the glorious Vajrasattva.
Grant your blessings to realize the Trekchö view.

Orgyen sindhu gyamtso chenpö ling
Rinchen barwa tsegpey khangpa ru
Trülku garab dorje la solwa deb
Yingrig tenla phebpar jingyi lob

On the island in the great Lake Sindhu of Uddiyana,
In the multi-storied mansion of Glowing Jewels,
I supplicate the nirmanakaya Garab Dorje.
Grant your blessings to establish certainty in awareness and space.

Ngamji durtrö tsangtsing trikpa ney
Yeshe mepung barwey phugpa ru
Lobpön jampal shenyen la solwa deb
Nyamnang gongdu phelwar jingyi lob

In the awesome charnel ground Dense Wilderness,
In the cave Blazing Mass of Wisdom Fire,
I supplicate the master Manjushrimitra.
Grant your blessings to increase vision and experience.

Durtrö silwa tsalgyi zhingkham su
Yeshe ö nga khyilwey gurkhang du
Rigdzin shiri singha la solwa deb
Rigpa tseyla phebpar jingyi lob

In the realm of Cool Grove charnel ground,
In the mansion of swirling five-colored wisdom light,
I supplicate the vidyadhara Shri Singha.
Grant your blessings to reach the fullness of awareness.

Lhonub ngayab palri tsemo ney
Pema ökyi phodrang chenpo ru
Lobpön pema jungney la solwa deb
Chönyi zeysar togpar jingyi lob

On the summit of the Glorious Mountain in southwestern
 Chamara,
In the vast palace of Lotus Light,
I supplicate the master Padmakara.
Grant your blessings to realize the stage of exhaustion in
 dharmata.

Dzamling bö-yül gangchen neykyi chog
Samye chimphü entsa gongma ru
Tsogyal lhasey yabyum la solwa deb
Dag gyü minching drölwar jingyi lob

In the supreme place of snowy Tibet on the Jambu continent,
In the upper retreat of Samye Chimphu,
I supplicate Tsogyal, the prince, and his consort.
Grant your blessings to ripen and free my nature.

Garzhug damchö yizhin jungwey ling
Sang ngag phodrang özer zhalyey su
Chokgyur dechen lingpa la solwa deb
Damtsig tsülzhin sungwar jingyi lob

Wherever you dwell is the site of the wishfulfilling true teaching,
A radiant mansion, the Palace of Secret Mantra.
I supplicate Chokgyur Dechen Lingpa.
Grant your blessings so that I correctly keep the samayas.

Dokham lawa kangchig namkha dzö
Lhochog yubal drag gi phugpa ru

Damchö künzang tuktig la solwa deb
Zabdön gongpa lönpar jingyi lob

At Lawa Kangchik, on Mount Namkhadzö in Dokham,
On the southern slope, in the Turquoise Cave,
I supplicate the sacred teaching, *Kunzang Tuktig.*
Grant your blessings so that I understand the profound meaning.

Chökhor korwey neychog tamchey du
Nyengyü beypey lhamo namdzong du
Tensung khandro chenmo la solwa deb
Tenpa ta ü khyabpar jingyi lob

In all the supreme places of turning the Wheel of Dharma,
The sky fortress of the goddess of secret oral transmission,
I supplicate the Great Dakini who guards the doctrine.
Grant your blessings for the teachings to spread everywhere.

Lamey lungten drubpey enney su
Ösal tagtu charwey phugpa ru
Cheydrog chödzey tamchey la solwa deb
Dagnang chogmey charwar jingyi lob

In the retreat places prophesied by the guru,
In caves where luminosity continuously shines forth,
I supplicate all practicing dharma friends.
Grant your blessings so that impartial pure perception may arise.

Kadrin chengyi lama dampa nam
Dag gi gyüla deydang sherab dang
Daljor nyeka chiwa mitag sog
Ngejung gyüla kyewar jingyi lob

All kind and sublime gurus,
Bless my mind with devotion and intelligence,
So that I realize the facts of death and impermanence and the
    rarity of freedoms and riches.
Grant your blessings so that renunciation takes birth in my being.

Lama könchog sumla lokhel ney
Drokün phamar sheypey nyingjey yi

Tsechig sangye drubpey tsöndrü den
Tsedang drubpa nyampar jingyi lob

To place my trust in the guru and the Three Jewels,
To have the compassion to regard all beings as my parents,
And the diligence to attain enlightenment in this very lifetime—
Grant your blessings so that I equalize life and practice.

Rangjung rangshar shitrö kyerim dzog
Nöchü phungkham tögal nangwa tog
Chöku yolang zang ngen panglang dral
Trekchö tawa togpar jingyi lob

Completing the development stage of self-existing, self-appearing
    peaceful and wrathful ones,
May I realize the world and beings, aggregates and elements, as
    Tögal display.
Free from accepting and rejecting the continuity of dharmakaya as
    good or bad,
Grant your blessings so that I realize the Treckchö view.

Chönyi dagpa togmey ngangdu shar
Redok meypa nyamnang gongdu phel
Rigpa tseypheb chönyi zeysar tog
Ku ngai ngangdu ngönpar sangye shog

Pure dharmata manifests in the continuity of nonthought.
Free from hope and fear, experiences increase.
Reaching the fullness of awareness and realizing the stage of
    exhaustion in dharmata,
May there be full awakening in the state of the five kayas.

*At the request of the perfectly diligent Pema Rangdröl, for words with such mean-
ing, I, Chokgyur Lingpa, composed this at glorious Lhasa. May all be auspicious!*

Mantra

Kunzang Tuktig Leyjang
The Manifest Essence

The General Practice Manual for the Peaceful and Wrathful Ones According to the Heart Essence of Samantabhadra, the Pure Gold Great Perfection

Padmasambhava, revealed by Chokgyur Lingpa

ཐུ་ཐཱུཿ

HOMAGE TO GURU SAMANTABHADRA!ཿ

With faith and karmic connection, having obtained empowerment,
    and possessing pure samayas,ཿ
This is how to carry out the practice:ཿ
In a place of solitude, take a comfortable seat.ཿ
Having prepared the mandala and gathered the practice materials,ཿ
Train in the preliminary, main, and concluding sections.ཿ
Samaya.ཿ

THE FIVE STAGES OF PRELIMINARIESཿ15

Namoཿ
Ngowo tongpa chökyi kuཿ
Rangshin salwa longchö dzogཿ
Tukje natsok trülku laཿ
Jangchub bardu kyabsu chiཿ

NAMOཿ
In the empty essence, dharmakaya,ཿ
In the cognizant nature, sambhogakaya,ཿ

207

And in the manifold capacity, nirmanakaya,§
I take refuge until enlightenment.§

Ho§
Khanyam drowa malü pa§
Sangye sala köpey chir§
Dzogpa chenpö man ngag gi§
Rangrig chöku tokpar ja§

HO§
In order to establish all beings equal to the sky§
In the state of buddhahood,§
I will realize dharmakaya of self-existing awareness,§
Through the teachings of the Great Perfection.[16]§

Hung§
Marig trulpey nyidzin gek§
Neydir madug zhendu deng§
Yeshe rangrig trogyal gyi§
Tokmey yingsu lagpar gyur§
Hung hung hung utsa taya phey§

HUNG§
Duality demons of ignorant confusion,§
Do not remain here, go elsewhere. §
The wrathful wisdom king of natural awareness§
Will crush you into the realm of nonthought.§
HUNG HUNG HUNG UCHATAYA PHAT[17]§

Hung§
Nangsi shitrö kusung tuk§
Madag gegkyi ming yang med§
Yeshe dorje mey yi gur§
Tsamchey diley mada shig§
Om ah hung bendza raksha raksha dhrum§

HUNG§
All that appears and exists is the body, speech, and mind of the
    peaceful and wrathful ones.§
There is not even the term "obstructing forces."§

This is the fiery dome of wisdom vajras.⸴
Do not cross the boundary line.⸴
OM AH HUNG VAJRA RAKSHA RAKSHA BHRUNG⸴

Hung⸴
Yeshe melung chutrö pey⸴
Ngöpor dzinpa tamchey jang⸴
Nöchü künzang chöpey trin⸴
Ying kyi bhandha yangpa ru⸴
Sha nga dütsi ödu shu⸴
Kusung tugkyi chüdrang tim⸴
Dechen rakta gyamtsor kyil⸴
Torma döyön gyamtsor gyur⸴
Om ah hung sarva pudza megha bendza sapha rana kham⸴

HUNG⸴
By sending forth wisdom fire, wind, and water,⸴
All fixation on concreteness is purified.⸴
The universe, with its contents, is a Samantabhadra
    offering-cloud.⸴
Within the vast skull cup of space,⸴
The five meats and nectars dissolve into light,⸴
Inviting and absorbing the essence of body, speech, and mind.⸴
The rakta of great bliss becomes a swirling ocean,⸴
The torma becomes an ocean of sense pleasures.⸴
OM AH HUNG SARVA PUJA MEGHA VAJRA SAPHARANA KHAM⸴

This pacifies obstructing forces, purifies your mindstream,⸴
And makes you a suitable vessel for accomplishment.⸴
Samaya.⸴

THE FIVE SAMADHIS OF THE MAIN SECTION⸴

Hung⸴
Chöku yeney tongpa nyi⸴
Rangshin yeshe künla kyab⸴

Rigpa kyemey aru sel
Ötrö nöchü dagpar jang

HUNG
Dharmakaya is the primordial state of emptiness.
Its wisdom nature is all-pervading.
Unborn awareness manifests as AH
Radiating light to purify the universe and beings.

Namdag yum ngai khalong du
Yeshe ngayi shelye khang
Gyendang köpa phünsum tsok
Shitrö phodrang teng og tsül

In the vast pure space of the five female buddhas,
Is the celestial mansion of the five wisdoms,
Abundant in perfect ornaments and designs.
This is the two-storied palace of the peaceful and wrathful ones.

Korlo tsibshi tewa ru
Sengtri pema nyidey teng
Lama küntu zangpo ting
Nyamshag chagya yumdang tril

In the middle of the four-spoked wheel,
Upon a lion throne, lotus, sun, and moon,
Is Guru Samantabhadra, deep blue,
With the hand gesture of equanimity, embracing his consort.

Ü-dang chokshi trichog la
Namnang yingchug korlo kar
Mikyö nyemma dorje ting
Rinjung chenma rinchen ser
Taye gökar pema mar
Döndrub drölma gyadram jang

On the supreme thrones in the center and in the four directions,
Are Vairochana and Dhatvishvari, white with a wheel,
Akshobhya and Vajratopa, blue with a vajra,
Ratnasambhava and Lochana, yellow with a jewel,

Amitabha and Pandara Vasini, red with a lotus,
And Amoghasiddhi and Tara, green with a vajra-cross.

Tsamshir pema nyidey teng
Sayi nyingpo gegma kar
Namkhai nyingpo trengma ser
Chenrey zigwang luma mar
Chagna dorje garma jang

In the four intermediate directions upon a lotus, sun,
    and moon,
Are Kshiti Garbha and Lasya, white,
Akasha Garbha and Mala, yellow,
Mighty Avalokiteshvara and Gita, red,
And Vajrapani and Nirti, green.

Druchay shila pedey teng
Jampa karser metog ma
Dribsel marser dugpö ma
Künzang marjang nangsel ma
Jampel jangkya jugpa ma
Künkyang tsendang pejey dzog
Dardang rinchen rüpey gyen
Taye özer trowa o

In the four corners of the square, upon lotus and moon,
Are Maitreya and Pushpa, white and yellow,
Nivarana Vishkambhin and Dhupa, red and yellow,
Samantabhadra and Aloka, red and green,
And Manjushri and Gandha, green and light green.

All have the complete major and minor marks.
Ornamented with silks, jewels, and bones,
They emanate boundless rays of light.

Kyamla tulku tubpa druk
Chagdral drowa dülwey tsül
Pekyang tengna shengpey tab
Goshir trogyal chenpo shi

Gargü nyamden yumdang tril
Durtrö cheygye kalmey bar

Along the sides are the six nirmanakaya munis.
Free from attachment, in the posture of taming beings,
They stand on single lotus flowers.

At the four gates are the four great wrathful kings.
In the ninefold dance postures, embracing their consorts,
They wear the eight charnel ground ornaments and blaze with the
flames of the kalpa.

Trowöi phodrang chenpö ü
Dragchen penyi rudrey teng
Palchen chemchog heruka
Tingnag yeykar yönmar shel
Yeysum dorje yöndung trag
Yumchen troti shorir tril

In the center of the great palace of the wrathful ones,
Upon a huge rock, lotus, sun, and Rudra,
Is the great and glorious Chemchok Heruka,
Dark blue, right face white and left face red.
In his three right hands are vajras, in the left ones skulls with
blood.
He embraces the great consort Krodhishvari.

Ü-dang chogshir penyi la
Buddha tragtung yab-yum mug
Bendza tragtung yab-yum ting
Ratna tragtung yab-yum ser
Pema tragtung yab-yum mar
Karma tragtung yab-yum jang
Trotsül nyishu rabtu bar
Paldang durtrö cheykyi gyen

In the center and in the four directions, upon lotus and sun, are
Maroon Buddha Heruka with consort,
Blue Vajra Heruka with consort,
Yellow Ratna Heruka with consort,

Red Padma Heruka with consort,
And green Karma Heruka with consort.
Adorned with the glorious attire and charnel ground ornaments,
They blaze in the twenty modes of wrath.

Druchey lobur rigshi la
Neykyi tromo chenmo gye
Kudog natsog shingla röl
Khyamla yülgyi tramen gye
Gonyen natsog jigpey zug

At the sides and corners of the four families
Are the eight, great wrathful ladies of the sacred places,
In various colors and standing on corpses.
Along the sides are the eight tramen of the sacred countries
With various heads and terrifying forms.

Goshir tarje goma shi
Gugching domnyö leydzey ching
Chikyam wangmo nyishu gye
Rigkyi dogchen chagtsen dzin

At the four gates are the four female gatekeepers, the annihilators,
Performing the acts of summoning, binding, chaining, and
    intoxicating.
In the outer yard are the twenty-eight ishvaris,
In the colors of their families, holding their attributes.

Rigdzin gyalwa seydang chey
Pawo khandro chökyong tsog
Nangsi tilgang shindu sel
Dorje kusung tugdang den
Yeshe ngayi ngowor dzog
Om ah hung
Om ah hung so ha

Vidyadharas, victorious ones with their sons,
And hosts of dakas, dakinis, and dharma protectors,
Are manifest, filling the phenomenal world like a full sesame pod.
Possessing the vajra body, speech, and mind,

They are perfect as the essence of the five wisdoms.⁞
OM AH HUNG, OM AH HUNG SVAHA⁞

Hung⁞
Chöying trödang dralwey shing⁞
Longchö dzogkü phodrang ney⁞
Gyalwa shitro kordang chey⁞
Tugdam wanggi shegsu sol⁞
Bendza samaya dza⁞
E haya hi Dzah hung bam ho⁞
Ka va tsi gyana bendza titra⁞
Atipu hoh Trati tsa hoh⁞

HUNG⁞
From the palace of sambhogakaya,
Within the unconstructed realm of dharmadhatu,
Peaceful and wrathful buddhas with your retinues,
By the power of your samaya, please come!
VAJRA SAMAYA JAH⁞
E HAYA HI, JAH HUNG BAM HOH⁞
KA VA CHI JNANA VAJRA TISHTA⁞
ATIPU HOH, PRATICCHA HOH⁞

Om ah hung⁞
Chiyi chöpa küntu zangpö trin⁞
Nanggi chöpa döyön dütsi men⁞
Sangwey chöpa dechen kadag ying⁞
Gyalwa shitro kordang cheyla bül⁞
Om bendza argham padeng püshpe dhupe aloke⁞
Gendhe niwente shabta trati tsa hoh⁞
Maha pendza amrita kharam khahi⁞
Om ah hung maha rakta kharam khahi⁞
Maha balingta kharam khahi⁞
Mahasukha gana pudza hoh⁞
Maha dharmadhatu tana pudza hoh⁞
Maha shunyata gyana pudza hoh⁞

OM AH HUNG

The outer offering is a Samantabhadra offering cloud.

The inner offering is sense-pleasures and amrita medicine.

The innermost offering is the primordially pure space of great bliss.

I offer these to the peaceful and wrathful victorious ones and their retinues.

OM VAJRA ARGHAM PADYAM PUSHPE DHUPE ALOKE GANDHE NAIVIDYA SHABTA PRATICCHA HOH

MAHA PANCHA AMRITA KHARAM KHAHI

OM AH HUNG MAHA RAKTA KHARAM KHAHI

MAHA BALINGTA KHARAM KHAHI

MAHA SUKHA GANA PUJA HOH

MAHA DHARMADHATU TANA PUJA HOH

MAHA SHUNYATA JNANA PUJA HOH

Om

Tsendang peyjey dzogpey ku

Chönyi rangdra dorjei sung

Migyur yeshe dorjei tug

Yönten trinlay samyey tö

OM

I praise your body, complete with the major and minor marks;

Your vajra speech, the natural sound of dharmata;

Your vajra mind, the unchanging wakefulness;

And your inconceivable qualities and activities.

Hung

Ngowo nyiley ma yö kyang

Düljey yül la trowöi ku

Trulpa chagnyen phonyar gye

Tabkey tugje chenla tö

HUNG

Though unmoved from the essence itself,

You appear in wrathful forms before those to be tamed,

Sending out emanations and attendants as envoys.

I praise your compassionate and skillful means.

Hung⁞
Nangwa tamchey shitrö ku⁞
Dragpa tamchey ngag-kyi yang⁞
Rigpa togmey ösel ying⁞
Chötrin gyamtsö shingnam kheng⁞
Trinlay dumey drowa tral⁞
Kagyab gyalwey kyilkor nyi⁞
Duma rochik ngangdu dzog⁞
Om bodhi tsitta mahasukha gyana dhatu ah⁞
Om rulu rulu hung joh hung⁞

HUNG⁞
All sights are the body of the peaceful and wrathful ones.⁞
All that is heard is the sound of mantra.⁞
Thoughtfree awareness is the space of luminosity.⁞
The ocean-wide realms are filled with clouds of offerings.⁞
Innumerable activities free all beings.⁞
This is the all-pervading mandala of the victorious ones;⁞
Everything is perfect in the continuity of one taste.⁞
OM BODHICHITTA MAHASUKHA JNANADHATU AH⁞
OM RULU RULU HUNG BHYOH HUNG⁞

Recite according to your ability while maintaining the view.⁞
All siddhis and activities will be accomplished.⁞
Samaya.⁞

THE FIVE CONCLUDING STAGES⁞

Hung hung hung⁞
Nangtong lhaku jatsön yingsu tim⁞
Dragtong sung yang drugdra khala yal⁞
Kyemey rigtong machö ngang-la shag⁞
Gongpa zangtal künzang ngang-la ney⁞

HUNG HUNG HUNG⁞
Apparent yet empty forms of deities dissolve like rainbows into
    space.⁞

Resounding yet empty sounds of speech vanish like thunder in the
  sky.
Leaving the empty nonarising awareness in its unfabricated state,
It abides in the unimpeded realization of Samantabhadra.

Ah Ah Ah
Lüsu nangwa yenay shitröi ku
Ngaggi dangkey yeney shitrö sung
Rangrig machö drenrig shitröi tuk
Yermey küntu zangpö tsal ley shar

A A A
Whatever appears as body is primordially the body of the peaceful
  and wrathful ones.
The sound of speech is primordially the speech of the peaceful and
  wrathful ones.
The mind of unfabricated awareness is the mind of the peaceful
  and wrathful ones.
Inseparable, they appear from the expression of Samantabhadra.

Om ah hung
Chinö yingkyi rangshin ö ngai shing
Nangchü kyedro rig nga yabdang yum
Tamchey yeshe nga yi rangzhin la
Küntu zangpö rölpar lhüngyi drub

OM AH HUNG
The external universe, the nature of space, is the realm of five-
  colored light.
The inner contents of sentient beings are the five male and female
  families.
Everything, in the nature of the five wisdoms,
Is spontaneously present as the display of Samantabhadra.

HOH
Künzang gyalwa shitro drubpa dang
Düsum sagpey gewa jinye pa
Domtey lamey jangchub chenpor ngo
Dagdang tayey semchen malü pa

Dribnyi künzey yönten kündzog ney
Zungjug dorje changdu sangye shog

HOH

This practice of Samantabhadra and the peaceful and wrathful
victorious ones,
And all the virtue gathered throughout the three times,
I add together and dedicate to unexcelled great enlightenment.
May I and all the infinite sentient beings
Exhaust the two obscurations, perfect all qualities,
And awaken as the unified state of Vajradhara.

OM

Ngowo tongpa chökü tashi shog
Rangshin salwa longkü tashi shog
Tugje natsog tulkü tashi shog
Yermey küntu zangpö tashi shog

OM

May there be the auspiciousness of the empty essence,
dharmakaya.
May there be the auspiciousness of the cognizant nature,
sambhogakaya.
May there be the auspiciousness of the manifold capacity,
nirmanakaya.
May there be the auspiciousness of their inseparability,
Samantabhadra.

The perfection of all activities is the fruition. Samaya, seal.

This activity practice, The Manifest Essence,
Which benefits whoever encounters it,
Will spread the heart-teaching of Samantabhadra
From the conclusion of the Dark Age until the end of this aeon.

By fully condensing the Dzogchen tantras
Into an easy method that is simple to carry out and bestows swift
blessings,

*I, Padma, made this excellent composition *

*As a meaningful encounter for the fortunate ones in that time. *

*Tsogyal respectfully recorded it, *

*And concealed it as a profound treasure. *

*May my fortunate son discover it. *

*Through his discovery, may this teaching flourish! *

*Samaya. Seal of treasure, seal of concealment, seal of profundity. *

I, Chokgyur Dechen Lingpa, extracted this from the Turquoise Cave on the southern slope of Namkhadzö in Dokham and translated it from the yellow parchment in Orgyen Samten Ling at Rudam Snow Range. May it be virtuous! May all be auspicious!

Chemchok Heruka

Short Dharmapala Petition

Hung࿇
Mahakala phogyü gönpö tsog࿇
Ekadzati mogyü mamo nam࿇
Lhachen palbar maning drekpey tsog࿇
Malü khordang cheypa tamchey kyi࿇
Damdzey shatrag torma dishe la࿇
Barchey drageg tamchey drelwa dang࿇
Trinley namshi tenpa sungwar dzö࿇

HUNG࿇
Mahakala and gathered protectors of the male class,࿇
Ekajati and mother deities of the female class,࿇
Lhachen Palbar, the non-dual class and all the gathered drekpas,࿇
All of you, without exception, together with your retinues,࿇
Accept this samaya substance of flesh, blood, and torma,࿇
Liberate all obstacle-makers, enemies, and obstructing forces,࿇
And protect the doctrine through the four activities.࿇

The Inexhaustible Garland of Lightning

Künzang Gyurmey Tsewang
Drakpa Ngedön Drubpey Dorje

HOMAGE TO SHRI SAMANTABHADRA!

Here is the invocation, offering, and praise to all the vajra guardians, supplicating their powerful activities to help the ones who one-pointedly exert themselves in the meaning of the instructions of simplicity. If you have gathered offering articles, consecrate them.

To consecrate the offering, repeat three times:

OM NAMA SARVA TATHAGATE BHAYO BISHO MUKHEBHE
SARVA THAKHAM UTGATE SAPARANA HIMAM GAGANA KHAM
    SOHA

A
Döney tongpa chenpö chotrül ley
Yingdang yeshe yermey mamö tso
Ney yül durtrö küngyi dagpo chog
Sangchen sabmö yang nying tartuk pa

AH
From the primordial magical display of the great emptiness,
Inseparable space and wisdom, Queen of the Mamos,
Supreme Lord of all the places, valleys, and charnel grounds,
Profound and ultimate Quintessence of the Great Secret,

Tegtse ati rangshin dzogpa chey
Kayi sungma eka dzati dang
Kyabjug chenpo tumchen rahula
Gyalwey tenkyong bendza sadhu tsal

Guardians of the teachings of the summit of the vehicles,
The natural Great Perfection, Ati,
Ekajati, Great Khyabjug, most ferocious Rahula,
And protector of the doctrine of the victorious ones, Vajrasadhu
Tsal,

Münrum lokgyu jishin dirjön la
Künzang dorsem sangwey dagpo ney
Rimjön tönpa chunyi la sokpey
Kasang meyjung damtsig dön la som

Come here like lightning flashing in dense darkness,
And think of your wonderful samayas of the secret teachings
Of the twelve teachers and others,
Which were successively transmitted through Samantabhadra,
Vajrasattva, and the Lord of Secrets.

Gangnang de ngor charwey chöpey trin
Nyampey shatrag dön nying nangtröl chey
Ngönpar tobbo trinley nyurdu drub
Chönyi tongpey rangdra dradrok dril
Sangwey ngeuchung chokchen damaru
Tensung chenpo kyenam dirgong shig

Whatever is seen, the offering clouds manifest in one's experience,
The flesh, blood, inner organs, and entrails of the violators,
I truly offer to you; swiftly fulfill the activities.
With the resounding bell of the empty, natural sound of dharmata,
The secret small drum, the great supreme damaru,
And the human bone trumpet possessing vajra songs, I exhort you.
Please listen, Great Guardians of the teachings.

Chöku lagchang tröpey tab chikpu
Rangshin trödrel sabdön dzogpa chey
Tawey yangtse namtog trekchö chey

Gompey tartuk ösel tögal chey
Chöpa dadral dzinmey jung gyal chey
Drebu gyurmey kudang yeshe chey

The single method of giving dharmakaya in the palm of the hand,
The deep meaning of natural simplicity, the Great Perfection,
The summit of views, the great cutting through thoughts,
The ultimate of meditations, the great luminous passing above,
The matchless action, the great unfixated spontaneity,
And the unchanging fruition, the great kayas and wisdoms,

Lamdu shugpey naljor dagchag la
Tsewa kündral dudzi enpa dang
Drubpa taru chinpey trinley dzö

For us yogins who have entered the path of these,
Perform the activities of being free from harm, devoid of
    distractions,
And reaching the perfection of practice.

Kyepar sabter diten chogdu kün
Tadün wangpo shintar kyabpa dang
Degom namkyang lüten denyi du
Chönyi seysar kyölwey trinley dzö

In particular, perform the activities so that through this profound
    treasure,
The teaching may pervade all directions and times like the sun
    disc,
And so that all who practice it may, in this very body,
Arrive at the level of dharmata exhaustion.

Dükyi logyur digchen gangdag gi
Gyalsung chödir shekur jepa dang
Lamgöl tönching sulum reychö je
Nyampa dünden namkyang drölwar dzö

Any evil person, influenced by Mara,
Who slanders or criticizes this teaching spoken by the victorious
    ones,

Who shows a perverted path, or is pretentious and false,
Anyone endowed with seven transgressions, please liberate.

Shenyang rimey tendzin shabten ching
Chokdang dükyi gendün trinley gye
Labsum gyichug tuktün trimtsang shing
Dronam deden samdön drubpar dzö

Moreover, extend the lives of the doctrine holders, without
  partiality.
Make the activities of the sangha spread throughout all directions.
Rich in the three trainings, in harmony, and in pure discipline,
Make all beings possess happiness and let wishes and aims be
  fulfilled.

Trinley chölja chölje chölwey yül
Loley deypa dömey shi soma
Yedröl gyalwey gongpa ma leypa
Danta nyidu tokpey trinley dzö[18]

The enjoined, the enjoiner, and the object of enjoining the activities
Are beyond concepts, the original fresh essence.
Perform the activity of realizing this very instant
The primordially free, uncorrupted mind of the victorious ones.

In response to the repeated request from Gyurmey Osel Dorje, stating the necessity of a petition offering to Ma, Za, and Dam, the teaching guardians of the Heart Essence of Samantabhadra, the profound great space instruction section, the Ati Great Perfection, which is like pure gold, this was composed in the style of five greatnesses by Künzang Gyurmey Tsewang Drakpa Ngedön Drubpey Dorje at the age of sixteen at the time of dwelling within the sphere of the Düpeydo practice. Vijyantu.

ENGLISH BIBLIOGRAPHY

Lingpa, Chokgyur. *The Ocean of Amrita*. Translated by Erik Pema Kunsang. Hong Kong: Rangjung Yeshe Publications, 2014.

Lingpa, Karma. *The Tibetan Book of the Dead*. Translated by Francesca Fremantle and Chogyam Trungpa. Boston: Shambhala Publications, 2000.

Rabjam, Longchen. *The Guhyagarbha Tantra, Secret Essence Definitive Nature Just As It Is*. Translated by Lama Chonam and Sangye Khandro. Ithaca: Snow Lion Publications, 2011.

Rabjam, Longchen. *The Precious Treasury of Philosophical Systems*. Translated by Richard Barron. Weaverville: Padma Publishing, 2008.

Schmidt, Marcia, comp. *Dzogchen Essentials, The Path That Clarifies Confusion*. Hong Kong: Rangjung Yeshe Publications, 2004.

Tulku Urgyen Rinpoche. *As It Is*, Volume I. Translated by Erik Pema Kunsang. Hong Kong: Rangjung Yeshe Publications, 1999.

Tulku Urgyen Rinpoche. *As It Is*, Volume II. Translated by Erik Pema Kunsang. Hong Kong: Rangjung Yeshe Publications, 2000.

TIBETAN SOURCE MATERIAL

Chokling Tersar

Volume KI: Author: Chokgyur Lingpa, *(mchog gyur gling pa)*, unless otherwise specified.

rdzogs pa chen po gser gyi zhun ma kun bzang thugs tig las thun mong zhi khro'i las byang snying po don gsal ldeb, pp. 63–70

Kunzang Tuktig Leyjang, The Manifest Essence.
rdzogs pa chen po gser gyi zhun ma kun bzang thugs tig las thun mong dbang gi rim pa sdig sgrib kun 'joms dang don dbang yid bzhin nor bu yid bzhin nor bu'i snying po bcas ldeb, pp. 63–70

The Destroyer of All Evil Deeds and Obscurations.
rdzogs pa chen po gser gyi zhun ma kun bzang thugs tig las thun mong zhi khro'i las byang zur rgyan nyams chag bshags skong dang tshogs mchod gshin po rjes 'dzin gyi cho ga bcas thugs rje'i phrin las ldeb, pp. 83–107

Zurgyen, The Compassionate Activity.
rdzogs pa chen po gser gyi zhun ma kun bzang thugs tig las thun mong zhi khro'i las byang zur rgyan nyams chag bshags skong dang tshogs mchod gshin po rjes 'dzin gyi cho ga bcas thugs rje'i phrin las ldeb, pp. 187–221

Döntri, Self-Luminous Wisdom Mind.
rdzogs pa chen po gser gyi zhun ma kun bzang thugs tig las don khrid yid bzhin nor bu'i snying po dgongs pa rang gsal ldeb, pp. 71–81

Karmey Khenpo Rinchen Dargye, *The Brilliant Concise Meaning.*
mchog gter kun bzang thugs tig gi zab khrid don bsdus rab gsal ldeb, pp. 227–261

Karmey Khenpo Rinchen Dargye, *The Excellent Path to True Goodness.*
rdzogs pa chen po gser gyi zhun gyi sngon 'gro nges legs lam bzang sdeb,
pp. 175–185

Chokgyur Lingpa, *Self-Manifest Luminosity.*
rdzogs pa chen po gser gyi zhun ma kun bzang thugs tig las bgyud 'ot gsal rang
shar ldeb, pp. 59–62

Extracted from *Padma sgar dbang.*
Short Dharmalapal Petition

Künzang Gyurmey Tsewang Drakpa Ngedön Drubpey Dorje,
The Inexhaustible Garland of Lightning.
rdzogs pa chen po gser gyi zhun ma kun bzang thugs tig gi bka' srung ma gza'
dam gsum gsol zhing mchod pa'i thabs mi zad glog gi phreng ba zhes bya ba
bzhugs so, pp. 223–235

Dilgo Khyentse Rinpoche, *Kunzang Gongyen, The Mind Ornament
of Samantrabhadra.*
Skyabs rje dil mgo mkhyenbrtse tin po che'i bka 'bum
The Collected Writings of Dilgo Khyentse Rinpoche, Volume Ba,
pp. 245–266

ENDNOTES

1   From: Tulku Urgyen Rinpoche. *Quintessential Dzogchen*. Translated by Erik Pema Kunsang. (Hong Kong: Rangjung Yeshe Publications, 2006). pp. 21–26.

2   Sense bases, *skye mched*, Tibetan, *ayatana*, Sanskrit. The five senses and their objects as well as the mental faculty and mental objects. Rangjung Yeshe Dictionary.

3   Padmasambhava, Chokgyur Lingpa, Jamyang Khyentse Wangpo, Jamgön Kongtrül, and Jamyang Drakpa. *Light of Wisdom*, Volume II. Translated from the Tibetan by Erik Pema Kunsang. (Hong Kong: Rangjung Yeshe Publications, 1998). p. 147.

All these phases of sadhana activities should be linked with the traditionally prescribed four gates of Secret Mantra. As is said,

> *The verbal gate of utterance is to remind of the ultimate.*
> *The secret gate of mantra is to invoke the samayas.*
> *The mental gate of samadhi is to keep one-pointed focus.*
> *The playful gate of mudra is to link gesture with meaning.*

Among these, the three of mantra, word, and samadhi, should be combined with all phases, while mudras are necessary for offerings and so forth.

4   Extracted from: Tulku Urgyen Rinpoche. *As It Is*, Volume I. Translated by Erik Pema Kunsang. (Hong Kong: Rangjung Yeshe Publications, 1999). pp. 190–202.

5   *Nangjang* training—literally, "training in refining experience"—is the personal process of resolving the nature of reality and experience, by means of the profound teachings of the Great Perfection. An extraordinary example of this method of practice is found in Dudjom Lingpa's *Buddhahood without Meditation*. Padma Publishing, 1994.

6   Karmey Khenpo Rinchen Dargye. *Self-Manifest Luminosity*.

7   Erik Pema Kunsang, trans. *Precious Songs of Awakening*. (Hong Kong: Rangjung Yeshe Publications, 2014). pp. 1–2.

8   op. cit.

9   This recording by Tulku Urgyen Rinpoche is available on the Lotus Treasure website, www.lotustreasure.com

10   The name and picture of the dead person is written on a piece of paper that is placed in front of the vajra master. He summons the consciousness of the deceased, purifies, teaches, empowers, and finally performs transference of consciousness, after which the paper is burned.

11   See Liturgies.

12   A dharmapala petition composed by Chokgyur Lingpa.

13   This verse is a play on Chokgyur Lingpa's full name, Chokgyur Dechen Shikpo Lingpa, meaning Sanctuary of Supreme Great Bliss Spontaneity.

14   Dilgo Khyentse Rinpoche, after the terma root verses of refuge and bodhichitta from the *Kunzang Tuktig,* extracts the other preliminary practice verses from the *Dzogchen Desum,* another terma of Chokgyur Lingpa.

15   During feast offering, prior to this, add the following:

> *Namo, rangnang yeshe kyi khorlo khakyab tu seypar gyur⋮*
> *The wisdom continuity of self-display is manifest, filling the sky.⋮*

16   During a feast, add here:

> *Dzah hung bam hoh Tsokshing nam rangla timpar gyur⋮*

> JAH HUNG BAM HOH, the entire field of accumulation dissolves into me.⋮

> Then add the gektor, torma for the obstructing spirits: ⋮

> *Ram yam kam, Tongpey ngang ley drung ley rinpochey nö yangshing gyachewey nangdu torma khadog driro nüpa phünsum tsogpar gyur.*

> OM AH HUNG⋮
> RAM YAM KHAM. From within emptiness, BHRUNG becomes an open and vast jeweled vessel, within which there is a torma with perfect color, smell, taste, and strength.

17   During a feast, add the Fourfold HUNG Mantra for the gektor:

> OM SUMBHANE SUMBHANE HUNG, GRIHANA GRIHANA HUNG, GRIHANA BHAYA GRIHANA BHAYA HUNG, AH NAYA HOH BHAGAVAN BRIYARAN DZAYA HUNG PHET⋮

18   This last verse is often repeated three times.

For information regarding video and audio recordings,
published teachings, and programs in the lineage of Chokling Tersar,
please access one of the following websites:

www.lotustreasure.com

www.rangjung.com
Rangjung Yeshe Publications and Translations

www.shedrub.org
Shedrub Development Mandala

www.rigpa.org
Sogyal Rinpoche's Centers and Activity

www.tsoknyirinpoche.org
Tsoknyi Rinpoche Activities and Teachings

www.CGLF.org
Chokgyur Lingpa Foundation

www.gomde.dk
Rangjung Yeshe Gomde, Denmark

www.erikpemakunsang.com
Works of Erik Pema Kunsang

www.tsadrafndn.org
Study and Practice of Tibetan Buddhism

www.nitartha.org
Digital Tibetan and educational programs

www.all-otr.org
Teachings of Orgyen Tobgyal Rinpoche